Race and Groupwork

Race and Groupwork

edited by

Tara Mistry and Allan Brown

Whiting & Birch Ltd
London
MCMXCVII

Published by Whiting & Birch Ltd, PO Box 872, Forest Hill, London SE23 3HL, England.
USA: Paul & Co, Publishers' Consortium Inc, PO Box 442, Concord, MA 017422.

British Library Cataloguing in Publication Data.
A CIP catalogue record ins available from the British Library

ISBN 1 86177 011 1 (cased)
ISBN 1 86177 010 3 (limp)

Printed in England by Watkiss Studios Ltd

Contents

Acknowledgements

Tara Mistry and Allan Brown:
An edited book of this kind involves frequent communication between editors and authors and we would like to express our warmest thanks to all our contributors. We are grateful for their acceptance of our editing which sometimes involved a number of redrafts and some editorial fussiness! We appreciated the care and commitment taken by all the authors, and particularly hope that those contributors writing for publication for the first time feel the effort has been worth it. Thank you to all the various groups and their group members for allowing us to learn from their struggles, their pain, their strength and their emancipation.

Tara Mistry:
A special thanks and love to my partner Peter and daughters Nalini and Sunita who continue to provide me with hope and inspiration for the future. Many thanks also to my family and to Tracy Martins, Eleanor Stone, Sharon North, Tony Churchill, Hilary Burgess, Margaret Boushel, Lyn Shorthouse, Bill Beaumont, Kate Lyons, Anne Antonelli, Janet Bardsley and Margaret Ball for their friendship and support especially during 1995/96. Finally thank you Allan for the years of professional collaboration and guidance.

Allan Brown:
I would like to express my love and thanks to my partner Celia for her support and understanding throughout this and many projects undertaken while we were both in very demanding jobs pre-retirement. From now on I am sure the groupwork will be mainly 'experiential' with our friends and neighbours in Greece!

Dedication

For Ba and in memory of Bapuji

T.M.

Introduction

TARA MISTRY AND ALLAN BROWN

For a long time we were struggling in the Social Work arenas, to understand what 'anti-racism' really meant in practice. We were concerned that discussions about 'culture' would lead to accusations of being multiculturalists who did not quite grasp the structural inequalities facing Black people in Britain. Indeed we had many heated exchanges over terminologies and the implications of definitions for our conceptualisation. They were, and still are important debates. However, in recent years there has been an increasing number of publications and discourses on 'race' and the relationship between 'race', 'culture' and the politics of 'difference' (for example see edited work by Donald and Rattansi, 1992; Malik, 1996). This has given us permission to acknowledge that the debate is changing and evolving alongside the experiences of the established and the newer Black and minority ethnic groups in Britain. The translation of these discourses into meaningful anti-racist practices for a range of Black and minority ethnic user groups is still problematic in many areas of Social welfare provisions and services.

In response to the difficulties in translating the discourses of 'Race' into policies and practices many new publications, from academics and practitioners have provided frameworks and guidelines for delivery of anti-racist (and more recently anti-oppressive) policies and practices. Thompson (1993) in his introduction highlights how the new Diploma in Social Work in 1989 emphasised 'combating discrimination' and focused on working in a multi-racial and multi-cultural society. With CCETSW ensuring 'that students are prepared not only for ethnically sensitive practice but also to challenge institutional and other forms of racism' (CCETSW, 1989, p.10 quoted in Thompson, 1993) the Diploma did pave the way for anti-discrimination to have what we would term a 'legitimate' place on the social work agencies wider agendas.

In certain areas of social work there have been greater theoretical and practice developments than in others. For example, some of the most contentious areas have been discourses within the child care field about the identity formation of black/ mixed parentage children, particularly in the context of transracial fostering and adoption (see for example Tizard and Phoenix, 1989).

What are the implications of the myriad of theoretical underpinnings for the delivery of quality child care services to Black families in Britain? In our view there is no simple answer to any of these questions relating to race whether in the field of child care, criminal justice, disability, health or other areas in social work. These issues become even more complex when we start to ask questions about how these services are delivered, i.e. what social work models and methods are being used and to what extent are they 'anti-racist' or just existing models dressed up to look as if they are anti-racist or anti-oppressive? For example, does consideration of 'race' and 'gender' within a social work model, or specifically say within the 'cognitive' approach widely used in work with offenders, make the model of practice anti-racist and anti-sexist if the theoretical basis of that approach does not shift?

A close look at groupwork used to deliver services to Black/ minority groups, would reveal that this can be just as oppressive and laden with eurocentric values as any other social work methods. It is true however, that some of the more recent developments in social groupwork are more receptive to questioning traditional thinking and practice. Examples of these include the Social Action models (Mullender and Ward, 1991); the Empowerment models (Lee, 1994); the Feminist models and practices (Butler and Wintram, 1991; Mistry, 1989). Also, the influence of Youth and Community Work principles in general has had a significant impact in the conceptualisation of some of the 'empowerment' approaches. Despite some encouraging progress, there is still a huge gap in the theory/practice development of race and groupwork in Britain, and hence in the literature available in this area of social work.

Indeed it was partly the recognition of this extensive gap in the literature on anti-racist groupwork which led us to seriously consider editing this book. As lecturers in social work, we were regularly confronted by the frustration of students and practitioners at the lack of material available on groupwork with specific Black and minority ethnic groups. At the same time, through our links with practice teachers in agencies and our consultation/training roles, we were hearing about various innovative practices by practitioners. In effect workers were developing their own models based sometimes on some theoretical discourses, but often purely as a response to a specific need of the user or the 'client group'.

We were both very keen to encourage practitioners and especially Black practitioners to relate some of their experiences:

> As Mullender and Ward (1985) point out, ' a practice wisdom' of innovatory groupwork may be built up and passed on between practitioners, by word of mouth, but its impact remains localised and short lived. Such pioneering developments need a wider audience to disseminate the practice skills, techniques and values which have emerged through trial and error (Butler and Wintram, 1991, p.18).

We also felt that there was an urgent need for more Black/ minority workers to have access to the theoretical development forums so that these 'practice wisdoms' could be integrated within more dynamic models for application for groupworkers, and indeed (as Butler and Wintram go on to say in the above quote)...across professions. These academic forums are relatively few and access is notoriously difficult (if not impossible) for most practitioners. An edited book seemed to us to be a tangible contribution towards providing that public access as well as potentially meeting the needs of groupworkers, service users and the general readership.

Of course, inviting a range of contributors using the above criteria did mean that we could attract perspectives which could potentially clash or contradict our own position. But we felt that this in itself would illustrate one of the central aims of this book - which is that the translation of anti-racist objectives into tangible practice will vary depending on the interpretation (of anti-racism) by the agency, the worker and the user group.

The decision to co-edit was easy because it was the natural extension of our joint writing/working relationship on race/gender issues in groupwork. As Black/white colleagues working in a university social work department, we had developed a shared framework of understanding of race and groupwork which we could build on through this publication. We had earlier collaborated on two joint articles on related themes, both of which are included in this book. These papers offer readers a practice-theory perspective which can also be detected in some of the other papers in this volume.

In many ways the process of planning and compiling this book, seemed to us analogous with co-working and facilitating a group!

As co-authors ('co-workers') we experienced some of the feelings of working with a live group. We were conscious of some of the issues of race and gender in our own co-editing relationship and with the authors (i.e. 'group members'). What we didn't have was face-to-face member interactions, as our planned meeting for contributors failed to materialise.

We did circulate a list of contributors with contact details in order to facilitate meetings/discussions, but whether or not this was used was left to the individual authors. (It is interesting in this context to reflect that group meetings may not be a prerequisite for bona fide groupwork, as illustrated in Marcia Spence's paper in this volume, and by the 'telephone groups' in Australia described by Regan (1996)).

PLANNING

In planning the book, we had a number of decisions to make about the overall parameters, not least the terms used in the title, 'Race' and 'Groupwork'.

We are well aware that 'Race' is an often vague and much debated concept and we do not intend to enter that discourse in these pages. We hope that the use of the term in the title makes clear to readers the general territory with which we are concerned, which also includes racism, oppression, ethnicity and culture. Earlier, we made references to how the discussions on these concepts are vital but we have also said that this book is as much about how the authors/workers and their user groups have chosen to interpret those concepts as about the similarities and differences in those interpretations. However, on 'culture' we were confident that any cultural analysis would be considered within the context of racism so as not to regress into the 'exotic' interpretation which would lead to what is often described as 'the sari, samosa and steel band' syndrome.

We have not confined the focus to African/Caribbean and Asian groups, but have included papers on Gypsies and Travellers, on Refugees and on 'Foreign Nationals'. Neither have we imposed a particular definition of 'Black' on our authors - to reflect the complexities of that definition in the 1990s.

We did not agonise over our use of the term Groupwork, not least because we think it has often been defined much too narrowly (and usually by white academics), and in terms that can deter innovative practice. In fact, a major objective of this book is to articulate group practices which are responsive to the actual needs and living experiences of members of different minority ethnic groups, rather than expecting group members and practitioners to adapt their work together to conform with some theoretical straitjacket.

Another consideration was the range and type of papers we would seek in the context of a structure for the book as a whole. We had a vision of it being divided into three sections: theoretical perspectives; practice accounts; and a more 'macro' section to address the role of organisations as groups. In the event, despite strenuous efforts on our part, we were unsuccessful in obtaining the papers we had sought for the third section. The learning for us as co-workers was that, as in 'real' groupwork - we could not meet all our objectives nor fully control what happened, but we must confess that like many groupworkers we experienced some strong feelings about this!

In establishing general principles for recruitment of authors ('members') our prerequisite was that we did not necessarily want to go for the 'big names' in the social groupwork/anti-racism field. We wanted rather to cast the net widely 'out there' for potential contributors who were engaging in day to day practice, and who may not have previously written about their work for publication. However, we were keen not to exclude some more established authors who have made valuable contributions in this area of groupwork, especially those involved in practice with minority ethnic groups, and/or multiracial groups. We wanted the majority of papers to be new material, with just a few 'reprints' being made available to a wider readership than hitherto. So in addition to the three already mentioned, we decided also to include Paul Taylor's earlier paper for the important things he has to say about issues of communication in international groups with different cultures and languages represented.

ANALOGY WITH GROUP PROCESS

Getting the membership

This was done mainly through networking with a range of colleagues and intermediaries who were people involved in work in specific settings or who had contacts with practitioners working with specific user groups. We explained that our aim was to edit a book on Race and Groupwork which would start to fill the gap we had identified, and hopefully provide a vehicle for exhibiting some of the innovative practices taking place. We wanted to include as wide a range of user groups and settings as possible, for example new arrivals coming to this country as Refugees, 'Foreign Nationals' in prison, and Gypsies and Travellers experiencing a specific form of racism: all constituencies which we feel have been sadly neglected.

In summary, in order to get the members we networked extensively, and made some direct contacts via letters/phone and personal approaches to colleagues. We also went outside Britain to invite Judith Lee and her colleagues to write a chapter about their work, after we experienced their simulation of a very dramatic empowerment approach at the Groupwork Symposium in Hartford, Connecticut, USA, in 1994.

Getting started

We divided up the task of contacting each potential contributor between us, trying to do it in such a way that would be most enabling for each individual we approached. We were purposely encouraging new practitioner authors, aware that some may feel daunted by the task of exposing their work to the public. We tried, for example, to think about the issues of race and gender in our initial contact with them. This involved some matching based around our own ethnicity, gender, interests, knowledge base, experience and so on.

Early revision of plans

Of course, as in all real life situations we were constrained by resource limitations (one of these being part-time employment) and by unforeseen circumstances (in this case sick leave). This meant a rearranging of our liaison roles with the contributors - equivalent perhaps to a sort of 'storming' and revision phase. Our carefully planned links divided on the basis already outlined had to be modified. Whilst both of us read the scripts and discussed them in depth; made suggestions and provided some guidance where it was deemed necessary, it fell to Allan after these meetings to communicate with all the contributors. This involved letters and phone discussions to discuss with them the content of our joint meetings, and dealing with any of the concerns or issues arising.

On occasions this caused us concerns, especially when Allan as a white man (with his editor's role) had to ask Black women to make certain changes in their scripts. We would have preferred Tara to take on that role with women authors because of the inherent power in Allan's position. Interestingly, sometimes it was Tara's comments on the scripts which Allan found harder to discuss with women authors. This was because as a Black woman some of Tara's observations had a 'legitimacy' (to challenge or question) which Allan did not feel he had especially when the issue was one arising from Tara's experiences.

We are not saying that black people cannot be challenged by white people or vice - versa, only that it is difficult (for a white man in this case) to represent accurately the views born out of experiences of being a Black Woman. Interestingly, the roles changed at a later stage where Allan's views were expressed through Tara in discussion with mainly women contributors. This felt reasonably comfortable but pressurised due to the impending deadlines! We were to some extent consciously and unconsciously aware of the race and gender dynamics in our interaction with the contributors ('members'). In compiling this book we hoped that our practice in our interactions mirrored our understanding and writing on this subject, but it is only the 'members' who can judge if this was so!

It is a fine balance between being sensitive, enabling, encouraging, and at the same time having to give deadlines and directions which at times can be seen as disempowering. We hope overall that there was a sense of working together especially with the newer writers, despite the disappointment of not being able actually to meet face-to-face as a 'group'.

Impact on the co-workers

As a group develops the co-workers are often profoundly affected by the members and what they bring, and so it was with us. During the process of reading the drafts and giving the authors feedback we felt very involved in the material, and at times we were very touched by the struggles of various groups and by the commitment and skill of the workers engaged in the groupwork - whatever the context. It became very important to encourage some of the contributors to persevere to the final draft stage, and not just for the sake of the book. Reading and re-reading their scripts made us realise just how significant their work was for other groupworkers, but it was even more important to share the determination and commitment of their group members to improve/live their lives as well as they could in a range of settings and often oppressive conditions.

The final stage of some of the chapters coming in resembled in some ways the classic feeling of many co- workers where some members come through despite the odds (and as a result helped us develop and grow through their determination), whilst others managed to produce/contribute/deliver more easily, thus making things smoother for us. Others, despite cajoling, fell by the wayside and that too is the natural - though often painful - part of any group membership.

As co-editors we are left wondering what the final product could have looked like and how it might have shaped the final project differently had the original members all been able to stay on board? For example, we ended up with no papers by black male authors, and few about groups with male members.

Ending and evaluation

As the co-workers, coming to the end of this 'group's life, we do feel that many of our aims have been met. In this collection of groupwork with Black and minority ethnic groups, newer and more experienced writers/contributors have been enabled to find a forum to share their inspiring groupwork practice with a wider audience. The reader will find a range of practices with diverse groups of people in a variety of settings; all in different degrees attempting to find groupwork approaches which meet the needs of that specific group as effectively as possible. A number of practice and theory 'outcomes' and issues can be identified:

• The pervasiveness of racism and oppression

Although none of the papers focuses primarily on the influence of the organisational or political context, paper after paper provides 'evidence' of the oppressive and eurocentric nature of both the societal context of group members' lives, and of those organisations /institutions which impinge on them - including social agencies. For Black women, the oppression is often compounded by sexism. Sakinna Dickinson articulates very clearly the ways in which these macro forces disempower young Asian women, and the need for what she calls 'developmental groups' which create a climate in which the women can take control and shape their own lives within their own terms. She is developing a potential model for this type of group.

• The community 'in' the group

'Community' emerges in several of these papers as a crucial variable in the group process and method. This applies equally to Asian women's groups (Bijay Minhas, Gita Patel, Sakinna

Dickinson) whose members are embedded in their communities, and to refugee (Jeremy Woodcock) and Foreign National groups (Liz Hales, Liz Dixon) whose members have been separated - often violently - from their family and community.

All three papers on Asian women's groups illustrate how the community is in the group as a variable at least as important as each individual and the group itself. Workers need special skills (rarely mentioned in groupwork textbooks) both to link effectively with communities and their leaders, and to create a safe environment in the group in which members are able to disclose difficult personal matters e.g. abuse, in ways which do not undermine community membership.

• The centrality of culture
In the political discourse of the last 15 years, there has been an unfortunate and simplistic schism between racism and culture: to concentrate on one and not the other is to obliterate the lived experience of Black people and other minority ethnic groups. This applies equally to monocultural groups and multi-cultural groups, as is devastatingly illustrated in these pages. Sarah Cemlyn's paper on Gypsies and Travellers concludes that 'the denial of cultural validity is a central feature of the persecution of travellers' making the crucial point that the empowerment model paradigm needs developing to include the centrality of culture in the personal-political duality. In the international multicultural context, Paul Taylor stresses not only the centrality of communication and language but also of attitudes to authority and other cultural variables.

• Groupwork with refugees
Jeremy Woodcock's sensitive account of groupwork with refugees in a therapeutic setting gives us some insight into the skills, methodology and issues involved when working with a membership who have suffered horrendous trauma and fracture from family and cultural roots. Cooking food, telling their stories and physical movement are some of the ways of communicating when there is no common language.

• 'Foreign nationals'
Foreign nationals are a hidden though substantial part of the male and female prison population in certain prisons in England. This name is given to men and women from other countries

(particularly in West Africa and South America) who are remanded or convicted in prison for offences concerned with drug smuggling, and who are eligible for deportation.

The papers by Liz Hales and Liz Dixon (on Wormwood Scrubs and Holloway prisons respectively) outline key factors in groupwork with this prisoner population, one of the most important being contact in the group with representatives of immigrant, legal and other outside organisations. The Holloway group demonstrated the power of the group to effect change in the institution by consciousness raising and facilitating the quite exceptional early release of a woman prisoner on compassionate grounds.

• Black user groups

It was not possible to include papers on groupwork with the whole range of Black user groups, but the one by Juliet Amoa, on work with people with learning difficulties - well illustrates both the struggles and the potential of such a group. The struggles included having to 'educate' a 'white' agency about the staffing needs of the group, and the potential is seen in the group exchanges about being Black and disabled.

• Groupwork and Black men

Most of the groups discussed in this book are groups for Black and other women from minority groups, and most of the writers are Black and white women. We did not plan it that way, and we know that important groupwork with Black men facilitated by Black men goes on, albeit on a much smaller scale. This unwanted and unintended marginalisation of Black men in the book, flags up an important 'Race and Groupwork' practice and theory area for urgent attention.

• Black/white worker relations

This issue resonates in several papers, and is the main focus in Aileen Alleyne's account of her training work with 'mixed' staff groups, using a psychodynamic methodology. It is approached from a different more structural perspective in our own paper on black/white co-working, and also in our brief process examination above of the significance of our Black woman/white man co-authorship relationship for ourselves and for its perception by others. In Judith Lee and colleagues' paper they frankly examine their own struggle as a multiracial staff group not only with race issues, but also the intersecting issues of class and sexual orientation oppressions.

• Black/white workers and training

The contributions well illustrate that all workers need, and should be engaged in anti-oppressive practices across the range of oppressions. However, what becomes apparent in some papers (in the context of race/ethnicity at least) is that being workers from the same/similar ethnic group does not necessarily equip the worker for all the skills required either as a groupworker or in some cases as an 'anti-racist'. All workers need the opportunity to develop their knowledge and skill base through staff development, training and regular supervision and, where appropriate, consultancy. Similarly, white workers working with a range of Black and minority ethnic groups have important training needs which in the climate of financial cuts, need to be safeguarded.

The above key points, and the many others evident when studying the papers in this book, all indicate the need for the parameters of social groupwork practice-theory to be reworked if they are to be responsive to the needs of group memberships from minority ethnic groups and those who facilitate such groups. We are not offering a new model or panacea, but we are saying that those working with 'Race and Groupwork', and their organisations, can learn much from this book about the need to create facilitating environments which take seriously racism, culture, community and oppression. The authors come with differing perspectives, experiences and backgrounds ,some which the readers will agree or identify with and others which we hope will stimulate further discussion and debates.

We thank our author colleagues for their inspiring accounts of their work, which offer hope and pointers for effective groupwork with disempowered 'Black' women and men. As with any group ending there is sadness that the project and certain bonds formed through the shared work have come to an end, coupled with expectation that the struggle has not and will not be in vain.

Groupwork with 'Mixed Membership' Groups: Issues of Race and Gender

ALLAN BROWN AND TARA MISTRY

This subject is beset with contentious definitional problems, and we start therefore with an attempt to clarify our use of terminology in this paper. By 'mixed' we mean a group membership with a composition which includes black and white people and/or women and men. Our use of the term 'black' is that used quite commonly in the political context in Britain to refer to people from those ethnic groups whose skin colour attracts a racist response in a predominantly white society. We are aware that in the USA 'black' refers to African-Americans and not to other ethnic groups, for example Hispanic or Indian. For clarity in the major argument we shall retain the inclusive term 'black', but when the occasion requires it - for example when cultural difference rather than racism is the issue - we shall refer to specific ethnic groupings.

'Sex' and 'gender' tend to be used interchangeably in the groupwork literature (as in Garvin and Reed, 1983). We shall use sex to refer to the biologically determined differences between women and men, and gender to refer to the socially constructed meanings associated with female and male. By 'anti-oppressive' we mean practice which in Philipson's words '...works to a model of empowerment and liberation and requires a fundamental rethinking of values, institutions and relationships' (1992, p.15). This paper concentrates on the in-group dimension of anti-oppressive practice. We are in full agreement with Breton's view that '...the times are such that social workers cannot afford the luxury of looking only at what goes on inside groups' (1991, p.46), but think that in-group anti-oppressive practice is an essential starting point for social groupworkers.

There are of course unfortunately many other oppressions besides those associated with race and gender. We have selected these because of their centrality in our own experience and understanding, and because we believe that many of the points made in this paper transfer directly to other oppressions in the social microcosm of the group. Our view is that ranking oppressions in order of hierarchical importance is itself an oppressive action, and we recognise that each oppression merits analysis in its own right.

There have been several theoretical, conceptual and ideological developments in the last decade, in Britain and in North America, which form the background to the rationale for this paper.

The sex and 'race' of groupworkers and group members has a profound effect on group behaviour and process
Although there is some disagreement on precisely what some of these effects are, there is overwhelming evidence from research to support the contention that there are major effects. Davis and Proctor (1989) combed the research literature exhaustively and produced substantial evidence of the salience of both race and gender in groups. Garvin, Reed and colleagues (1983), in a special issue of this journal on gender and groupwork, demonstrated the pervasiveness of gender influence on the differential experience of men and women in same-sex and mixed groups. In one of the few studies that examines the intersection of gender and race in leadership in groups, Brower et al. (1984) conclude '...the gender and ethnicity of the groupworker (and all leaders) have an impact on group situations that may be of equal force to the variables we customarily seek to affect such as programme , leadership technique, group composition, and so forth' (p.147). In Britain, practice-based articles refer to the powerful influence of race and gender on group process and the feelings of the workers and the members (see Rhule, 1988; Mistry, 1989, both articles by black women practitioners).

Groups are a social microcosm of the wider society
For some time we have thought of a small group as a social microcosm, on the basis that any small group will replicate the social-structural-political status and power relationships that are evident in the wider society (see Brown, 1992, p.154). This view is based not only on research-based theory, but equally on our own separate and shared experiences as a black woman and white man in numerous 'mixed' groups. It was therefore with much interest that we recently read Shapiro's article 'The social work group as social microcosm' (1990) and noted his views on

the implications for group practice.

In his paper Shapiro conceptualises group members as entering a group, each with her or his own personal/social frame of reference. The effects of this are analysed on the two dimensions 'Familiarly/Stranger' (inclusion and intimacy) and 'Horizontal/ Vertical' (status and power), with group members experiencing society as both their in-group and external environment. Shapiro envisages group formation as the intersection of these individual frames of reference, and goes on to say:

> Social groupworkers have a particular responsibility - and opportunity - to help members engage sensitively with both the content and context of their frames of reference and, through this engagement, to shape the structure and development of their own group as a 'person/group/structure-sensitive' task (p.18).

We find Shapiro's conceptualisation helpful, but it does not address explicitly the 'fit' between different member's socially determined frames of reference. For example, part of the black person's frame of reference is that they experience living each day in a racist society controlled by white people, and the white person's frame of reference takes for granted their superior status and power as a white person in relation to black people and all those from minority ethnic groups. Similarly, the social microcosm frame of reference of the woman group member is likely to be infused with her experience of male oppression, and that of her male counterpart in the group to be based on a gendered view of the roles and relative power of men and women in the wider society (but see later comments on the positions of black men and white women in relation to sexism in a white patriarchal society).

This 'fit' between socially determined frames of reference is fundamental to the evolution of both group content and process. The latter will reflect the external oppressive dynamic unless the worker's perspectives and interventions are specifically designed to develop and nurture an 'alternative' culture of empowerment.

There is widespread evidence of the efficacy of same-sex and same-race groups for women and black people, respectively

The groupwork literature is replete with accounts of the advantages of same-sex groups for women, at least when the group task is associated with issues of personal identity, social oppression and empowerment. In addition to the research-based work of Garvin and Reed (1983) and Davis and Proctor (1989), there are other recent publications (for example Home, 1991; Butler and Wintram, 1991) emphasising the strengths of women-only groups. Home makes a very convincing argument that for women to experience groups which can combine both personal and political change, they need to be without men. She supports this by demonstrating how in community work groups men have often assumed leadership and control, and been dismissive of women's concerns, for example about child care and violence, as 'private matters'. The men have a 'macho' ethos emphasising ends and not means, using 'male' language, and a group culture which is antithetical to the collective decision-making, power-sharing model generally preferred by women.

In *Feminist Groupwork*, Butler and Wintram (1991) have drawn extensively on their experiences of groupwork in two English Social Services Departments with socially/politically disadvantaged, isolated and oppressed women. They demonstrate how the groups focused on women's understanding of themselves and their experiences, and how feminist groupwork can lead to potentially liberating interpretations with profound consequences for participants' lives and social actions. To have had any men in this type of group would have been both a contradiction and counter-productive.

Research (see Garvin and Reed, 1983) suggests that whereas women are frequently disadvantaged in mixed groups because their needs tend to get subordinated to those of men (the social microcosm again), men often prefer and actively benefit from being in mixed groups. One reason for this differential experience is that the presence of women is 'used' by men, often unconsciously, to enable them to be more expressive and in touch with their feelings than they normally can be in groups of men. We say normally because there are now some men's groups which are specifically designed to facilitate men working at their own issues. Some of these are consciousness-raising and to facilitate expression of feeling and caring as an alternative to the competitive status-conscious ethos that typically prevails in all male groups (Sternbach, 1990; McLeod and Pemberton, 1987). Other men's groups focus directly on male violence and aggression (Canton et al., 1992).

Turning to race, the formal evidence (Davis and Proctor, 1989) is less extensive, but points in the same direction: that for many purposes an all-black or ethnic-specific group is both preferred by black members, and more productive, certainly when issues of racial identity, racism and culture are central to the task. Other sources of 'evidence' in Britain include: the campaign to create black sections in the Labour Party; the establishment of 'black only' organisations of social workers and probation officers; and support groups for black social work students on qualifying courses.

The views of white people about respective membership of all white and mixed race groups are not well documented, and probably vary in different contexts. Our experience in social work training is that white students tend to favour 'mixed' groups 'to learn from each other', whereas black students accept mixed groups for general learning purposes but prefer their own groups when racism and white oppression are likely to be high on the agenda.

The message from this research and practice 'evidence' suggests that the grouping of choice, in many circumstances and for many purposes, for women is women-only groups, and for black people is black-only groups. Two points follow from this. First, in order to meet both gender and race criteria, we are talking about four types of preferred group composition for black people and women: homogeneous groups of white women, black women, black men and white men respectively. Within the black population as defined inclusively, the choice between black groups of mixed sex, black men's groups, black women's groups and gender-specific/ethnic specific groups (e.g. Chinese women or Jamaican men) will depend on group purpose, political perspectives and cultural traditions. Secondly, the positions of black men and white women, who are both at one level oppressor and oppressed, should not be thought of as symmetrical - as we explain below.

In practice there will be some situations where workers are in a position to influence 'mixed or not' decisions about how group services are offered, and they need to take into account the above points. There will also, however, be numerous situations where lack of resources, the context, and/or the task, result in groups of mixed composition, by race or sex or both.

Composition is often, and quite properly, not controlled either by groupworkers or group members (for example in small residential units, and groups whose membership is self-selecting from advertisement). Furthermore, to exclude someone from a group on grounds of their race or sex when no alternative is available because of a resources deficit, and/or when they themselves wish to be a member (and many women and black people prefer to be in mixed groups), can be both oppressive and discriminatory.

Social action groups and empowerment

In recent years there has been a resurgence of interest in social action groupwork on both sides of the Atlantic. As stated earlier, Breton (1990, 1991) has strongly asserted that it is no longer good enough for social groupworkers to concentrate on empowerment within the group, for example when working with disempowered disadvantaged women. She argues that internal process must be coupled with an external agenda of collective social action - for example in alliance with community groups - not only by group members but also by groupworkers.

In Britain, Mullender and Ward (1991), with other colleagues, have developed a model of *Self-Directed Groupwork* which as the name suggests is predicated on group members being in charge of their own group agenda and process, with help from a group facilitator. The group task is to identify agendas external to the group in which the members have a common interest. Empowerment is developed as the groupwork method as well as being the underlying principle.

These social action approaches being developed by Breton, Mullender and Ward, and others, understandably tend to play down the importance of group process relative to the external goals of the group. However, as we think those authors would agree, attention to process is integral to successful goal achievement. It would indeed be ironic to have an oppression-ridden group seeking anti-oppressive external goals! Many social action groups will by definition have homogeneous membership and their process falls outside the terms of reference of this paper. Many other social action groups are, however, of mixed race and/or sex composition, requiring the careful attention to internal group process suggested here.

The intersection of race and gender in groups

A further complexity already anticipated is the interaction of race and gender issues in the same group. There is not much on this important subject in the groupwork literature, and we do not have space to make more than one or two points here.

One of the issues is the potential and actual conflict that can occur between these two oppressions. Many black women reacted critically to the white dominated feminist movement in the earlier days when it was demonstrably racist in its 'white assumption' and failure to address the racism which is central to the experience of all black women. The positions of black women and white men can in one respect be distinguished from those of black men and white women. For the former the oppressed/ oppressor dimensions point in the same direction, whereas for the later they are in opposing directions. Thus in a group composed entirely of white men and black women the dynamic is clearer than in a group with white women and black men. It is interesting to note that in the research of Brower et al. (1987) into (white) group member reactions to leaders of varying ethnicity and sex, there was more positive feedback about their experience of black women and white men leaders than either black men or white women leaders.

It would however be a mistake to treat the oppression position of black men and white women as symmetrical in Britain and North America. As Day (1991, p.19) records, black women writers (Carby, 1982; hooks, 1982) have pointed out that the dominance of black men cannot be equated with the dominance of white men because only the latter is part of the patriarchal-capitalist inheritance. Day goes on to say that black women are not denying that black men are sexist, but that some black women identify their position as one where they 'struggle together with black men against racism, while we also struggle with black men, about sexism' (in Day, quoted from Carby, 1982).

Anti-oppressive groupwork

Anti-oppressive groupwork is about feelings as well as ideology and theoretical formulations. Inevitably much of the groupwork literature (with notable exceptions, see Rhule, 1988) on race and gender in groups is theoretical and objectified and does not begin to communicate the strength of personal feeling that for all of us surrounds the issues of race and gender. It is therefore very important when developing a mixed-group practice methodology to 'keep alive' these deep-rooted feelings in both workers and members (see, for example, Brummer and Simmonds' reference to the hatred associated with racism, 1992) - though not to the point where the group climate becomes disabling and dysfunctional.

SUMMARY

There is extensive evidence that the structurally determined oppressions of racism and sexism are replicated as a powerful dynamic in small groups of 'mixed' membership. For this reason, among others, there are many group purposes which, for women and black people and others from minority ethnic groups, are best served in homogeneous 'not-mixed' groups. There are also numerous groups, including some social action groups, whose composition, whether by choice or circumstance, is mixed racially and/or by sex.

We shall now therefore consider some of the practice principles and methodology which are essential if groupwork is to counteract the replication of social oppression in the small group, and facilitate the empowerment of all group members.

PRACTICE PRINCIPLES FOR ANTI-OPPRESSIVE GROUPWORK

The familiar 'good practice' groupwork principles go some way towards an anti-oppressive approach, but they mostly do not incorporate the implications of the group as social microcosm. They underestimate - or more likely ignore - the reality that, in a 'mixed' group, members enter the group inequal in power, structurally and interpersonally. The homeostatic assumption of systems theory does not allow for these structural inequalities. Anti-oppressive practice demands not only specific worker actions towards equalising the power and position of group members, but constant awareness and vigilance to ensure a consistent approach to all aspects of the groupwork process. In what follows we have necessarily been selective in our choice of which worker activities to concentrate on to illustrate the approach.

Agency context

While it is possible to work anti-oppressively with a group in an oppressive agency setting, this contradiction makes it both stressful and problematic. Workers who are empowered themselves by an agency which is serious about equality and shared decision-making, are in a much better position to facilitate the empowerment of those with whom they work. For disadvantaged and disempowered potential group members, their perception of how the agency regards them will be a crucial factor in whether or not they seek to join a group (see Breton, 1991).

Group composition and structure

The general principles governing group composition for members have been well rehearsed elsewhere (Bertcher and Maple, 1977), and we have already discussed the importance of the initial decision on mixed/non-mixed membership. In mixed groups, a 'balanced' group membership (for example at least four black members in a group of ten) makes an enormous difference to the potential for an anti-oppressive dynamic. Conversely, the singleton member is prone to marginalisation and stereotyping, and the worker needs to take action both inside and outside the group to create conditions which offer that member equal opportunity in the group.

Worker composition is an issue that attracts surprisingly little attention in the literature. The case for two workers is particularly strong in mixed groups (see Brown, 1992, chapter 3). As a general principle it is helpful to a minority group member to have at least one worker of similar sex and/or ethnicity. There is also the opportunity for the two workers to model an anti-oppressive, equal relationship between a man and a woman and/or between a black and white person. In 'Black/white co-working in groups' (Mistry and Brown, 1991) these issues are examined in more detail, including the severe resource limitations on choice of workers.

The preparation stage
As in all groupwork, careful preparation is the essence of good anti-oppressive practice. Five aspects of preparation are particularly relevant:

1. a location for the group which offers equal access to the group for all members;
2. a group programme which is at least in part negotiable, which in both content and methods does not replicate the dominant ethos of the wider society; and which is reflective of all members' cultural perspectives and interests;
3. ground rules which incorporate anti-oppressive principles about relationships and behaviour in the group;
4. worker(s) preparation;
5. preparing responses to oppressive/discriminatory behaviour.

The last two are now considered in more detail.

The personal preparation of workers (especially men and white people) undertaking groupwork with groups of mixed membership is essential. Theoretical understanding is necessary, but needs to be integrated with experiential learning which requires the worker to examine his/her own history and attitudes, and make a self-assessment of what he/she needs to do (for example for a white man to listen to what women and black people are saying about their experience, and for a black woman to learn how to cope with the feelings evoked by racism/sexism in the group).

With two co-workers, male/female and or black/white, the usual preparation for working together (see Hodge, 1985) takes on the additional dimension of acknowledging the significance of socially determined inequality in the relationship (Mistry and Brown, 1991). Especially in a new partnership, there is much work to do in honest sharing of feelings about working together, and discussing the implications of co-working with a mixed membership group. Sometimes a consultant's questions are needed to facilitate co-worker communications: for example, 'what feelings and anxieties do you, a white/black person, have about working with a black/white colleague in a group in which racism may surface?' The pair need to work out together how they can organise themselves as a partnership in a way that neither perpetuates oppression nor overcompensates for it. Examples of the latter are when a male worker takes less than his equal share of responsibility in the group through fear of being seen as replicating the dominant male stereotype; or when a white co-worker is unable to query a black partner's actions for fear of being seen as racist.

The other preparation issue is anticipating how to respond in the group if and when sexism or racism - or indeed other oppressive behaviour - occurs. It is clear that the worker(s) will have to be active and interventionist, particularly in the early stages, in affirming an anti-oppressive approach. Overt racist or sexist behaviour is sometimes easier to deal with than the subtler forms of oppression, just because it is so obviously unacceptable - though often very painful. An example of one of the subtler forms of oppression is the gradual domination, often unconsciously, by men/white people of group interaction and decision-making, in the process marginalising the contributions of women/black group members. With 'mixed' co-workers, the man/white person carries particular responsibility for challenging oppressive behaviour, whether obvious or subtle, and not leaving it to the woman or black person to be the one who exposes the oppressive behaviour. All these issues need discussion in the pair as part of preparation, with the expectation of revision according to what actually happens in the group.

Anti-oppressive work in the group: saying, being and doing

From the moment the group first meets, the worker(s) needs to start establishing an empowering anti-oppressive climate based on trust. How they do this will vary to some extent according to the particular group model and purpose. Certain tangible steps on approach to programme, ground rules, and the co-working relationship, have already been mentioned. However, though what the worker says is always important, the membership is likely to be influenced much more by how it is said, and even more by what they observe of the worker's non-verbal behaviour - his or her being and doing.

For example, for a male worker to make 'impressive' anti-sexist ground rule statements in the group, and then proceed to develop an alliance with the male members, tacitly rewarding their tendency to dominate the group, is simply to replicate the social microcosm effect of male dominance. Similarly, for a white worker to emphasise verbally to the group the need to be anti-racist, and then, quite possibly unconsciously, to undermine their black co-worker colleague's equal status role, is oppressive and disempowering of her colleague and of other black members of the group. It is a not uncommon experience in staff groups with just one black member, for that person to find him/herself marginalised by a cultural dynamic which makes it difficult to participate to his/her full potential. This can happen where there is a genuine staff group commitment to an anti-oppressive policy, and may be exacerbated by associated factors to do with gender, class and part-time/temporary employment status.

Research (Davis and Proctor, 1989) and personal experience both suggest that mixed groups - especially those with a gender and race mix - are likely to 'import' distrustful attitudes from women/black people towards men/white people, born out of a life-time's experience of oppression. This challenges the worker(s) to take steps early on in the group to demonstrate their commitment to race and gender being high on the agenda. Some of the most important steps are quite difficult to articulate because they are less obvious. They include: communicating non-verbally and empathetically with individual members - particularly those in minority positions - through the kind of eye-contact that conveys recognition, awareness and feeling; being 'comfortable' in talking about, and the use of language about, race, gender, racism, sexism, and other oppressions; relating to a co-worker of different race or gender in a mutually respectful and equal way, without suggesting that anti-oppressive behaviour is only a matter of good personal relationships; being prepared to challenge, and not defend, oppressive agency policies and attitudes; listening to and validating what group members are saying and expressing non-verbally; being quite open about recognising power issues in the group, including professional power; being open and ready to acknowledge one's own oppressive or insensitive behaviour when this occurs; acknowledging the reality of the social conditions prevailing in group members' localities, and so on.

Another anti-oppressive practice skill is recognising and responding to the cultural diversity of members. This does not necessarily mean accepting, much less celebrating, some culture-based views (for example, religious beliefs that homosexual relations are 'abnormal'; the practice of genital mutilation). What it does mean is 'doing your homework' on the cultural perspectives of group members, and this includes class-based attitudes. Chau (1990) has made a major contribution to the literature on ethnicity, cultural difference and groupwork; and in the Hong Kong context, Pearson (1991), has drawn attention to some of the fundamental differences between Chinese culture and the ethnocentric cultural assumptions of much 'Western' groupwork practice-theory.

When workers have put their own anti-oppressive house in order, one of the most difficult tasks is knowing how to intervene when members are oppressive to one another in the group. The agreed ground rules provide a benchmark, but the worker(s) still has to make delicate judgements about when and how to intervene between members. As outlined elsewhere (Mistry and Brown, 1991) the tendency is for white and male workers, in respect of racism and sexism respectively, to prevaricate if not collude; whereas workers identified with the recipients of sexist/ racist behaviour often feel the pain and anger personally.

In both situations the challenge to the worker is to intervene in a way which is strong and unequivocal, yet without provoking an angry defensive response which exacerbates the situation and disempowers both the perpetrator and the 'victim'. Part of the skill is learning how to expose oppressive behaviour in a way which is not so confrontative that it creates a defensive reinforcing reaction. Wade and Macpherson (1992), who work with young male offenders in a day centre in Inner London, describe the dilemma they faced in approaching anti-racism, in a mixed race group, with working-class whites who feel themselves to be powerless and worse off than their black counterparts. After discovering that direct early confrontation which did not recognise white men's feelings was destructive to all concerned, they developed a gradualist approach which included some separate sessions for black and white men on racism and prejudice, and which later in the mixed group enabled a more considered discussion in which anti-racist peer challenges began to occur. As in groupwork practice generally, one way forward is to make the issue 'group business' in the hope that working it through - painful as that may be - can be a source of learning and empowerment for all group members.

Links with the external environment of the group

In mixed groups, with primarily internal aims, an important practice issue is how to link in-group anti-oppressive practice with the external oppressive reality of many group members' lives. A particularly effective way in which this can be achieved is when the group as a whole has contact with the outside world as an group outings and in activity groups.

Mistry has described elsewhere (1991) an example of the power of shared experience on a group outing. The occasion was a three day residential visit of nine group members (black and white women offenders) and their six children to a holiday camp. Mistry was the only worker able to go:

> One evening I attended a dance with other women in the group and we were set upon by white women holidaymakers. I was terrified, but the other black women (having always been on the receiving end of this type of behaviour) dealt with it in the most skilful way possible. It demonstrated to the white women in our group how racism worked against the black women... and much of this shared experience formed an important focus for group discussion in the next twelve months in the group (p.152).

Another way in which the internal/external links may develop is when in discussion of racism and sexism in the group, examples are shared of the external oppressive reality of group members' lives. This in turn may generate external agendas for individuals, the group as a collective, and/or the workers and the agency.

Consultation

We are well aware that it is much easier to write about anti-oppressive group practice than to do it! Anti-oppressive work is personally demanding, and evokes strong feelings in workers, whether black or white, male or female, associated with personal identity, emotional pain and past experience of oppressing and being oppressed. The sheer complexity and strength of feeling can confuse perceptions and practice judgements, and sessions with a consultant can be a great help, particularly for inexperienced workers and for 'mixed' co-workers (see Brown, 1988).

In choosing a consultant, not only is their general suitability and competence important, but also their race and sex, depending on that of the group members and groupworkers, and the purpose of the group. As a general principle, in mixed groups a black and/ or female consultant may be preferred, because they can provide both a support for black/female workers, and be more likely to recognise unconscious worker collusion with oppressive developments in the group.

A poignant example of the need for a same-race consultant is the account by Rhule (1988), a black woman groupworker, of a group for white women bringing up black (mixed parentage) children. Rhule co-worked with a white woman colleague, and was the only black person in the group. The oppressive racism of the women in the group was such that although she had a racially aware and supportive white colleague she desperately needed to talk through what she was experiencing, on a one-to-one basis with a black consultant - quite separate from any consultancy for the workers as a pair. In Britain there are real practical problems of finding and paying for suitable consultants in these kinds of situations.

FURTHER WORK

This article has taken an overview of issues of race and gender in groupwork, and discussed some of the ingredients of anti-oppressive practice in 'mixed' groups. What we have not done is broaden the framework to include and discuss the particularities of other oppressions, such as disablism and heterosexism, nor have we done more than touch on the complexities of the intersection of race and gender in groups. These are subjects meriting further papers in their own right.

This chapter was first published in Social Work with Groups *17(3), 1994.*

Black/White Co-Working in Groups

TARA MISTRY AND ALLAN BROWN

INTRODUCTION

The subject of black/white co-working would seem to be one of considerable importance in the theory and practice of social groupwork, yet the practitioner or student searching the groupwork literature for some guidance will almost certainly be disappointed. Why is there such a deafening silence on this topic? One explanation is that it is only in the last few years that the topic of 'race' has appeared at all seriously on the groupwork agenda. In Britain this may be partly because until quite recently there were very few black groupworkers and it has taken their presence in greater numbers to raise the consciousness of white workers about this issue. It may also be that the topic of black/white co-working is still considered by some to be unimportant (the 'colour-blind' approach), uninteresting, problematic or 'too hot to handle'. Whatever the explanation, there is undoubtedly a need to address the issue, which is the purpose of this paper.

Two points need to be made on terminology. In the literature and in practice parlance 'co-leadership' and 'co-working' are often used almost interchangeably, with co-working becoming the preferred contemporary term, at least in Britain. We use co-working here in recognition that all group members share the leadership. The second point is our use of the terms 'white' and 'black'. We are using them in the way they are generally used in the UK in political discussions about racism and related issues i.e. 'white' refers to the majority caucasian population in Britain, and 'black' to minority ethnic groups whose skin colour being 'non-white' results in them experiencing racism. In opting to use 'black' in this way, we are aware that it is an umbrella term for people from a wide range of different ethnic groups, cultures and traditions. For the main purpose of this article, black/white will suffice, but where the different ethnicities of non-white people in groups is central to the argument, the distinctions will be made.

In a recent USA text based on an exhaustive literature review, Davis and Proctor comment:

> Surprisingly, the issue of race and co-leadership has received almost no attention.... The absence of attention to race and co-leadership is even apparent in works that have been exclusively devoted to reviewing the literature on race and groupwork practice (Davis and Proctor, 1989, p.101).

To check this finding against the UK as well as the North American groupwork literature, our brief review has been divided into:

1. general groupwork texts;
2. the co-working/co-leadership literature;
3. the 'race and groupwork' literature.

General groupwork texts

Firstly a sample of established North American texts was examined. Yalom (1975), Garvin (1981) and Shulman (1984) make no mention of race and have very little to say on co-working. Balgopal and Vassil (1983) refer to institutional racism but not to race in the co-working relationship. Henry (1981) has a substantial section on co-working and refers to race as a major factor in co-worker composition.

Secondly, most of the major British texts were scrutinised. The majority of these (Douglas, 1976; Douglas, 1978; Whitaker, 1985; Heap, 1985; Benson, 1987; Preston-Shoot, 1987; Aveline and Dryden, 1988; Thompson and Kahn, 1988) make no significant mention of race or ethnicity in groupwork, although all to a greater or lesser extent address general issues of co-working/co-leadership in groups. Some do consider gender and co-working, but with an emphasis on role-models and psychological aspects, not on sexism and structural factors. Brown (1986) discusses race briefly in a section on group composition, but in his section on co-working he does no more than refer to race as one of a number of co-worker differences which may argue for having two workers. In Douglas's book on Group Living (1986) there are two pages on race (mostly based on 20 year old USA articles), but the co-leading section refers only to gender. Brown and Clough's edited book (1989) *Groups and Groupings: Life and Work in Day and Residential Centres* addresses the issue of race throughout the text, but nowhere is the significance of black/white co-working or indeed multiracial staff groups in those settings considered.

A volume edited by Triseliotis (1988), *Groupwork in Adoption and Foster Care,* does make significant reference to race and co-working in each of the three chapters on racial dimensions. Chapter Five on preparatory training groups for black foster parents notes that agency policy is now to have at least one black co-worker; that selection of 'co-leaders' is very important; and that with black/white co-workers it is essential to counteract any unconscious assumptions that authority and power rest with the white worker. An account of groupwork with black children in white foster homes (Chap 9) makes it clear that all the groupworkers were black, offering a range of black role-models for the children. The final chapter (14) on groupwork with white transracial foster parents comments that there were two black and one white co-workers, partly to meet 'the possibly stereotyped view' of white foster parents that 'all black social workers would be somehow against them'.

The co-working literature

An early special issue of the journal *Social Work with Groups* (1980) was devoted to the topic of 'co-leadership'. Much of the content is devoted to the pros and cons of co-working. In an otherwise excellent article by Galinsky & Schopler (1980) the only reference to race is in a section on co-leader composition (p61) when race is listed as one of a number of 'extrinsic' factors which are important in the matching of co-leaders. The best known British publication on co-working is Hodge's booklet *Planning for Co-leadership* (1985). Much of his material and guidelines offer general principles on co-working which are directly relevant to black/white co-working, but unlike gender, neither race nor ethnicity are mentioned. None of three articles in *Social Work with Groups* (Waldman, 1980; Starak, 1981; Shilkoff, 1983), which address co-working, mention race, although two address gender issues.

The 'race and groupwork' literature

Social Work with Groups published a special issue on 'Ethnicity in social groupwork practice' (Davis, 1984). Several of the articles in that issue, and two others in different issues of the same journal (Delgado, 1980; Freeman and McRoy, 1986), all address the racial composition of 'co-leadership' as an important practice issue. It may be significant that several of these authors are themselves black, and therefore people for whom 'race' is of ever present significance in their practice and their daily experience. In some minority ethnic groups an all-black leadership was preferred (e.g. Comaz-Diaz, 1984; Brown, J.A., 1984; Freeman and McRoy 1986), whereas others chose combined black/white, male/female pairings (e.g. Edwards and Edwards, 1984; Delgado and Siff, 1980). Delgado and Delgado (1984) reviewed the literature on groupwork with Hispanics and discovered a whole range of leadership and co-leadership patterns.

Several articles addressing race and groupwork issues have appeared in the journal *Groupwork* (Muston and Weinstein, 1988; Rhule, 1988: Mullender, 1988; Lebacq and Shah, 1989; Mistry, 1989). Muston and Weinstein suggest that in a racially mixed group there needs to be black/white co-workers. Rhule, a black worker who co-worked with a white colleague in a group for white women with black children, focusing on anti-racist child-rearing, makes some telling points about her experiences as the only black person in that group. She emphasises the need for black consultancy, and speculates on whether in this type of group there should be two black and one white co-workers. Lebacq and Shah, who co-worked with an ethnically mixed group of sexually abused children of both sexes, stress the value to the children of seeing black and white adults working together on an equal basis. Mistry reflects on her co-working experience with a white woman colleague in a multi-racial women's probation group, commenting on the complexity of the mix of class, gender and race, and her identification with her colleague as another woman probation officer, but also with the black working class women in the group.

Conclusions from the literature review

This survey confirms that, with a few exceptions, Davis and Proctor's comment (1989, p.101) on the absence of writing on black/white co-working is true for the UK as well as the USA.

PRACTICE EXPERIENCE

(Note: In this section we are referring to the UK context which is the one we know best and the one from which we draw most of our experience. We appreciate that circumstances are different in other parts of the world, although we find it difficult to envisage any society in which some form of racism is not a factor in groupwork.)

Reflection on the practices and experiences of black co-workers over the last ten years highlights some very interesting but complex factors along with some of the pain and angst which accompanies that type of reflection. Many black co-workers have been involved in leading all white groups with a white co-worker, where issues of race and racism have arisen. Often the black worker was left either to challenge this unsupported, or where the white worker's lack of awareness on race and gender issues was such that the black worker has had to put up with intolerable experiences in the name of groupwork! In the earlier days of groupwork, inexperience and lack of training was an additional burden for black workers especially as the use of black consultants was such a rare occurrence (particularly in areas where black workers were and still are a small minority). In our experience, this is still an issue in various parts of Britain.

Our view is that a black/white co-worker pairing is usually desirable where the group is racially mixed and there are potential benefits associated with joint working. However, the reader's own ideological perspective on race and racism will affect his/her views on the general acceptability or otherwise of black/white co-working whether with mixed, all-white or all-black groups. For example, in Britain some black people hold a political perspective which questions the acceptability of black/white co-working under any circumstances.

The complexities arising from different types of groups with a variety of clientele, structure, functions and focus pose challenges for co-workers. For example, race issues for co-workers and group members are very different where the focus of the group is anti-racism compared to groups with a focus on some other specific topic, say coping with addiction. Similarly, co-working with children or adolescents raises issues which are different from work with adults. The interesting interplay of race and gender issues further complicates the co-working relationship. We shall briefly return to 'cross cutting factors' such as age, gender, voluntary/statutory, culture, ethnicity, mixed/same race membership, at the end of this section.

We shall now focus primarily on the black/white co-working experience and the basic dilemmas, principles and issues which may arise and need special attention. Much of this is gleaned from the experiences of the authors as black and white co-workers (mostly not with each other) in social work agencies and educational establishments. Some comments are also drawn from discussion with social work colleagues about their experiences.

To explore the dynamics of the co-working relationship, we have selected two basic aspects of groupwork: focus and structure. For each of these aspects two different kinds of groups are identified for illustrative purposes. We shall firstly compare the significance for black/white co-working of groups whose primary focus is on anti-racism per se with those which have a very different main focus - for example, caring for others, anger management, social skills, or sexual abuse - but in which issues of race and racism nevertheless arise. For the second aspect, group structure, we shall examine some of the differences for black/white co-workers when working with highly structured closed membership groups for example, offending behaviour groups, as compared with unstructured often open membership groups, e.g. women's groups concerned with mutual support and empowerment.

FOCUS

Groups with a focus on anti-racism

The contrasting experience of (generally) white people as perpetuators of racism and black people as recipients means that these two racial groups have very different needs, perspectives and agendas when anti-racism is the main focus. For this reason separate groups with an all-white or all-black membership are usually preferred. All-black anti-racism groups normally have black co-workers, but all-white groups may have black/black, white/white or black/white pairings. We shall now consider the black/white co-working issues in an all-white membership anti-racism group, highlighting particularly the pressures on the black worker. To illustrate the different experience for black workers we shall also consider all black anti-racism groups with black co-workers.

Black / white co-workers in a white membership anti-racism group

1. Black workers may have a higher status because it is assumed that they will have specialist knowledge and validation of personal experience of racism.
2. The black worker can be an object of anger if the group is challenged or feels threatened.
3. If the black co-worker has an assertive style members may see this as a positive or negative trait depending on their

experience and interpretation.

4. If the black worker has a 'laid back' style or is fairly inexperienced, white members may see their presence as a token gesture to bring in a black worker because of their colour and not for their expertise.

5. The white worker may be seen as deferring to the black co-worker if group members feel that the white worker is playing a passive role.

6. If both workers share a common understanding of the structural and political context of racism they are likely to be able to demonstrate a consistent model of co-working. Conversely if there are major political differences the group may attempt to use this to divide the workers who will then experience a 'battering'.

7. Some white workers are able to take risks and challenge the members. Others tend to leave this responsibility inappropriately to their black colleague. The extent to which members challenge each other varies in different groups and over the life of a group.

8. Our experience suggests that where white/black co-workers have established their relationship over some time, they are more successful in countering the membership's possible testing out of the positive co-working partnership they are modelling.

Black / black co-workers in a black membership anti-racism group

1. Black workers are often viewed in a very positive light by black group members because they are seen to understand the position of black participants not only in the group but also in the wider society.

2. The co-working relationship improves with previous shared experiences just as it does with black/white co-working; if co-working is not shared equally or one worker takes on a dynamic radical role, the other worker may become less 'visible' and feel sidelined.

3. Black groups will have a greater commitment to explore the effects of racism on their performance and will want to ensure that they leave with some useful strategies for coping; this (usually) makes the co-working relationship a very constructive experience.

4. If the group has a mixed ethnic composition (e.g. Afro-Caribbean/ Asian) and the ethnic mix of the co-workers reflects these differences, an affinity often develops between

group members and the co-worker who shares the same ethnic background. This ethnic mix can then be a positive rather than a negative experience for all the group members, especially if the co-workers model a united relationship in the struggle against racism. Where co-workers are of the same ethnic origin but the black membership is of mixed ethnic composition, the programme content and exercises need to be ethnically sensitive: otherwise those of different ethnicity will feel their needs have been marginalised.

In anti-racism groups, perhaps not surprisingly, black co-working relationships in groups for black members tend to produce a more satisfying experience than black/white co-working with white groups. However, in both contexts the usual groupwork co-working issues, such as shared values and compatible styles, apply (see Hodge, 1985).

Groups whose main focus is not anti-racism
When the focus of the group programme is not anti-racism but another topic such as being a foster-parent, black/white co-workers in mixed groups face some of the issues already identified for anti-racism groups, but also others arising from the fact that race is not the 'official' topic.

1. The co-workers may or may not be aware of the interplay between structural racism which gets imported into the group, and the main topic. The effects of this will disadvantage the black members unless it is anticipated, addressed and counteracted in both group content and process.
2. When, as quite often happens, the black worker is the only one to identify these issues, for example the needs of a black child in a transracial fostering arrangement, or racism in the stereotyping of black males' propensity towards violence in an anger management group, the significance of racism is likely to be marginalised and the black co-worker will likewise be marginalised as 'only being interested in the race issue'.
3. Often the issue of how far to challenge the introduction of racist stereotypes or unrelated racist comment in the group raises interesting discussions. Our experience is that white co-workers tend to talk about the choice whereas for black co-workers there is no choice but to challenge in the group - although different black workers have developed different methods of approach.

STRUCTURE

Highly structured groups

When groups are very structured the membership is usually closed and focused on a specific task. In statutory agencies, for example the probation service, the task of structured groups is frequently concerned with seeking some behavioural change like tackling offending behaviour, or with an educational purpose as in alcohol education groups. In these examples the controlling power of a state agency with its dominant values and culture can be an influential factor, and the co-workers - both black and white - are likely to conform with the values embodied in the set group programme or 'package'. Somewhere in the programme there may be a space for considering racism and its effect on black individuals in the group, but this is often peripheral to the main social control and/or educational purpose.

There are several factors to consider in the black/white co-working relationship in structured groups with a racially mixed membership:

1. The structured style and programme content will help both workers to share the task of co-working more equally - often because it is pre-planned.
2. The difficulties for co-workers may be in how to allocate group space between the primary task of the group with its set programme, and the process issues such as 'race' which may arise and need urgent attention. Structure is sometimes used positively to ensure important matters like race are on the agenda, but often a highly structured and planned content can serve as a protection against opening up the wider more difficult issues. Co-workers do not always have a shared understanding about 'diverting' from the main task to confront race issues.
3. For the black co-worker and black group members in a mixed race group a highly structured format often causes frustration when debate is stifled. An example of this in a group on offending behaviour is the exclusion of the structural and black perspective needed for understanding how black and white people are treated differentially in the criminal justice system.

Unstructured groups

In an 'unstructured' group where the membership is more likely to be open, and the aims and objectives of the group to be supportive and empowering (e.g. women's groups), and where there are no pre-planned programme topics, issues of race and racism are more likely to be exposed and to surface in all sorts of ways. In these groups co-working style and relationship are more central and instant because co-workers need to respond flexibly to often unforeseen issues as they arise.

1. For black and white co-workers there can be areas of shared experience as, for example, in a women's group where gender, socialisation, relationships, motherhood, class and oppression can bind the female co-workers and group members together. However the additional dimension of race may need responses which white workers may be unable to deliver. In unstructured groups the ascribed power and control of the co-workers may be secondary to what emerges in group process, so the level of understanding the white workers have about racism will be of central importance. In the example of a mixed women's group the white female co-worker needs to understand the position of black women in the wider society and how that is reflected in the co-working relationship with her black colleague, even though their gender is the same.

2. In an unstructured group setting where the focus is on support and empowering, our experiences indicate that both workers may develop quite a close bond with the group members and with each other. Whether due to some shared experiences or other affinity, this intimacy and sharing may lead to some collusion in the co-working relationship which may make challenging the racism or prejudice which surfaces harder for both white and black workers.

Having explored some of the particular co-working issues associated with differences in group focus and structure, it is apparent that some issues are common to all types and structures of group whereas others are specific to a particular focus and degree of structure. In this rather simplistic and crude formulation there are however a number of quite complex cross-cutting factors which have not been explored. Gender has already been mentioned, but when the gender and race dimensions in black/white co-working with mixed race groups are combined with other important variables like open/closed, adults/adolescents/children, ethnicity, statutory/voluntary agencies, 'client' based/community based orientation, we are faced with more complex co-working group process issues.

For example, Tara has had the experience of being a black female co-worker of Asian origin running a mixed gender group for black (African-Caribbean) and white adolescents with a white male co-worker using a semi-structured group programme! Not surprisingly this experience produced all kinds of co-working issues, including the following:

1. Reproduction of sexist stereotypes in the way the black woman worker became more dominant in discussion based sessions and the white worker more dominant in activity based sessions.
2. Group members dividing the co-workers on gender and racially, thus isolating them from each other. This is especially likely where the ethnicity of the black female co-worker is different from that of the black members.
3. Issues of adolescent behaviour/acting out were confused at times with racial/gender issues. The white male worker needs to be particularly aware of how racism and sexism occur with adolescents.
4. It is difficult if not impossible to deal with all these permutations with just two workers of different race and gender. Should there be say four workers modelling a variety of perspectives, styles, views and behaviour?

Whatever the context, our experience is that major demands will always be made on black co-workers especially if they are women and the group membership is predominantly male. We have only been able to touch briefly on cross-cutting factors in this paper, but note that for the co-workers each combination of factors produces its own challenges which can only be responded to effectively when both workers have sufficient awareness of race, class, gender and other forms of discrimination.

Drawing on the experiences and issues outlined in this section we now suggest some guidelines for black/white co-working practice.

PRACTICE GUIDELINES

If the general principles for good co-working practice are followed (as in Hodge, 1985) these will cover many of the points to be considered in black/white co-working. Rather than reiterate these and then add on points particular to black/white co-working, we will suggest our own practice guidelines for the latter in the awareness that many of them are no more than the application of good co-working practice. We appreciate that some of the guidelines which follow may appear idealistic to workers in teams which are under-staffed, under-resourced and overworked, but it seems to us essential to start with high standards in the knowledge that these sometimes have to be compromised for reasons beyond the control of the practitioner.

The decision to work together

There are three decisions to be taken: whether to have one, two or more workers; whether a black/white pairing is appropriate; and whether a particular pair of black and white colleagues are personally compatible for working together. Assuming that co-working is preferred, decisions about a black/white pairing are likely to depend on the composition and purpose of the group.

The essential task of testing for co-worker compatibility is particularly important for black/white co-working. Of the various factors listed by Hodge (1985) as 'conditions necessary for effective co-leadership', four are particularly relevant here: congruence on theory, values and practice principles; the nature of each worker's authority vis-a-vis the other; ability to deal with conflict; and risktaking with regard to self-disclosure. If the two workers do not have previous experience of co-working together they will have a lot of checking out to do, and may need the help of a third person. For example if one of them has a worked out anti-racist perspective and expects race and racism to be central issues in their work together, and the other sees these as peripheral taking the view that 'the important thing is that we get on well together and have good group skills', this is likely to be a contraindication for co-working unless there is mutual acceptance of these fundamental differences, and race issues are unlikely to be a major factor in the group. If the group members are all white and the white co-worker does not understand the expressed need of her black colleague to have a black consultant for herself this is also likely to be a contra-indication. A readiness and ability to talk about the race dimension in the co-working relationship is a prerequisite.

Preparation for co-working

Having established that there is a sound basis for working together and having agreed to do so, the next stage is preparation. The 'usual' discussion about how to work together, including sharing responsibilities in and out of the group, sharing feelings and values relevant to the group and its purpose, and so on, needs to be permeated by preparation for the race dimension in both the co-working and the groupwork. For example what ground rules to have on racism, how racism will be responded to in the group, how to respond to any attempts by group members to cast the white worker as the 'senior partner', how to respond to any attempts to divide and split the co-workers, and explicit agreement that in consultation/review sessions race as a component of the co-working relationship and the group process will be regularly discussed.

Consultation arrangements

In our view consultancy is nearly always a potential benefit for co-workers and their groupwork, and one of us has discussed this elsewhere (Brown, A., 1984; 1988). The arguments for consultation, whether outside or inside supervision (see Manor, 1989), become increasingly strong when the workers are inexperienced and in unstructured groups where process is especially important. Also, when there are potentially difficult race issues which co-workers may find almost impossible to discuss without the facilitation skills of a third person. In black/white co-working two other factors arise. The first is whether a black or white consultant is preferred, and the second is whether in addition to consultancy for the co-worker pair, individual consultancy, probably from another consultant, is needed for one or both of the workers.

The type and purpose of the group will be crucial. Whether the membership is racially mixed, all black or all white, a black consultant may be preferred because of incipient racism and to counteract the tendency of the white co-worker and/or white members to either assume or be attributed greater power than the black co-worker and/or black members. As Rhule (1988) has pointed out, however understanding a white partner may be, when a black/white pair work with an all white group, the black worker is likely to need an individual black consultant to help her cope with the inevitable isolation and racism. This would be in addition to consultancy for the co-workers as a pair which in these circumstances could be from either a black or white consultant. Conversely, when a white co-worker is in an all black group she may benefit from having her own consultant, either black or white, to help her manage any issues arising from her racism and white perspective.

These issues are quite complex and readers may not agree with our views, based as they are on our personal perspectives and experience rather than formal research. The most important guideline is that frank discussions about choice of consultant - where choice exists! - should occur taking these factors into account. For some co-working pairs, factors other than racial identity may be considered more important in a consultant, for example their gender or the sheer quality of their skills and capacity to instil confidence in the co-workers.

Group contract and ground rules

In any group, whatever the composition of the members and the workers, there needs to be a clear ground rule about the unacceptability of anyone in the group treating anyone else in a discriminatory or derogatory way because of their personal characteristics. Increasingly social work offices and day/ residential centres have publicly stated policies and ground rules along these lines which automatically apply to groups in those settings. With black/white co-working no additional ground rule may be necessary except perhaps a particular emphasis on the rules applying equally to the workers both in how they are treated and how they treat others in the group. When ground rules are stated at the beginning of a group they are often not fully understood and only become meaningful at the point something happens in the group which is in breach of them. This is the opportunity for the co-workers to help the members understand the rules experientially. This may be particularly important in groups where there are a number of cross-cutting factors.

Structuring leadership responsibility on a 50:50 basis

Groups are likely to behave as though the white co-worker is the senior partner, reflecting social attitudes and expectations. This makes it important that not only do the co-workers arrange to share group tasks on an equal basis, but that they ensure they carry approximately equal responsibility in their response to unstructured situations, and counteract any group behaviours which seek to cast them in stereotypical roles. This means avoiding both white dominance on the one hand, and placing the major burden of responsibility on the black worker on the other.

The above guideline is based on the assumption that both workers have roughly equivalent levels of experience and ability. There will of course be situations where either the black or the white worker is considerably more experienced and/or skilled than their co-worker, and a 50:50 model may not be appropriate.

In these circumstances, as in all good co-working practice, it is important that firstly the workers themselves clarify how they are going to work together in a way which reflects their different levels of experience, skill and ability, and secondly that they convey this to the group members in an appropriate way. If the black worker is the 'senior partner' there is a danger that the white worker's racism may make it difficult for them to validate their partner's role; and when the white worker is the more experienced the pair need to be very careful that this difference is not reinforced by acting out the racist stereotypes. In both instances good practice requires that the co-workers behave in ways that maximise the opportunities for the 'junior partner' to develop her abilities and skills.

Modelling an effective black / white co-working relationship
Consciously or unconsciously group members are going to be aware and often very interested in how the pair work and relate together. They will detect factors like degree of mutual respect; comfortableness together; honesty and openness particularly about race, ethnicity and racism; shared assumptions and values, and so on. The more sophisticated group members will notice to what extent the co-workers support each other (helpful) or have a need to protect each other. Protection of a colleague is sometimes necessary and helpful, but more often unhelpful, indicating lack of confidence in the other's personal resources and skills, or it can be a patronising form of racism.

Inevitably there will be times when one co-worker 'gets it wrong' and their colleague feels either unsupported or overprotected. Co-workers often find it very difficult to offer their colleague the necessary feedback about what they experienced and this deprives the other person of the opportunity to learn from what happened and improve their own practice and co-working skills. Race anxieties may further inhibit the frank sharing necessary for developing positive practice in this area, and consultation with a third person will often be necessary to facilitate honest and open exchange.

Some group members, black or white but for different reasons, may find the presence of a close productive black/white relationship uncomfortable or threatening, and may try in various ways to sabotage it by splitting the co-workers, for example by attacking one where they are most vulnerable and aligning with the other. This kind of behaviour can be a severe test of the work relationship necessitating consultancy outside the group and perhaps explicit feedback to members in the group about what they are doing coupled with some attempt to understand and relate it to purpose and process. This is not easy, not least because of the strong feelings aroused, and can be quite a severe test of the confidence the two workers have in each other and their different perspectives on racism. Pressure of this kind is likely to be particularly great on a couple working together for the first time, and like all of these guidelines it may be affected by other non-race factors and characteristics.

Challenging racism and other race issues in the group

When racism occurs in groups, white people frequently look to the black person or persons to take up the challenge and make the response. This is often a form of abdication of responsibility, a 'cop-out', placing a quite inappropriate responsibility on the black person for challenging what essentially is very often a 'white problem'. It is therefore essential that black/white co-workers are aware of this and have worked out strategies for responding based on an understanding that the white co-worker has a responsibility to play a central role in the intervention. Sometimes the white worker gives the response 'I'm doing my best' which places the black worker in a difficult position. Another task of consultation is that of empowering the white worker as well as his or her black colleague. This may be particularly important when challenging racism in the group is the issue and the white worker needs help in gaining the confidence to take risks and be assertive.

CONCLUSION

The expansion and development of the groupwork method in Britain since the late 1970s has been paralleled by a slow but steady growth of interest in an anti-discriminatory approach to social work practice. The latest and perhaps most significant indicator has been its centrality in the requirements for the new UK social work qualifying award, the Diploma in Social Work (DipSW) (CCETSW, 1989). During this period, groups have been central to both the raising of consciousness and the taking of social action on discrimination arising from race, gender, age, disability, sexual orientation and class. There has been much debate about the aims and ideology of these groups but little, at least in published form, on the process and leadership issues.

Our survey of the mainstream groupwork and co-working/co-leadership literature confirms both how little the general issue of race and racism is addressed in groupwork texts and articles (although this is now changing), and the almost complete absence of discussion on the specific issue of black/white co-working practice. The published material available on the latter issue literally has to be dug out of the few articles in which it is embedded.

This paper is an attempt to begin to identify some of the conceptual and practice issues which need to be addressed when considering black/white co-working. We are very aware that this is only a beginning, and that there are gaps and oversimplification. What we hope is that this beginning will stimulate discussion and exploration of ways of developing an anti-racist groupwork practice which goes beyond polemic to identifiable strategies and skills. We have concentrated on the enhancement of black/white co-working skills which in turn can enable more fruitful group experiences for members and workers from different ethnic and racial backgrounds. At a personal level, writing this article together as a black woman and a white man with contrasting life and co-working experiences, has opened up rewarding insights into our own practice!

This chapter was first published in Groupwork *4(2), 1991.*

The Linguistic and Cultural Barriers to Cross-National Groupwork

PAUL TAYLOR

INTRODUCTION

The question posed by this Symposium, 'Survival and Success in Groupwork in the 1990s', reflects the enormous political and social changes which have come about in Europe in the last two years and which concern us directly. This Europe of the future will require us more and more to have professional competencies in multi-lingual and multi- cultural groups. Without the frontiers of the past, Europeans have a cultural, social, economic and political mobility which previous generations have never known. We will therefore find ourselves in a new group dynamic, in both social and task groups, where there will be no single, dominant cultural or national norm. It is therefore most opportune that we look carefully behind the jargon of groupwork 'without frontiers' in the new, open Europe which exists, because of or despite Mastricht, since January, 1993.

In proposing this reflection on the barriers to such cross-national work created by the way people speak, by the way they think and the way they behave, it is critically important that I move both beyond simple anecdote and over refined stereotypes to offer a more rigorous analysis of some of the criteria by which we differentiate cultures and national identity.

First, however, we need to consider the more permanent, insidious, blockages that drastically limit or even prevent an approach to creative groupwork.

The most evident of these blockages is cultural tourism. We know that a host country or culture often has a vested interest in exploiting what the tourist wants to see (traditional dress, dances, music, recipes), but that this exploitative nostalgia is a collusion in highlighting what is quaint, exotic, historic or folkloric. Both host and tourist know that such cultural stereotyping does not represent the reality of contemporary, ordinary life. As many anti-racism campaigns have discovered, cultural tourism creates a false image of the society or culture because it remains a profoundly ethnocentric way of looking at what is different. It is a voyeurism, a consumerism of the dominant myths, reinforcing prejudice. As Levi-Strauss indicates[1], we cannot respect what we feel to be quaint. Cultural tourism gives us refracted knowledge without responsibility.

Our personal moral system often provides a different form of mind-guarding, a more insidious blockage. Morality substitutes for knowledge: I have no need to know more about the other because I have already decided the degree to which she or he is compatible with my own moral values. Morality is of course important, but it cannot replace understanding. It is in many ways like a frontier: we are morally open or closed, allowing ourselves a more or less restricted passage of values and opinions. Is the Russian or Chinese culture more just or more democratic than the British? Are Scandinavian cultures more permissive or less sexist than the French or German? Are women in Arab cultures less free than women in Europe or North America?

These are not flippant, stereotyped questions. They appear regularly today, for example, in the debates about immigration, the right to asylum, citizenship and the right to vote which are currently occupying many European parliaments in their struggle to define national identity. They represent a view of complex cross-cultural, cross-national problems, seen through the simplifying lens of a certain morality. It is as much a distorting lens as is the third form of blockage - the view from a distance caused by a *surfeit of tolerance*.

At best tolerance is a necessary virtue, at worst it is a refined system of self-defence, a half measure. It is a substitute for real confrontation, a genuine meeting, a going beyond the 'what lies between us'. If we only tolerate, if we each respect the territory of the other, we will never have to cross the barriers or frontiers which divide us.

The plea for more tolerance is often only a political ploy, at a personal or national level, to ensure that there will be no change. Implicit in the statement 'I am willing to tolerate you, I accept you as you are' is the reverse appeal: 'You must accept me as I am, let me be'. I will tolerate you but on condition that I do not have to change.

Tolerance avoids or pre-empts conflict. Yet cross-national groupwork demands that we confront each other (literally, confront means to 'stand face to face with someone'), honestly and authentically, otherwise there will be no group or group life. We need to engage in constructive, cultural opposition which goes far beyond the simplicity of liberal toleration (Demorgon, 1993).

Culture

If the preconditions of cross-national groupwork are that we should not be seduced by the attractiveness of different cultures, should not export our own moral judgments nor import a confining tolerance, then where do we begin? There are two very different ways to start looking at another culture -from the inside as it is lived, or from the outside as it is thought to be lived. Obviously the new arrival who adopts a given culture, who is trying to be culturally integrated, does not see that culture in the same way as someone who has been born and bred into it, for whom it is completely natural, first nature. This is the key 'insider-outsider' analysis of Pike and Harris (Headland et al., 1990) about emics and etics which has so much to offer our discussion. It exposes the differences between what is essential (emic) to a culture and what is changeable (etic), between what is learnt consciously (etic) about a culture and what is acquired subconsciously (emic).

What is fascinating is that the insider's view, the emic analysis, is not necessarily more authentic or accurate than the etic view of the outsider (Reiss, 1990). This is because we learn culture, or at least our primary culture, mostly unconsciously through the acquiring of personal, social and moral values and behaviour.

The groupworker/community worker is most often, almost necessarily from the outside, someone for whom the culture of the group is not a natural, first instinct, but which she or he has to learn by active observation and reflection. How then do we look at such a group, especially when that group is of a different nationality, inhabits a culture which is foreign[2] and even speaks a different language?

Their culture, any culture, is effectively a collective mental programming, a way of thinking and behaving that distinguishes one group from another. Many differing scales (national, regional, local, social group, task group) of programming are possible, all inter-related and more or less mutually coherent.

An etic description of a given culture allows for the discovery of patterns of thinking or behaviour within this collective mental programming which are unavailable to us through emic descriptions. Harris (1979) firmly asserts that the observer's competence (linguistic or cultural fluency) is sufficient to enable him or her to have a valid etic mental understanding of a culture, that is, to be able to identify a rule or principle of that culture. This is not the same as saying, however, that the observer is thereby immediately capable of acting or reacting in accordance with that culture.

An example might be useful here: I might have observed where, how and when the French or the British shake hands. I can formulate a rule that in such or such a circumstance, shaking hands is the correct thing to do, and, given the necessary circumstances, I may be able to behave appropriately and so express my understanding of, and acceptance of, those cultural norms.

In another culture, I may be able to observe with the same correctness and accuracy that the law and social customs of a society require that certain criminals are subjected to a public flogging. However, although the circumstances of a particular crime may be clear and beyond doubt, I may not be able to collude with this form of punishment. At best, my non-conformity would express my understanding of, but rejection of, what others would consider to be normal, acceptable behaviour.

Both these examples, but particularly the latter, expose the fact that both emic and etic perceptions are essentially ethnocentric: in fact, they cannot be otherwise. Ethnocentrism is a natural, psychological reaction, which is inextricably linked to a sense of identity and of belonging. The processes of enculturation, integration and socialisation all seek to provide each individual, group or community with an ethnic or cultural centre. We learn to belong, we learn to centre ourselves on a given culture, to have roots and to recognise those who share those roots and those who do not (Tajfel, 1979).

This acquired, passive ethnocentrism is not the same as the active, exclusive ethnocentrism which lies at the heart of positive xenophobia or conscious racism. It is rather a way of drawing attention to the fact that ethnocentrism is to society what egocentrism is to the individual. I have to start with the fact that I am who I am. I can only look honestly at another culture or another individual if I know genuinely what it means to be Me.

One notes time and time again, therefore, that what happens across the cross-cultural boundaries has more to do with what happens within those national cultures that it has to do with any great spontaneity or dynamic produced at the moment of encounter. The participants of any mixed national group tend[3] overwhelmingly to express themselves on issues of power, control, sexuality, agreement and disagreement based on their normative behaviour within their own separate cultures.

Let us take a light-hearted example. In no matter what culture they find themselves, the English tend to form a queue for anything: the French do not. The Dutch, like the French, greet strangers when they enter the confined spaces, for example, of a shop, a lift or an office: the Belgians do not, be they French or Flemish speaking. Austrians on foot wait for green before crossing a main road: never the Italians. Swiss drivers and even pedestrians are voluble if you mistake a road sign or impede the flow of traffic: Swedish people are much more tolerant and forgiving (Tixier, 1992).

These specific examples of national differences are not in themselves important, but the question which lies behind them is critical: how is it that differing cultures, in situations which are common to all, prefer a particular response which is often quite at odds with that of their neighbour? The striking fact that we need to analyse is that our European neighbours, despite being Europeans, are all very different. That is what makes our reflection on cross-national groupwork exciting. We have no need to hide behind the liberal pluriculturalism which claims that all peoples and all cultures are different and that, therefore, cultural comparisons are odious or useless. On the contrary, we can exploit and better appreciate that diversity and difference: we can observe, as a phenomenon which we have all experienced, that there are specific characteristics which create typologies of national identity. These are founded on the differing cultural, climatic, historic, economic, social and educational variables (which ethnomethodology (Handel, 1982) defines as 'indexical' factors) which give rise to each nation's sense of identity.

THE DIVERSE CULTURAL BARRIERS TO CROSS-NATIONAL GROUPWORK

These typologies, embedded in history, schooling and collective moralities, just as much as in present social, political and commercial behaviour, reveal five barriers which a cross-national group must confront before it can work effectively together: language, hierarchy, individualism, gender and uncertainty.

Language

From Saussure (1974) to Barthes (1986) to Lacan (1977), many anthropologists and linguists, as observers of groups and cultures, have argued that all human beings and all cultures are essentially a product of language. Fascinating then that not all languages have words to describe even ordinary things that human beings might take for granted. Some languages do not have words to distinguish blue from green in a rainbow, others have no word for brown. We describe time differently and accordingly behave differently: 'half-eight' in English is thirty minutes after eight o'clock. In German, it is thirty minutes before eight, that is, half-seven. Some languages do not distinguish 'mother' and 'aunt', reflecting a particular construction of family life, while some Scandinavian languages have separate words to distinguish maternal and paternal grandparents.

As educators or social and community workers, we have to confront the problem created by the fact that, for example, the British idea of Community Education does not translate into German, that the French *Animation* does not translate into English, nor the German *Bildung* into French. Core groupwork concepts like empowerment, leadership, achievement, accountability, and self-assessment cannot easily be expressed, for example, in French. The words do not exist, so what does one do faced with the question of team-building and group identity? We may at least begin to suspect that standard groupwork theory as taught in the U.K., heavily American as it is, cannot be translated sufficiently accurately in order to provide us with a coherent base on which to develop cross-national groupwork.

In some cultures, contrary to Asch (1956) and Milgram (1963) for example, it is more important to be polite than to be seen to be right or forthrightly honest. The Japanese rarely say 'no', with the result that their 'yes' is not necessarily the same as *ja, oui, si*, or even *si*. They also do not have a word for 'decision-making', despite their very commercial culture. It is this kind of observation, of which there are numerous examples, which helps us appreciate that cross-national groupwork is not simply a question of translating words which we could all understand by agreeing to some kind of international glossary of useful terms. It is rather the more complex process of interpreting the connotation of words[4] within the cultural context of the other person (Demorgon, 1989, p.127).

An illustration is perhaps useful: if we ask in any given language 'what is the word for inedible?', we can find that word in a simple dictionary. I know of no language that does not have such a word. However, if we ask 'What do they mean by inedible?', the dictionary is no help. We would need to understand the religious, historical, geographic, social and economic context which results in one culture defining as inedible what another culture may think is a great delicacy. One person's poison is another person's fish, just as one person's morality is another's barbarism (Hurstel, 1988).

The translation/interpretation of relationships provides us with another potential stumbling block. English is habituated to a number of extended and restricted codes, often highly nuanced (Bernstein, 1971), but its generic *you* loses the important distinctions of the two forms of you which we find in many European languages, e.g. *tu/vous*, *du/sie*, and which identify both the singular and plural 'you' and a continuum of formal and non-formal relationships. Here, in ordinary everyday language, as in the *thee* and *thou* of yore, much is made implicitly and explicitly of the different degrees of relationship and familiarity, indicating a respect for older people or solidarity with a peer group, the status of an individual, a professional distance, an invitation to a closer relationship or the marking of a solemn moment. The problem for English speakers is how to transit from one culture to another, how to learn to use correctly these complex interpersonal modes of communication which, in English, are not marked by the verb but rather more subtly by the use of adjectives or a particular tone of voice. The converse is that it is not surprising that those whose first language is not English often find the British address them in a style which is cold and lacking in sensitivity. Interesting that *sang froid* might be a product not of heredity but of language?

Hierarchical distance

No anthropologist has ever found a society that was not marked by inequalities. That is simply another way of saying sociologically that any society that values difference over homogeneity ends up by structuring the disparities which cut society vertically by family and clan and horizontally by status and power.

What interests the cross-national groupworker is how a given society or culture perceives the degrees of inequality or distance between those who hold power and those who are subject to that power. Bollinger and Hofstede (1987, p.73) clearly argue that this perception differs from country to country.

In measuring the continuum of power, establishing the psychological and social dynamic that exists in a given group, we are able to calculate a figure for any country's 'relative hierarchical distance' (RHD).

Within the observed behaviour of a group, we can note the frequency with which leaders consult or value another opinion; whether the group seeks to personalise task activities rather than resting at a functional level where detailed directives would be sufficiently effective; whether the group collectively requests or demands an increased level of participation rather than 'accepting its place' in the hierarchy of things.

The groupworker needs to know how the group interprets the concepts of leadership and hierarchy, and its preference for modes of communication and interaction which are a-autocratic, b-paternalistic, c-consultative or d-democratic. Generally, in countries with a high RHD, that is where differences in hierarchy and power structures are clearly marked, the preference for the group culture is for a-b; in countries where hierarchical status is less evident, (low RHD) the preference is for c-d.

In that the culture of a group will naturally reflect the overall national culture, the consequences of differing RHDs for potential cross-national groupwork are significant. We observe that, generally, the Latin European countries (Italy, France, Spain, Greece) have a high RHD, a tendency confirmed by other countries nearer the equator. Germanic Europe (Germany, Scandinavia and the U.K.) tends towards a low RHD.

Table 1
Relative Hierarchical Distances

Relative ranking of each country		RHD Score*
1	Malaysia	104
14	Brazil	69
16	France	68
19	Turkey	66
20	Belgium	65
27	Greece	60
31	Spain	57
33	Japan	54
34	Italy	50
38	USA	40
40	Holland	38
43	Germany	35
44	UK	35
45	Switzerland	35
48	Sweden	31
52	Israel	13
53	Austria	11

* *110 = high RHD*   *0 = low RHD*
(*Source:* Bollinger and Hofstede, *1987*)

Clearly geography and particularly nearness to the equator is an important element, but technology is also an indexical factor. Countries with a high level of technological culture tend to have low RHD, perhaps because technology is a major equalising, levelling force in society. Conversely, poorer countries tend to distinguish more between the rich and the poor, the powerful and the powerless and this shows in their RHD.

The impact of such culture on the group is clear. Unless the groupworker places the group's preferences for styles of leadership and management within its own cultural context, the standard questions about authoritarian, *laissez faire* or democratic communications within groups will yield only misleading responses. A high RHD, where social stratification and access to power is clearly marked, creates a culture of latent conflict, tension, and competitive rivalry. Power is invested in the individual who leads either because of their charisma or because of their unquestioned role. Power is a pendulum between left and right, and change is founded, therefore, on conflict.

In a group culture of low RHD, change is more evolutionary, even though more slow because of the constant balancing mechanisms which prevent one person power. Power lies in the group, even in the team, where the internal politics tend to disguise or disregard the latent inequalities in the group.

Individualism

Different societies construct the continuum 'society-community-family-individual' in different ways. Anthropologists distinguish those that are dominantly communal societies from those that are individualistic. The former identifies the individual with their personal moral involvement in the society and in a given group. The social unit is the 'we of me', the individual whose place is firmly within a network of intercommunications. Immigration into, or emigration out of, such a group in extremely difficult.

The latter mode prioritises a person's professional contribution in society, their role and function rather than their personality. Individual convictions count more than collective identity. The social unity is the 'me of me', the individual who stands on his or her own two feet, but who is fundamentally no better nor no worse than the next person. Consequently, the tendency to individualise is compensated by tendencies to depersonalise, homogenise. Such 'equality of opportunity' makes immigration fairly easy.

Obviously there is a high correlation between the richness of a country and the value which it places on individualism. The standard americanised, 'Thatcherised' theory is that it is the individual, the entrepreneur, the self-employed who create a thriving economy and individual wealth. However, another ideological explanation may also be possible: that only in the rich countries can one afford to be self-centred and individualistic.

Table 2
Degree of Individualism

Relative ranking of each country		Score*
1	USA	91
3	UK	89
5	Holland	80
7	Italy	76
8	Belgium	75
10	Sweden	71
11	France	71
12	Ireland	70
14	Switzerland	68
15	Germany	67
19	Israel	54
20	Spain	51
22	Japan	46
35	Portugal	27
47	Pakistan	14
50	Venezuela	12
52	Ecuador	8
53	Guatemala	6

* *100 = individualistic society   0 = communal society*
(Source: Bollinger and Hofstede, 1987)

This index is useful in assessing whether a group is more likely to create a culture of cooperation or competition (Ladmiral and Lipiansky, 1989). Communal societies avoid major swings in power and government: for someone to lose face or honour or standing is a collective loss, their failure a collective failure. Relationships are founded on a social morality as they represent an investment in the social fabric in which all gain or lose. Professional life is integrated with personal life.

This is much less true in the *Gemeinschaft* societies where individualism flourishes. The pendulum of power can swing radically as certain individuals become more or less dominant. Relationships are founded on utility, calculated to advantage: useless relationships, familial or social, are discontinued. There is a marked separation between the personal and the professional.

Groupworkers in the U.K. will be used to working with the kind of group which is essentially a collection of individuals, but there are clearly situations, for example with minority ethnic groups, where a sensitive analysis of this indexical factor of individuality would be crucial to the proper functioning of the group.

Gender

It is this kind of setting that highlights another important barrier to groupwork, viz., that sexual differentiation is not the same in all countries. In some countries, high status roles are automatically masculine and, where there is role differentiation, it is nearly always the male who is advantaged. Without entering the sexism/sexist debate, although it is clearly associated, we can define a masculine culture as one where there is clear male/female role differentiation and a feminine culture as one where there is role equality and interchangeability.

It is interesting to reflect that Catholic countries in Europe are more male dominant than those more influenced by Protestantism. There is a marked correlation between that and the ideologies and style of social policy making, for example, which is itself an indexical factor for evaluating a given culture. Compare, in this light, Italy and Ireland with the Scandinavian countries.

The importance of this barrier for groupwork is that masculine cultures tend to be competitive, status aware, product oriented but technology dependent. Feminine cultures, particularly in small groups, tend to be process oriented, pay more attention to the ambience of the group that will facilitate cooperation and exchange, are competence rather than status aware, and exploit more its human rather than its technological resources. Within this whole debate, it is certainly my experience that British groupworkers express and impose their view about the gendering of culture and of group dynamics much more than their continental European counterparts. This despite the fact that English is not fundamentally a gender differentiated language. The definite article, adjectives, participles, nouns and pronouns do not have to accord in the same way that other languages (*le /*

la, der/die, el/la) have to reflect grammatical gender. The paradox is that, in grammatically differentiated language, e.g. French, the dominantly masculine form renders women less visible. British groupworkers may well find that much of what they take for granted as anti-sexist language does not translate directly into other European languages. Indeed, despite the dominance of English as a language (Lafont, 1991), the exporting of, or the insisting upon, anti-sexist language or codes of practice may well represent a neo-colonial form of cultural invasion. At least English speakers may need to think through the relationship between biological gender and arbitrary grammatical gender.

Table 3
Degree of Gender Demarcation

Relative ranking of each country		Score*
1	Japan	95
2	Austria	79
4	Italy	70
7	Ireland	68
8	Jamaica	68
9	UK	66
10	Germany	66
18	Greece	57
21	India	56
26	Pakistan	50
27	Brazil	49
29	Israel	47
36	France	43
37	Spain	42
41	S. Korea	39
45	Portugal	31
50	Denmark	16
51	Holland	14
52	Norway	8
53	Sweden	5

* *100 = masculine culture*   *0 = feminine culture*
(Source: Bollinger and Hofstede, 1987)

Managing uncertainty

The final barrier to cross-national groupwork is crucial to any form of change. How do we see the future? How do we cope with uncertainty? These simple questions influence each and every form of communication that goes on with a group, but needless to say, not all countries or cultures respond in the same way.

Table 4
Management of Uncertainty

Relative ranking of each country		Score*
1	Greece	112
2	Portugal	104
5	Belgium	94
7	Japan	92
10	France	86
11	Chile	86
12	Spain	86
19	Israel	81
23	Italy	75
29	Germany	65
33	Switzerland	58
35	Holland	53
43	USA	46
47	UK	35
48	Ireland	35
50	Sweden	39
53	Singapore	8

* *120 = threatened by uncertainty, seeks to control it*
0 = liberated by uncertainty, seeks to exploit it
(Source: Bollinger and Hofstede, 1987)

More than the other three indexical elements which we have already touched upon, the responses to the management of uncertainty are more evidently polarised. Some countries and cultures seek to limit disruptive insecurity by the existence of written constitutions, identity cards for every adult[5], passes, permits, and other controls. No-one is anonymous. Groups, in turn, insist on formal roles, written structures, conventions, rules and clear processes to avoid misunderstanding. Whatever the issue, whatever the context, the first court of appeal is 'What do the regulations say?'

Where countries seek to control uncertainty, there is often a belief that technology can provide safeguards, that rules can define behaviour and that religion and/or politics have access to some form of absolute truth. Complex ritualising curtails uncertainty: meetings are verified by reports and minutes rather than by results; planning prefers clear aims and objectives to preclude the unforeseen; experts and consultants are appointed to control rogue practice; and precise rules define responsibility and limit initiative.

Imagine, therefore, a meeting where participants are from, just for example, the U.K., the United States, France and Germany and we can see immediately why the GATT negotiations were so difficult.

Countries and groups which exploit uncertainty, as in Britain or in America, are more outward looking, less tolerant of aggression within the group, more able to take personal risks and rely on intuition. They are ill at ease within a culture that relies on logic, objectivity and insists on consensus. It is deeply significant that the expression 'non-directive groupwork' has its origins deep within the English speaking world: to many Europeans, it is a contradiction in terms.

Conclusion

Inevitably, language remains the major barrier to cross- national groupwork[6]. Nonetheless, in hoping to bring about change, we know that cultural norms, be they of a group or of a society, change rarely by the adoption of external values but rather because new conditions or situations arise within the group which facilitate necessary change. Cultural change always has more to link it to the known past than to a desired future.

Secondly, in order to change ideas we need to change behaviour. For me that means that we need to have more and more contact with other national groups and cultures, as a result of which our ideas will change. It is no good hoping for a change in patterns of thinking, new ideologies, and new groupwork practice so that, at some future but ill defined date, cross-national groupwork might be possible.

One cannot learn to swim in a library: nor can one learn the theory or the practice of cross-national groupwork in a mono-cultural or mono-national environment.

The values which we cherish as groupworkers have a clear intensity and direction. Our interventions in groups, as in society, are not neutral. We need to avoid the homogenising attraction of 'political correctness' which is often merely a thin disguise for 'cultural cleansing'. Only then can we confront the vibrant cultural differences within our own national and social identities, and push out the frontiers of social work and groupwork. The barriers to cross-national groupwork begin here, this side of the frontier and not in some other far off place. Perhaps the only real barrier to international groupwork is the frontier we build around ourselves.

Notes

1. The tension which exists between tourism, ethnology and ordinary life is well explored in Claude Levi- Strauss, *Tristes Tropiques*, Paris, Plon, 1955.
2. Someone who is foreign, a foreigner, is simply someone who, by definition (Latin: *foras, foris* = outside, not at home, from without) regards me, as I regard him or her, from a distance. It is necessarily an etic regard, a view from an 'other' perspective.
3. I have kept the word 'tend' here because, happily, there will always be individuals who do not conform to the norm. However that does not invalidate the norm or the typology. At the individual level, we are all different and inhabit our own specific 'culture'. Nonetheless, the constitutive variables of identity are sufficiently distinguishable for us to recognise national characteristics which give rise, at the macro-level, to verifiable typologies.
4. This point itself is dependent on the particular, indexical language of this article, i.e. the English nuance of the words 'translating' and 'interpreting'. French and German have the same words (*traduire / ubersetzen: interpreter / verdolmetschen*) but not necessarily the same connative or indexical usage.
5. Austria, Belgium, France, Germany, Italy, and Switzerland have identity cards; Denmark, Finland, Holland, Ireland, Norway, Sweden and the UK do not.
6. It is an important illusion of liberal cultural studies that learning a language necessarily helps a person understand the culture of that country. Language that is learnt/taught mechanically, simply as translated information, cannot transmit the qualitative value system of the culture.

This chapter is the substantive text of the paper given at the Third European Groupwork Symposium which was held at Goldsmiths' College, London, 15-16 1993, under the auspices of the publishers Whiting and Birch. It was first published in Groupwork 7(1), 1994.

Groupwork and Black Women Viewing Networks as Groups: Black Women Meeting Together for Affirmation and Empowerment

MARCIA FRANCIS-SPENCE

INTRODUCTION

This paper is not about an actual groupwork session but rather raises wider groupwork issues for discussion. What I aim to do is offer a personal, reflective (and reflexive) account of the relationship between Black women and groupwork. In so doing, I use a wide interpretation of groupwork. I will look at whether counselling or therapy plays a part in Black women's lives and, again, I will be interpreting counselling and therapy in very wide terms. For the purpose of this paper, Black women in the UK are taken as one with an acknowledgement, but no close analysis of, for example, social class differences. This is because, however successful or powerful Black women are in this society, many still carry an inner longing for affirmation of their worth and for respect, which is habitually denied them. The commonality of this experience gives Black women a shared bond, which in groups and networks may act more powerfully than the differences between them.

The intention in this paper is to raise awareness amongst practitioners to help them to understand not only why Black women can never forget about racism but also why the majority of Black women refuse to be confined by it and how this is achieved. It will consider some of the day-to-day actions that Black women use as a safety valve to combat racism. Racism is alive and well and there is little doubt it is a growing industry. Nevertheless, the chief highlight here will be on empowerment and affirmation, and on reminding readers that - contrary to popular belief - the majority of Black people (and certainly Black women) do not sit around and allow their lives to be confined by racism. Unfortunately, practice accounts and student essays alike too often choose to focus on the negative aspects of being Black, portraying Black people as passive dependent victims who are merely done to and take no control over their own lives. This paper will attempt to provide a counter-balance to this perspective.

WHY GROUPWORK IS IMPORTANT TO BLACK WOMEN

Usually when groupwork is mentioned, the tendency is to view it in relation to clients and practitioners. Rarely do we think of it in terms of professional groups or individuals who simply want support. Black practitioners have only fairly recently started to become involved in groupwork and my experience as a practitioner has been that Black women (like Black people generally) are reluctant to become involved in 'organised' groupwork with practitioners. However, it is not unusual to see groups of Black women talking regularly together and offering support to each other, be they social work/probation clients, unemployed women, women in mundane jobs, or professional women.

I would argue that groupwork is of utmost importance to Black women, in particular Black women who are raising children alone or undertaking other caring roles. This usually results in women adopting dual roles, which entails juggling caring responsibilities and full-time employment as well as, in some cases, part-time study as they try to provide a better future for themselves and their dependents. This inevitably leaves very little spare time and can lead to isolation. The double *day* has, however, long been an established feature of Black women's working lives (Bryan et al., 1985, p.18). Many Black women, it would appear, exist by recreating the networks which have been a feature of the history of their families in Africa, the Caribbean and Asia.

According to bell hooks, the vast majority of Black women in this society receive substantial care from other Black women, and she states that she is not talking about only lesbian women (hooks, 1992, p.42). Black women tend not to have a history of seeking therapy or counselling, in the formal sense, but I would argue that they do receive therapy and counselling through their interaction with other Black women.

This therapy can take several forms, for example, the grooming of hair is an important feature of Black women's lives. Many Black women choose to wear their hair in plaits - sitting for 8 or

9 hours whilst this is done is not unusual. For those who choose chemically-treated styles, it still takes about half this time. These hours for the majority represent the only space they have that is totally theirs and it is a time when they have the opportunity to discuss issues with other Black women. These issues could be to do with their children, partners, politics, aspirations, parents, their health problems - in fact, anything. More recently an increasing number of Black women have become economically independent and therefore reached a position whereby they have the luxury of acting on the recognition that stress is a danger to their lives. My experience has been that many women now take advantage of leisure centres, enjoying for example Turkish baths or saunas on weekends or evenings and engaging in similar discussion to that at the hairdressers. These women would be appalled if anyone tried to suggest that they were in effect participating in groupwork.

Black women have long recognised the damage that stress does to their lives. To be in a position whereby you are able to do anything about the pressures in your life is quite a privilege for the majority of women even more so for Black women. The pressure remains the same be they part of the so-called underclass or part of a more economically advantaged group. As we look towards the professions, we see Black women making strides, in spite of the barriers, so much so that reports abound of how they are leaving Black men behind and how White women feel threatened by their rapid progress. The presence of stress is not a new phenomenon to Black women's lives but for a long time they did not have the history of recognising or naming it as affecting their lives. 'Getting on', however, does not reduce the stress suffered by Black women; in fact it can be argued that the stress and isolation is increased the higher up the ladder they climb. In many cases this is the result of trying to straddle two worlds.

To cope with stress and isolation, Black women, in particular those who move from their community, often draw on the support of other Black women. For professional women the 'phone often becomes a life-line resulting in enormous bills as they reach out to other Black women for support. This support provides them with a safety-valve by enabling them to air and discuss issues they cannot share with others in the arena in which they are working.

BLACK WOMEN'S GROUPS AS A SOURCE OF EMPOWERMENT

'... self empowerment is the most deeply political work there is, and the most difficult' (Lorde, 1984, p.170). Audre Lorde therefore advocates that Black women should seek empowerment. The majority of Black women are in agreement and are actually engaged in doing just that. Black women's 'groups' can and do provide an opportunity for empowerment, enabling participants to look at their situation from their own perspective and as a result discover strategies to empower each other to improve their situation. We live in a world that does not respect people who do not fight for what is rightfully theirs. Black women's survival in a hostile environment has been a result of such a fight. Black women need to continue to use the opportunities to learn about and share their different experiences, in effect to drop the outer layer and get to the core of themselves.

We cannot make radical interventions that will fundamentally alter our situation unless we do this. We do, however, need the support of each other. It is when we get together as Black women that the other oppressions affecting us are addressed, because usually we are confined to responding only to racism. A feature of Black women's groups is that they allow women to articulate the differences between women, for example by age, class and sexual identity. When Black women come together, either by letters, the 'phone, or face to face, that is when we begin to acknowledge the other oppressions which are so much a feature of our lives. For example, homophobia, which is endemic in wider society, also has roots in the Black community, thus hindering lesbian women from being frank and open about their lives. The plight of elders is also a cause of concern for Black women. A large number of Black elders have arrived at retirement with the unfulfilled dream of returning 'home', having never had enough disposable income to make it financially viable for them to do so. Children are also a source of concern, in particular the way their future is blighted by the unfair treatment many of them receive in school. There are concerns as to the numbers being forced into under-achievement while others are absenting themselves from the employment market, perceiving their prospects as so dire they see little point in trying. They see failure as inevitable and try to cushion themselves from the humiliation of rejection by opting out altogether. It appears the only time these issues can be discussed constructively is when Black women come together.

Black women are starting to transform the images of

Blackness; the ways of looking at themselves, of being seen. Many Black women are busy trying to ensure that a truer image of Black womanhood is presented to society. There are, however, many barriers. Even those of us who are committed - who feel we have decolonised our minds - often find it hard to speak our experiences. Indeed '... the more painful the issues we confront the greater our inarticulateness' (hooks, 1992, p.2). Fighting against white culture which does not accept the unique experiences of Black women and continues to impose its standards and values, ensures that what we really want only emerges when we get into groups. We are only able to articulate this when we come together in groups.

Meeting and coming together in whatever way is a great source of support; being there for each other when things get difficult or appear impossible as they invariably do. It is not uncommon to see Black women nurturing each other, providing encouragement to continue the struggle, reminding each other to hold on to their dreams and goals.

When I was offered my current job, I was overwhelmed with apprehension about the area I was entering but friends told me 'don't worry, we want you to go; in fact we need you to go and we will provide you with the necessary support to enable you to at least give it a try'. At the time I was sceptical and could not see how they could give me the support I was convinced I would require given that I was going so far. To their credit, I can honestly say that they have kept their promise. It is that support, in the shape of 'phone calls, letters, cards, visits, which has kept me going and two years later still keeps me going. I know my situation is far from unique. I, as well as my friends, provide the same support for others; this support is not confined to a national basis but works equally well on an international level.

As stated earlier, it is my belief that groupwork is part of many Black women's culture. The interaction they have is, however, not called or viewed as groupwork, but only by understanding this history of interaction can practitioners understand how to approach groupwork with Black women. Like so many other aspects of life in the Black communities, for example volunteering, we do it without necessarily putting a name to it. One reason for this is that, often, what we bring is not seen as valuable, we abandon it and try to adopt the more formal style familiar to this society rather than adapt what we bring to fit in with and complement what is already present. An analogy can be drawn here with Black social work trainees. Social work programmes have for some time recognised the need to ensure the barriers are removed to enable Black students to take up training. However, as there is little value placed on what they bring they are usually required to discard the values and beliefs they hold and instead adopt what is in effect a Eurocentric perspective, which leaves them in a situation where they are unable to draw on their inner resources and areas of greatest strength.

IMPLICATIONS FOR PRACTICE

Practitioners must question not only their own practice but also that of their departments if they are to recognise the importance of Black people coming together. The experience of living in a predominantly white society has a detrimental effect on most Black women's lives, both at the personal and professional levels. Their thoughts and ideas are more likely to be dismissed than acknowledged. In order to redress this, practitioners must listen to Black women and enable them to define their experience. Recognition should be given to the fact that Black women are not just consumers of services. Dominant culture does not allow for individuality between Black women and fails to recognise that they do not all have the same needs. Differences need to be acknowledged but must not be used to divide us.

If we accept that talking about our problems can lead to strategies for curing them, and that it is important that those listening understand, then we must appreciate that Black women need the opportunity to talk to each other. This talking together is necessary for well-being and becomes more so for those caught up in the system as clients of social services departments, the criminal justice system, or mental health services. These women often have multiple issues impinging on their lives - issues which they cannot easily explain - and the opportunity to share with each other by drawing from each other's experience could help to make sense of it all.

The opportunity for creative dialogue is already available for many groups: for example within the probation service it is not unusual for there to be various groups meeting, for example young offenders, and groups for women offenders. Given that Black people are the ones denied power, however, it is paramount that they are given space to examine their realities which includes naming their pain, expressing their grief as well as asserting their strength - in a forum where understanding and consequently healing can begin to take place. Practitioners often underestimate the impact of racism and how, for example, it inhibits Black and white women from sharing fully in groupwork together. The nature of racism ensures skin colour has an overwhelming impact on both Black and white people. It is not unusual to witness the latter benefiting, while for the former the experience is a painful one as they attempt to share with individuals who are afraid to witness their pain. As a result, Black women in these groups tend to remain silent.

Support does not necessarily have to come from someone of the same gender or race. Black and white women can and do provide and offer support to each other. This happens all the time and, living in a society where they are outnumbered, Black women could not continue to function adequately without also having some support from white women. It can, however, be more meaningful, and especially affirming for individuals to share with someone who is like them. After all, racism and sexism hurt.

Practitioners therefore need to be aware of these factors and to act on them when working with Black women. In the probation service, for example, consideration needs to be given as to whether one-to-one work is always the most appropriate method or whether joint groupwork with Black and white women is necessarily the best way to work on female offending behaviour. Practitioners may benefit from re-examining the way they approach their work. This, in turn, may result in their looking service-wide and being prepared to co-ordinate groups for Black women offenders addressing a wide range of issues if they are to arrive at the root of their offending. In the mental health field, if Black women have been diagnosed as mentally ill, again they should have the opportunity to come together to discuss their problems, which could lead them to examine their route to their present situation and develop strategies to deal with the root of their problems.

What hinders groupwork with Black and white women from developing and being productive for both sets of participants is usually the issues being discussed. Some of the issues may appear identical but their impact, and consequently the importance placed on them differs. Black women have different experiences and thus interpret situations differently. For many of them their lives are ingrained with stress for reasons which may have additional and more complex causes to them than that experienced by white women.

CONCLUSION

Above all, we should never underestimate the stress that is generated by living in a society that does not appreciate you, that tells you in so many ways that you are unimportant, that you are not valued, that you do not have a stake here - implying over and over again that it does not matter where or how you live or how your children are brought up. The stress of being denied the opportunity to achieve your potential can lead directly to an absorption of the hostility and of the racist values on which it is grounded; bell hooks states that: 'Militancy is an alternative to madness. And many of us are daily entering the realm of the insane' (hooks, 1992, p.6). In an attempt to avoid the latter, Black women *are* reasserting themselves in a myriad of hidden groups and networks.

This chapter was first published in Groupwork *7(2), 1994.*

Reflections on Empowerment Groupwork Across Racial Lines: My Sisters' Place

JUDITH A.B. LEE, RUTH R. MARTIN, JUDITH A. BEAUMONT,
ROSALIND MOORE-BECKHAM, GAIL BOURDON, CHRISTY KING,
JEAN KONON, EVELYN THORPE

INTRODUCTION

This Chapter is written by a group of colleagues and friends who struggle for empowerment, transformation and liberation in American society. We are women of different ages , cultures and class backgrounds. We are black and white and gay and straight, lay women and religious, single, married, with and without partners and children. The lines that divide us in society have given us different statuses and titles which we do not use with each other except to recognise hard won accomplishments on occasion, but will include here so the reader will understand the work we are doing together with the concepts usually used to explain relationships. We are educators\consultants, Directors, social workers and group members\clients who utilise the empowerment group approach to grow in empathy, critical consciousness and activism to transform ourselves and our socio-economic-political structures and achieve justice for all people.

The context of the work we describe here is an agency serving homeless and formerly homeless women and children in a mid-size inner city setting. The agency has three programmes: My Sisters' Place, an emergency shelter where women and children can stay up to several months; My Sisters' Place II, a transitional living facility where families have their own apartments and can stay up to two years; and My Sisters' Place III, a permanent scattered site residential programme for formerly homeless women with mental illness. Due to the location of the agency, the women served are mostly women of colour, African-American and Afro-Caribbean, with some Hispanics/Latinas and whites. Nation-wide, homeless women and families are mostly white although people of colour are highly overrepresented in the ranks of the homeless due to the double jeopardy of racism and poverty (Johnson and Lee, 1994). It is estimated that there are over three million people who are homeless at any given time in America. Obviously an affluent society that permits this shame is dominated by a small and wealthy power elite that effects the quality of life for Americans of all descriptions. Empowerment work seeks to liberate the oppressed, the oppressor, and those who stand by and, perhaps without full awareness, permit injustice to thrive in what is ideally a democratic society in which each person has a voice. It is the dialogue, or multilogue that occurs in small groups that forms the building blocks of true democracy and human liberation (Coyle, 1930; Freire, 1973; Lee, 1994; Wood and Middleman, 1995.)

As we write this account of our work together we are strongly aware of the opportunities we have had which enhanced our own life chances and options, including the option to live and work across racial lines and other lines that divide us and yet continue to love and appreciate our own cultures and groups. Class, caste and race and difference most often lock people into a ghettoised existence from which few escape. Our personal and professional lives are congruent in the multicultural and multiracial relationships in small groups that have nourished us and encouraged our growth. The practice of social work we discuss here includes some of our life experiences for the authentic use of self is ultimately all we have to share with others in our mutual empowerment. The approach to practice is the empowerment approach developed by Lee (1994) in dialogue with the women and Staff at My Sisters' Place and others. The empowerment group is the heart of this approach.[1] Individual, family and community work which is both personal and political, clinically and structurally aimed are also important.

This Chapter will take the reader through objective and subjective experiences of women, workers and group members, black and white working together as they enter into dialogue in and about the empowerment process. The actual strands of our reflections will be woven together. Judy Lee will do the weaving and provide a theoretical basis for the reflections which are written by each of the co-authors. Ruth Martin will conclude with reflections on theory and practice and African American history. To set the stage for our practice we will first discuss the issue of race in the United States and some thinking on groupwork and race. Then we will present the empowerment approach as it is used at My Sisters' Place and present the viewpoints and experiences of those entering into the dialogue including examples from empowerment group meetings. We will include the strengths, problems and contradictions of empowerment group practice across race, class and other lines.

RACE MATTERS

> Everything now, we must assume is in our hands...If we – and now I mean the relatively conscious whites and the relatively conscious blacks, who must, like lovers, insist on , or create, the consciousness of the others – do not falter in our duty now, we may be able, handful that we are, to end the racial nightmare, and achieve our country, and change the history of the world. If we do not now dare everything, the fulfilment of that prophecy, recreated from the Bible in song by a slave, is upon us: GOD GAVE NOAH THE RAINBOW SIGN, NO MORE WATER, THE FIRE NEXT TIME! (Baldwin, 1963).

James Baldwin's prophetic passage is quoted by Cornel West, America's preeminent African -American male intellectual in his ground breaking work *Race Matters* (1993). As we reflect with West on the gains and losses of the thirty years between Baldwin and West we recognise the gains of the Civil Rights Movement in the changing of cruel discriminatory laws and the creation of new opportunities. We are saddened that the raised hopes of equality have been dashed upon the rocks of continued prejudice and reactionary conservative politics and cutbacks of services which especially affect low income minorities of colour in America. Despite the presence of a more liberal Democratic President, Clinton, who exists in constant struggle with a right-wing Republican Congress, the Reagan-Bush era had a snowballing effect on destroying social policies and programmes which offered a modicum of optimism . In 1989, Allan Brown described the effects of Thatcherism in Britain as 'a time of unparalleled polarisation with the law abiding, deserving, moral majority' on the one side, and 'the deviant, feckless, minority ' on the other. He saw social work practice as mirroring dichotomised 'behaviour changing and social action approaches to groupwork'. He called for a unity of the two approaches to include both personal responsibility for change and challenges to structural inequity (Brown, 1990). It is remarkable that parallel processes were occurring in the American and Canadian socioeconomic and social work scenes and that minorities of colour faced the worst consequences of this thinking (Lee, 1989; Breton, 1992).

Prominent African American social work theorist Larry Davis noted in 1983 that W.E.B. Dubois had predicted early in the twentieth century that the colour line would be 'the problem of the century'. He said:

> ...despite the many factors which affect individual Americans-
> such as income, education; gender and age, etc.- none has as
> clearly nor as consistently demonstrated its potency as has skin
> color. Color remains one of the best predictors of a population
> being 'at risk'...and in the greatest need of services frequently
> provided by groupworkers (1984a, p.3).

Sadly, with West and Davis, we must agree that race matters. We must also project it as a major issue of the twenty-first century along with the violence predicted by Baldwin in 1963, unless racism, classism and all other destructive isms are courageously and adequately addressed by the power of people joining together.

West wrote his incisive book after the 1992 'Los Angeles Riots' (mass violence, burning property and looting) precipitated by police brutality towards a black man, Rodney King. Yet, West points out, only 36 per cent of those arrested were black as the rioting was a 'multiracial, trans-class, and largely male display of justified social rage [caused by] economic decline, cultural decay and political lethargy in American life' (1993, p.1). West sees the malignancy of racism as part of the fabric of an American society that has lost its rudder and is adrift in a sea of anomie regarding positive cultural values. While the hope is that Americans will achieve a multiracial, multi-class democracy, the reality is that economic and political power is located in the hands of one per cent of America's richest white males. This one per cent controls 37 per cent of the wealth and the top ten per cent of wealthy white men control 86 per cent of the wealth (West, 1993, p.6). In stark contrast is the fact that young black men lead the nation in suicide and the rate of incarceration is also phenomenal (West, 1993, p.15). West notes that being black in America includes being subject to white supremacist abuse yet heir to the rich heritage of a community that has struggled against that abuse (1993, p.25). He challenges people with raised consciousness to go beyond 'neat' and simplistic packages like 'liberalism' 'conservatism' or even 'Afro-centrism' to formulations which embrace the humanity of all human beings as the destiny of any democratic multiethnic country includes interracial interdependence and common dreams. This destiny is destroyed by racial hierarchy and moral and economic impoverishment. This is particularly manifested in the 'chocolate cities and vanilla suburbs' phenomena in America as the industrial base of cities which has provided employment and some stability corrodes under the onslaught of cheaper labour markets elsewhere, housing policies which discriminate against the poor, white fear, and the influx of poor people. Post-modern culture, according to West, is:

> ...(a) market culture dominated by gangster mentalities and self-destructive wantonness...the Los Angeles upheaval was an expression of utter fragmentation by a powerless citizenry that includes not just the poor but all of us (1993:5-6).

It is exactly this powerlessness that the empowerment approach to social work practice addresses (Lee, 1994).

bell hooks, America's leading African-American postmodern feminist writer argues to include black women's unique struggles and triumphs in the definitions of what it means to be black in America. She also challenges us to go beyond choosing racism as the sole battleground if we wish to achieve a world society free of domination by the elite powerful:

> If we are to live in a less violent and more just society, then we must engage in anti-sexist and anti-racist work. We desperately need to explore and understand the connections between racism and sexism. And we need to teach everyone about those connections so that they can be critically aware and socially alive...(p.63).

The empowerment groupwork we will discuss here embraces this objective for the groupworker and group member alike.

Coms-Diaz and Greene (1994) note that the ability of the social worker to address multicultural and gender-informed contexts is paramount in today's world. They enjoin the worker to appreciate the complex needs of heterogeneous women of colour who are often pivotal caretakers in their families, communities and groups and often not in tune with their own needs. They see women of colour as 'culturally and emotionally distinct' from white women. For women of colour, racism engenders empathy for males who are emasculated by white society. This may lead many to tolerate and deal with oppression at the hands of men in ways that are different than their white counterparts. Racial and gender oppression facilitates bonds between multicultural women of colour. The worker must also appreciate group differences as well as similarities and develop appropriate interventive strategies.

hooks also adds the politics of 'difference' into this equation : 'Any individual committed to resisting politics of domination...understands the importance of not promoting an either/or competition between the oppressive systems' (p.64). Patriarchy, she notes, is the context of all exercise of privilege enacted against people of colour, women, gay men and lesbian women and all people of difference who can construct a bond of unity and common struggle. hooks is optimistic that postmodern society contains the potential for the construction of empathy:

> The overall impact of postmodernism is that many other groups now share with black folks a sense of deep alienation, despair, uncertainty, loss, of a sense of grounding even if it is not informed by shared circumstance. Radical post-modernism calls attention to those shared sensibilities which cross the boundaries of class, gender, race, etc. that could be fertile ground for the construction of empathy-ties that would promote recognition of common commitments, and serve as a base for solidarity and coalition (1993, p.27).

The writers of this chapter seek to construct such bonds, between themselves as co-workers and group members and among group members who represent a variety of black, white and Latino groups.

RACE AND THE EMPOWERMENT GROUP APPROACH
RACE AND GROUPWORK

Davis (1984) suggests that there are several essential components to meaningful groupwork practice with black Americans (African-Americans). These include : knowledge of black Americans as a people and as a 'treatment' population; knowledge of group dynamics pertinent to groups that contain black members and; the importance of models that have a strong person-environment focus. Davis's principles are for both black and white groupworkers to utilise. He stresses that workers should have knowledge of the historical and current struggle of blacks in this society . This knowledge can come from interpersonal contact and from reading good sources. Blacks often prefer black workers but are mixed on their preference for homogeneous group composition. Sometimes black workers with an all black group are devalued as 'not good enough' to work with a mixed group. It is interesting to note that African-Americans usually prefer at least a 50-50 racial mix in group composition while whites prefer a majority of whites and up to 20 percent blacks. There should be at least two persons of difference in any group to avoid tokenism and provide a reality check. Groupworkers must acknowledge the salience of race early in the group's existence even though members may or may not immediately pick up on the invitation. The discussion of race in racially heterogeneous groups is usually a turning point in the group's work and development of intimacy. Workers must also cope with the absence of initial trust in the group. All African-American or mixed groups may distrust the sponsoring agency and its representative, the groupworker. They may perceive the non-black members or worker, and possibly even some blacks, as not understanding the social realities of black people. Workers need patience and openness in building trust. A lack of participation may also be a problem of trust. The worker needs to remain attuned to the rate of participation of each member and gently encourage full participation. Maintaining an overly individually focused group purpose and levels of intervention fails to recognise the societal complexity and oppression experienced by blacks (Davis, 1984). A person: environment focus encourages faith in the group process and worker.

Mullender's discussion of bicultural groupwork in the Ebony Project with black youth and white carers in Nottingham illustrates the use of racial heritage strategies and the workers' abilities to use a variety of methods to stimulate dialogue and develop knowledge about racial difference (1990). It is important to note that all did not run smoothly as issues of trust and knowledge were encountered. The ability of Mullender and her students/ workers to openly discuss their reactions and feelings in this process was a critical factor in the success of the groups. This was an effort in critical education as well as mutual aid and action. Chau (1990a) advises us that groupwork these days is likely to be multiethnic and multicultural as well as mixed racially. Groupworkers therefore need to aim toward multicultural competence even as they recognise the perils of living in a racist society. Interventions that help group members appreciate their own and each others cultural backgrounds help groups develop intimacy and freedom to do the work of the group.

Delgado and Humm-Delgado (1984a) focus on groupwork with Hispanic\Latino populations. Recognising the different Latin cultures members may represent enhances the bonding process. Women are more likely to give groups a chance and not mixing ages to include adolescents and older women recognises cultural norms. The worker must also attend to levels of acculturation and to the difficulties in the acculturation process. The worker might use group activities; focus on problem-solving in the here and now; share one's own thoughts and feelings at times; and encourage a comfortable cooperative atmosphere that upholds cultural values. It is also helpful to take the time to get to know members and use 'personalismo' (being a real and open person) and authenticity which minimises worker/client distance. Gopaul-McNicol (1993) discusses strategies that are effective in working with West Indians. She suggests that workers must appreciate the differences between African-Americans and West Indians in the United States due to their different histories. For example, if West Indians do not speak up in groups it may be due to embarrassment or a perception of gender roles while African-Americans may have learned adaptive wariness. West Indians also value working two or more menial jobs to sustain their families here and in the West Indies while African-Americans may be more assertive about 'good jobs' and working conditions. West Indian women may also marvel at the independence of African American women. African-Americans may also feel that preferential treatment is given to African-Caribbeans by dominant Americans. Once West Indians are in this country long enough to understand US race relations they identify more with African-Americans. Highlighting the different and similar historical contexts and perceptions may help the two groups to engage in honest and meaningful dialogue as they discover common ground. A focus on reclaiming pride in African heritage as well as an appreciation of different group histories and individual uniqueness is helpful.

All of the above principles and insights were useful to us in developing the model of the empowerment group and working with the women of My Sisters' Place. The groups were composed of mostly African-American members though several different Afro-Caribbean cultures and regional differences among American blacks were also represented in the groups. Many groups were all black but some were also mixed with whites and a variety of Hispanic/Latino women. Some of the groups had racially and culturally different workers, some had white workers and some had black workers. The common ground of homelessness or being formerly homeless helped bridge differences. There were also other areas of common ground in some groups, such as being persons 'in transition,' or parents, or, in My Sisters' Place III, persons with mental illness. But the workers' abilities to put race and cultural differences at play in the group process and the dual focus on personal and political/ structural change in a racist, classist, and sexist society were also critical to the success of the groups. This is also part of the empowerment approach we now describe.

THE EMPOWERMENT APPROACH AND THE EMPOWERMENT GROUP

The empowerment approach (Lee, 1994) makes connections between social and economic injustice and individual pain and suffering. Utilising empowerment theory as a unifying framework it presents an integrative, holistic approach to meeting the needs of members of oppressed groups. It adapts an ecological perspective as advanced by Carel Germain, which helps us to see the interdependence and connection of all living and non-living systems and the transactional nature of relationship (1980, 1991). It does not deny the possibility of nonviolent conflict as one of the means to releasing the potentialities of people and environments. But this dual view of function needs an additional component: that people/clients themselves actively work to change the oppressive environment and mitigate the effects of internalised oppression. A side-by-side stance of worker and client is needed to release potentialities. Potentialities are the power bases that are developed in all of us when there is a 'goodness of fit' between people and environments. By definition, poor people and oppressed groups seldom have this 'fit' as injustice stifles human potential. To change this unfavourable equation, people must examine the forces of oppression, name them, face them and join together to challenge them as they have been internalised and encountered in external power structures. The greatest potentiality to tap is the power of collectivity, people joining together to act, reflect and act again in the process of praxis fuelled by mutual caring and support.

The assumption about people in this approach is that they are fully capable of solving immediate problems and moving beyond them to analyse institutionalised oppression and the structures that maintain it as well as its effects upon themselves. They are able to strengthen internal resources, work collaboratively in their families, groups, and communities to change and empower themselves in order to challenge the very conditions that oppress.

The basic principle of this approach is that 'people empower themselves' through individual empowerment work, empowerment oriented groupwork, community action and political knowledge and skill. The approach sees people as capable of praxis: action-reflection – and action, action-in-reflection and dialogue.

A unitary conception of person: environment prevents us from victim blaming on the one hand and naivete regarding the panacea of environmental change on the other. It leads toward developing helping 'technologies' (strategies, methods, knowledge and skills) that are both clinical and political. It necessitates 'both and' conceptualisations of practice (Bricker-Jenkins and Hooyman, 1986). People can and must take themselves and their environments in hand to attain empowerment. To envision social change that comes about without the full efforts of oppressed people is to envision a Machiavellian Utopia. To envision oppressed people making this effort without changing themselves: to refuse oppression, to actualise potentialities, and to actively struggle to obtain resources is to negate the effects of oppression in the lives of the oppressed. Both changed societies and changed people are the goal of empowerment. The ultimate aim of empowerment work goes beyond meeting individual needs for growth and power to empowering communities and developing a strong people.

FIFOCAL VISION

Five perspectives are used to develop an empowerment practice framework. This multifocal or 'fifocal vision' also determines the view of the client:

1. the historical perspective – learning a group's history of oppression including a critical-historical analysis of related social policy;
2. an ecological perspective – including a stress-coping paradigm and other concepts related to coping (a transactional view of ego functioning which takes oppression into account, problem solving and cognitive restructuring of the false beliefs engendered with internalised oppression);
3. ethclass;
4. feminist perspectives which appreciate the ceilings and lowering floors imposed by class and race and gender;
5. a critical perspective, analysing the status quo.

Our vision is sharpened in particular areas yet clearly focused with these lenses. In addition to this fifocal perspective the empowerment approach is based on values, principles, processes and skills which are integrated into an overall conceptual framework. Helping processes include the support of strengths and ego functioning; dialogue; challenging false beliefs; challenging external obstacles and unjust systems; developing pride in peoplehood; problem solving and problem posing; consciousness raising and building collectivity. The uniqueness of this approach is the integration of the personal/clinical and the political in a direct practice approach relevant to poor and oppressed people. The reader is referred to Lee (1994) for further detail.

THE EMPOWERMENT GROUP

The empowerment group is a particular type of group which is consistent with the empowerment approach. Many groups may help people empower themselves. The empowerment group has challenging internalised and external oppressive conditions as an explicit focus along with other foci chosen by the group. For example, the empowerment groups at My Sisters' Place addressed personal and systemic issues related to homelessness. A blending of critical education and conscientisation group methods (Freire, 1973, 1990, 1994) with the interactionist and mainstream models, particularly the development of the group as a mutual aid system (Schwartz, 1974; Papell and Rothman, 1980) form a foundation for the empowerment group (Lee, 1994).

Empowerment is an outcome and a process which comes initially through validation of peers and a perception of commonality (Parsons, 1991). Groups may have consciousness raising, help to individuals, social action, social support and the development of skills and competence as their overlapping foci in order to help members facing oppression gain equality and justice (Garvin, 1985). Mullender and Ward (1991), major British theorists, stress that empowerment groupwork must be a self-directed (not worker directed) process. Although there are some differences, the self directed group approach is highly compatible with the empowerment group approach. Parsons (1991) identifies empowerment as: a developmental process which begins with individual growth, and may culminate in social change; a psychological state marked by heightened feelings of self esteem, efficacy, and control; and liberation: The empowerment approach unites these three kinds of empowerment.

Empowerment group skills include: making a clear mutual contract that bridges the personal and the political; establishing the common ground and common cause among members; challenging the obstacles to the group's work; lending a vision; and reaching for each member's fullest possible participation in the process. These are a variation on Schwartz's tasks of the groupworker (1974). The worker will also skilfully pose critical questions and develop codes to focus the group's work (Freire, 1973). Codes are themes chosen by the group for analysis. Codes are conveyed artistically, poetically, musically or in powerful ways not solely dependent on words. Combined, these become 'empowerment group' method.

A WORKER REFLECTS ON EMPOWERMENT GROUP METHOD

Evelyn Thorpe is an older, well experienced African-Caribbean-American worker (first generation American of Barbadian parents) who is also the Residential Director of My Sisters' Place II. Here she reflects on utilising the empowerment group method in her own style of working:

> I approach empowerment work with a desire to have people express who they think they are and how they feel about where they fit into the wider society. I have members of the group sit as closely as possible to each other so as to generate some feeling of unity. I sit within the group so as to become one of its members sharing in the feelings they articulate. I ask each group member to describe/relate an oppressive experience that had an impact on their self esteem or confidence. These experiences could be with family, welfare, school, employment, personal relationships, etc. In this way, the validity of oppression is established. The easy part of developing the work of the group is in establishing that there are possibilities and resources within the group, also that choices were made, evidenced by each member electing to come into a transitional setting. I will then define the word transition so that people may understand that the process has negative as well as positive aspects. The difficult part is in determining which parts of the discussion are being processed, to take that part and move with it towards internalisation. Motivating the group to work is the most difficult part of the work. As transitioning residents tend to be locked into personal conflicts to the exclusion of their groupmates, it is sometimes difficult to focus on a set purpose. It is challenging to

break the cliches of individual concerns and direct the group, through words, phrases, visual or verbal expressions , or compassionate exchanges, to a shared commonality. It is also difficult to channel free expression on imminent issues concerning programme structure. In these instances, I must maintain objectivity and project compassion and understanding on an individual basis; however, I also make clear to the group that structure is important and commitment even more so.

EVELYN CONTINUES ON GROUP PROCESS AND RACE

Issues of race are ever present, though perhaps unspoken, in groups of racial diversity. When a level of comfortability is set, group members are more apt to reveal personal innuendos regarding race. I can recall when a Hispanic and a white client made reference to African-American historical aspects that did not include them. In working each year on presenting a Black History programme, I was able to depict how each person present is included in Black/multi-racial evolution. In the ensuing dialogue, each of these clients revealed how it felt being a minority within the group. Another client spoke up and said, 'Well, you're here now, you're with us now'.

I was then able to assign roles that typified white and Latino contributions to freedom from slavery and oppression.

I view as a plus the sharings of American-Americans in the individual or group setting. The concerns of Afro-American women run the gamut from hope of survival for their children, prospects of upliftment from an oppressive condition, stability of family, to evidences of distrust, despair and paranoia. In the various levels of exchange, one cannot remain 'separate and unequal' due to various life experiences and conditionings. Life-long biases rise to the top and create a rich ground from which empowerment issues can be explored. Minuses are: distrust, disbelief, paranoia, superstition and intra-racial differences as they impact clients' awareness of making breakthroughs to progress.

Bridges are made to Latino and White ethnic clients through conveying an understanding of the dilemmas of language and cultural barriers. The dilemma holds true for the White as well as Latino client, for each one shares a language/vernacular, cultural difference apart from that of the Afro-American. These bridges are constructed and crossed by sharing some of my life experiences and language modifications which allow me to shape myself to fit many moulds.

In many instances the Afro-Caribbean clients views herself as apart from the Afro-American. This is true, granted that the Caribbean cultural experience is based on differences in class, language and mores. In discussions I will ask group members to discuss some of their differences, relate feelings to these differences, also to describe how the crossover experience has affected them. I might then sensitise the subject of racial heritage. Group members identify themselves by adding the suffix AN or IAN to the country or island of origin. One biracial client stated that her mother was British, but could or would not give a racial term.

In groups I share life experiences, I introduce myself as an Afro-American woman, proud—who has known interpersonal relationships with family and the emotional stresses attendant to the 'cross-over' cultural experience. People then often respond with their own stories.

One day the group played a word game with words beginning with the prefix de. A Latino resident chose the word dead. There followed a profound silence and exchange of looks in the group. I asked the client what she meant. She responded with a smile and said, 'yes, dead is what I mean'. She further explained that prior to coming to the programme, she felt dead, in despair, but now felt secure and safe. The group broke into smiles then laughter, for it undoubtedly raised similar feelings. To me, 'meaty' work is doing the circle, holding hands to left and right, creating energy and the power of peace.

Having been a person who has had a good share of authority conditioning, I view my authority position carefully. I have the greatest respect for authority and encourage respect by presenting as a positive role model. Difficulties arise when clients challenge authority or where authority seems unfair. This must be worked through and sometimes we have to compromise. Working with a variety of co-workers of diverse backgrounds is rewarding and enlightening. Each of us handles authority differently.

I am glad that I am at MSP II. Here I can give back a lot of what I have learned through life experiences. I am glad to share in the development of empowerment groupwork'.

To illustrate the empowerment group approach in action, we will present excerpts of empowerment groupwork at My Sisters' Place (MSP). We will reflect now on the 'Successful Women's Group'. Judy Lee and Judy Beaumont were the co-workers for this group which became a protypic group for the development of the empowerment approach. Christy King was a member of this group. She will reflect on the experience after group meetings are shared, as will Judy Lee and Judy Beaumont.

THE 'SUCCESSFUL WOMEN'S GROUP'
FORMING THE GROUP

Membership in an empowerment group is a matter of personal choice based on knowledge of the experience. We found that a 'try it and see' philosophy helps members who share common ground understand what it is like to be in such a group. In forming an empowerment group for women who had 'graduated' from the shelter, the co-workers began by inviting large groups of 'alumnae' to six evening get-togethers. This approximated Freire's culture circle. The codes and themes for the empowerment work would emerge from these six meetings as would a nucleus of women interested in pursuing empowerment together. The format of the evening which took place in the homey atmosphere of the shelter included a dinner where an informal style of sharing mutual concerns could take place, and then a formal period of group discussion when empowerment notions were introduced. Many attended national and local protest activities regarding affordable housing which coincided with these meetings. Seven African-American women, ages 22-34, decided to become the 'Alumnae Empowerment Group'.

The co-workers started off as more central to the process in helping the group develop a structure and maintain a focus on issues of empowerment but they soon took on a more advisory role. Within four months the group developed a club-style structure with a President who called the meetings and maintained the work focus. They chose the meeting nights, time, frequency (biweekly) and the content of the meetings. The workers bolstered the leadership structure and continued to contribute information and to assist in guiding praxis and reflecting on feelings and facts to deepen the work. The group existed for two years though members continue to be there for each other. This is an excerpt from a meeting nine months into the life of the group in which they name themselves:

> Tracey, the President, said 'Alumnae' just don't get it. Who are we? asked Vesalie? We are successful women said Tracey. Yeah, said Latoya, 'The Successful Women's Group'. No, said Vesalie, we can't call ourselves that. Why? Shandra asked. Vesalie strongly replied, it implies too much power, that we are powerful. The worker asked if they felt powerful? Vesalie said, yes we are more powerful now – we've got good jobs, we're good mothers, we help others who are homeless, we are meeting our goals, but we haven't gotten there yet. The worker asked, when you get there, then you have power? Tracey replied, but that's just it, we need that power to get there, and we're on our way. Let's convey that we are powerful women, we are successful women, let's take that name and make it ours. We deserve to walk with that name! The others strongly agreed. Vesalie thoughtfully accepted this and the name Successful Women was enthusiastically adopted.

Names mean a great deal. The worker's questions here are consciousness raising questions.

This renaming after nine months of meeting represents a 360 degree turn in self-esteem, group pride and conscientisation. The use of codes helped the group achieve this new image.

In the Successful Women's Group, two themes were codified; one was 'barriers to success' and the other was 'African American womanhood'. On the first theme the worker asked the group members to define success. It was defined as personal achievement and 'people centred' accomplishments (giving back to the community). The Wall of Barriers was the code:

> The members were asked to imagine and dramatically act out climbing and pulling bricks down from a wall which represented barriers. *The worker posed the question: What are the barriers to young African-American women getting over the wall to success for themselves and their people?* Amika was first to try to dramatise it. She said the wall is over there, I'm going toward it. OOPS...she said as she slipped and fell with a great thud, they greased the ground, I can't even get to the wall. Forget it! Everyone roared as Amika, a large heavily build woman, dramatised falling down in disarray. Tracey said, it isn't really funny. Amika is right, some of us can't even get to the wall. The grease is prejudice and racism. And sexism Ves added, don't

forget that. Shandra said, yeah, but determination makes you try and you reach the wall. Like you finish High School and you think you're somewhere, but you didn't take the right courses to go to college so you got to start all over again. Tracey said, I was angry too when I found out my diploma meant so little...

Shandra got up and started using a hammer and a chisel saying, and this one you got to strike at, its prejudice on the job. You get the job, but they treat you like you're stupid just because you're black. She told of how she was treated by a nurse she worked with...She unwedged the brick and threw it down hard. Everyone applauded. Ves said, OK. Watch out! I'm driving this bulldozer right into the wall. Later for brick by brick, or climbing, the whole thing is coming down. Slam, crash. Everyone cheered her on. Wait said Latoya, a brick hit me, I'm hurt. She wiped imagined blood from her head, its the brick of hating myself because I believed 'if you're black stand back' and I stood back and didn't go for even what you all went for, a real job and all. But I survived and stand here to tell it, I'm going to get me some too! Everyone encouraged her...

The use of humour by African-Americans and other oppressed groups is an adaptive mechanism. But no one should mistake the seriousness of the meanings in this dramatic enactment and decoding which was at once both therapeutic and political - leading to a variety of actions.

The next codification on African-American womanhood was the reading together of Ntozake Shange's Choreopoem 'For Colored Girls Who Have Considered Suicide When The Rainbow Is Enuf (1977).

After several readings of selected poems and their discussion, Tracey, who had committed some to memory, concluded:

These are our lives. It could have gone either way for us, we too could have died, or chosen paths that lead to death of our spirits and our bodies. But, we didn't because we found other women who was feeling what we were feeling and living what we was living. I will always see myself in Shandra. I will always be there for her. We found true Shelter and we found each other, and we found God in ourselves, like the poem says. Yes, said Ves and we found the truth about our struggles too. And we are free, no turning back.

Christy King was a member of the Successful Women's empowerment group and she continues in her association with the agency for individual empowerment work. She also continues her relationships with some members of that group and its workers, sometimes joining in empowerment actions. Her name is disguised in the group meeting presented above to protect the particulars of her life . She sees that group experience as formative in catalysing an ongoing empowerment process. Today she is a woman who uses her voice to speak up on behalf of herself and others. She has examined the effects of internalised racism and external obstacles and has taken actions based on seeing herself as entitled to ' the best in life'. She has moved to a town of her choice which is integrated ,safe, and offers good schools and recreation for her five year old son. While she initially felt isolated in the new town, she joined a local 'Women of Colour Support Group' which helped her to make friends and continue the empowerment process. She completed a cosmetology course and works part time while attending a nearby college to pursue legal studies. These are her reflections and the sharing of some of her current thoughts on empowerment:

The Successful Women's group was a great source of support and empowerment for me. It was a way to reach out to other women like myself with similar issues. The group empowered me to cope with my issues. Getting acquainted with other group members was inspiring and encouraging to me. The best thing about the group was the 'coming together' and having that support system we needed. Moreover, being able to express what was on my mind and not have others be so judgmental.

Being an African-American in the United States is somewhat oppressing because I feel limited in obtaining employment, education and public services. I feel some sense of prejudice in the community or work force. Talking about racism and being oppressed helps me deal with others and their differences. Being able to understand the issues helps me relate more. The racial differences of Judy and Judy B. helped the group feel more secure with white people. Some may have felt inferior with whites as a result of believing prejudice. Another issue is trusting white people. Black women, especially young black women, may have a hard time opening up to white people because they may feel intimidated. They learned from their parents not to trust white people or tell family business. Sometimes not trusting is with good reason. Once I trusted a white male social worker at a Clinic and he told my abusive step father what I said. I didn't think I could ever trust one again. But the group with Judy and Judy B. provided a different experience of white people as I learned I could trust them and that some white people can be trusted, and that not all are prejudiced.

I would like to see more people of 'difference' work with an empowerment group so the women involved can learn about various backgrounds and experiences of others. Since we are involved with a variety of people every day of our lives we should involve them as workers or as part of the group. We should share our differences to help others understand our issues. All minorities should learn about each others' cultures so they can be united against oppression. Lack of knowledge makes people quick to buy stereotypes and to judge people. We should not be afraid of each other. We face common issues. Recently, my College Professor took the class on a trip to the Schomberg Center in Harlem, in New York City. I learned a lot of things you would never find in a history book. One exhibit showed how our ancestors came over on boats and how they were chained together, suffering from many diseases. I learned we were inventors, craftsmen, politicians and so much more. I was so touched that I started to cry. The man giving the tour told me he cried too when he first saw this, and that his tour guide had cried too, as had many taking the tour. Its good to be able to share these feelings with those who share a common bond and to teach our children our history.

I am presently in a Women of Colour support group. Although I feel more could be done in the group , its a way for me to get support and relief from stress. Being able to share and give to others as well as receive makes for a stronger me. This is a poem for my sisters:

Strive For The Best

You should insist on the best,
Because you deserve the best.
If we want the best, then
We can have the best.
You have to believe in the best
In order to receive the best.
So always remember now,
Don't settle for less!

Working with Christy is a profound experience and one that is inspiring to her workers. She teaches us more than she learns. Christy has included us in her extended family. Our empowerment is mutual. Yet, we reflect, for every Christy there were some we lost. Some could not trust us as white women, and some were too damaged by racism to 'open up' ,as Christy says. A few were also painfully homophobic: one or two started a malicious rumour mill we had to deal with. This scapegoating of gay staff and/or clients crops up from time to time. It is never easy to experience. Sometimes we share our feelings and discuss the folly in oppressed groups oppressing each other.

There were times in sharing with Christy and the other group members that we had to come to grips with the vestigial remains of our own racism and exorcise it. We also had to be careful of the age difference and the educational differences so that we did not take on the role of experts on lives that were not our own. We needed to remain intently interested in what they thought and what they hoped to do about the problems they faced . We also felt vulnerable as we made ourselves real and available during and after hours in response to individual requests.

Yet 'going the second mile' also engendered trust as did sharing some of our own experiences with poverty and oppression. Most relationships with the women of My Sisters' Place were gratified with trust and mutual respect as we crossed bridges to each other.

As Executive Director and Agency Consultant as well as direct practitioners , the first hand experience with this and other groups was critical to our growth in understanding and responding with appropriate services. We are dedicated to mentoring, educating and hiring social workers of colour to work with this population. The agency staff reflects this commitment. But we have also heard Christy and believe that white workers can also make the bridges necessary when they act out of knowledge, compassion and raised consciousness, and that there is something to be gained in this configuration too. Ideally , we could assess the needs of each group and assign same race or mixed race individual workers or co-workers depending on the member's needs. While initially we had mainly white workers, we are now fortunate in having a number of African-American and white workers and student social workers in the agency so that group members can get the exposure and build the trust

Christy discusses. It is always important to discuss the race, class, age and any other difference of the worker and be open to members responses. The administrators of the three programmes and the Board of Directors are also a diverse group of women. Sometimes walking the road together meets with obstacles but open dialogue helps to keep the paths open and the focus on the common purpose of empowerment. We will now present reflections of other white and black staff members on the experience of working together with the women of MSP toward empowerment.

BUILDING AN EMPOWERING AGENCY STRUCTURE

As we have noted, the composition of the Administration and Staff is multiracial in order to provide role models for empowerment and models of communicating and working together in a multiracial society. Whenever possible MSP involves clients in the hiring of a Staff or Administration member. In this section Rosalind Moore-Beckham reflects on working with the empowerment group at MSPII after they participated in the hiring process, helping to choose her as the Programme Director. She also shares how she used her own experiences with the group. She is an older African-American woman who was actually raised, and continues to live, in the community where the facility is located.

REFLECTIONS OF MSP II PROGRAMME DIRECTOR

I still remember my first empowerment group at MSP II. I reminded the women that they were instrumental in hiring me. I told them how proud I was that they had made a wise choice. They chuckled instantly recognising my humour. I asked how it felt for them to be on that 'side of the table'. Their response was 'great'. I reminded them that I worked for and with them.

We talked briefly about other people, fire persons, police officers, teachers, social workers who work for the citizens. This allowed for discussion about police brutality, teachers who don't teach, social workers who are too nosey and the list goes on. The question was raised about how we can make people more accountable. I shared a personal experience of the early days of Head Start (a pre-school programme) when we, as Head Start parents, were encouraged to spontaneously visit our children's class rooms, go to the board of education meetings and attend City Council meetings. The emphasis was on involvement which leads to political empowerment...and sometimes to employment. Again on the personal level my involvement as a volunteer in the Head Start programme led to a part-time, then a full-time position with a career ladder in place. For a while the door of opportunity stayed open long enough for me to get an undergraduate degree and much later, a Master's degree in social work. Sharing the above information made it easy to stress the importance of volunteer work as a means of gaining experience and being considered for a job. This was to give the women ideas on how some doors, not all, can be successfully opened through volunteerism. The women agreed and enthusiastically shared accounts of their being in the right place at the right time. One woman told how she helped to develop a parent advisory committee to review class room material and when a grant was approved she was given a stipend for her participation. The women agreed that participation on that level does much to raise self esteem and gives a boost to self confidence. One woman commented that she had never been paid for using her brain...Some one said 'go sistuh, there's no place to go but up'.

I'm reminded of a Yoruba proverb: 'For no man/woman can be blessed without the acceptance of his/her own head. I bless the spirit of my head'. I am including an excerpt from *Acts of Faith: Daily Meditations for People of Color* which I used with the group to encourage valuing their intellect and wisdom.

The wise Africans knew and understood the power of the mind. People can only be as good as their thoughts, as successful as mental patterns, as progressive as their ideas. Africans did not rely on books, relative theories or postulative quotations. They listened to their thoughts, prayed for divine guidance, followed the intuitive urging...

I touched my head and said, 'I bless the spirit of my head,' and the group members did the same. Then I shared that I could remember as an adolescent, my wise mother constantly advising us to: use our heads for something else besides a hat rack. They had heard this too! We connected and made a strong beginning.

As I think of my empowerment, I'm reminded of how often I had asked my mother to make a decision for me (so I could say to my peers – my mother won't let me). Well, she fixed my 'little red wagon' and responded like this. 'Use your own good judgement'. So for the rest of my life I'll continue to use my own good judgement. The good judgement has led me to some interesting experiences like my second career as Programme Director of MSP II. It is also the challenge of a lifetime!

REFLECTIONS OF MSP III PROGRAMME DIRECTOR

Here Gail Bourdon reflects on the consciousness raising experiences in her own life and the ways in which race and class relate to her practice with formerly homeless women with a history of chronic mental illness.

Gail is an early middle-aged woman from a rural, small town, French Canadian-American working class background. Like all of MSP's administrators, she also does direct practice in the programme. She is a Sister of St. Joseph and is pursuing her doctorate in social work. Administrators, the consultant, and staff members do share a Christian faith commitment that is in common with most clients served as well. At times faith discussions are part of the empowerment process for all of us. All faiths are respected and valued.

Gail writes:

I see the raising of my consciousness as being a lifelong process with roots in numerous experiences, relationships and faith. Some critical experiences that helped to lay and nurture an empowerment foundation for me include:

• My relationship with my grandmother, the family matriarch, who exemplifies to me the strength of women in the midst of a traditional patriarchal environment.
• Accounts given by my seventh grade teacher during the 1960s of the demolition of housing and displacement of many poor, predominantly African-American families in Washington, D.C.
• My experiences working with an activist inner-city priest during the late 1970s in a poor, predominately African-American neighbourhood. Through these experiences I came to know and deeply care about many persons who lived lives very different from my own such as homeless alcoholics, prostitutes, and persons of many races who lived on the margin of society. It was during this time that I came to know 'the person behind the label'. As a result of this experience, I began to use my anger about injustices and compassion for oppressed persons to take political action. Until this time I had suppressed most of my desires to be politically active due to my fear of my family's disapproval of some of my political stands and activities. I

learned during this period that I could withstand my family's responses if I were true to my beliefs. Being faithful to these beliefs was to me to follow God's call to 'break the bonds of oppression'.

• My personal experiences of being dismissed or seen as less than capable as a female in a patriarchal society and as a religious woman in a patriarchal (and often discriminatory) Catholic Church.

• My experiences with the Sisters of St. Joseph, the religious community of which I am a member as we strive to change unjust structures and realities.

• The empowerment trainings and groups at My Sisters' Place.

• The stories of and experiences with people who are poor, often of colour, and/or persons who are stigmatised by the label of mental illness. Through their lives I have come to learn about the oppression that they experience. This second-hand but very powerful knowledge stirs an intolerance within me that demands a response of work for social change.

I am keenly aware of the difference in my experiences as a white woman from those of women of colour. My attempts to make a bridge to clients of colour often focus on acknowledging the oppression that they experience and sharing my sense of the pain and anger this causes. I also share my feelings regarding the lack of dignity and respect they are given due to their colour or psychiatric disability and join them in identifying how we, as women, can work together to challenge the discriminations that we face in our daily contact and in the larger society. I also find that taking political action with them, as sisters, (e.g. non-violent demonstrations like the 1991 Housing Now March on Washington, DC and providing legislative testimony) is a critical means by which bridges may be created. Standing together is a way of demonstrating that the empathy and commitment that I feel are not just words but are supported with action.

Although bridges are often made with clients of colour, I sometimes feel that, as a white social worker in an agency that serves a high percentage of persons of colour, my difference remains obvious. As a middle-class white person, I have had many opportunities that were not available to most of the clients whom we serve. I sometimes feel this difference is even more pronounced by my position as a worker and their position as clients. These positions mirror the power relationships that clients of colour experience in a white dominated society. While there are many ways to diminish the unequal distribution of power in the worker: client relationship, the worker retains a unique experience of power that is inherent in the role of worker. This power differential is particularly present with regard to involuntary hospitalisations. It is one of the necessary contradictions in social work with clients whose judgment is severely impaired by a psychiatric illness. This is a power differential that I recognise and one which I constantly strive to find ways of reducing in how the work is done. One way that MSP III tries to diminish this differential use is to involve the clients in the hiring and training processes of new staff members. Here we rely upon their expertise in describing what they and the programme need in new workers. Their input is an important part of these processes.

Probably the most challenging aspect of empowerment groupwork that I have experienced is maintaining the dual focus on the personal and political levels of work. I find it is an art to blend these two aspects in a manner that nurtures the particular level of work at hand without neglecting the other level. Sometimes the integration of levels occurs naturally, while other times the integration may feel more disjointed. Finding the right moment and manner in which to make the connection to the other level requires a skill that comes only with sufficient practice.

In addition to this challenge, I find that empowerment groups with persons who are mentally ill present a unique challenge. While my attention and energy as a groupworker is focused on the usual tasks of keeping a focus and deepening the work, I must also attend to the simultaneous task of 'weaving in' the sometimes loose connections of delusional clients. (See Lee, (1994) for examples of this work). In these groups, I work to process group information to help further the work while I am simultaneously sorting through often confused remarks of a group member to find the theme or common ground that connects to the work of the rest of the group. While this is demanding work, I have often found that even the contributions of delusional members have contributed much the group's process of empowerment.

I experience working within a woman-based agency structure to be both freeing and challenging. It is freeing in that male dominance is not experienced within the agency. The challenging aspect is that, as a women's organisation, there is an expectation that we run the agency in a manner that is consistent with a feminist approach and that we do not replicate many of the oppressive conditions found in many male-dominated organisations. This may mean we are held to higher standards and, as individuals with human frailties, living up to these standards can be difficult. In MSP III the women are involved at every level of the hiring process. We also use a collegial team approach. The staff is now bi-racial and clients experience us as a caring team considerate of them and each other. Sometimes they see us as interchangeable but the African-American workers are especially important in role modelling for the clients.

A WHITE WORKER REFLECTS ON USING HER OWN EXPERIENCES TO MAKE BRIDGES
Jean Konon is a divorced, Anglo-Saxon mother of two children who was raised in suburban Connecticut. She is an experienced social worker who has worked and supervised MSW students in two programmes at MSP, the Shelter and the Transitional Living Facility. She feels that her own empowerment continues to grow as she works with staff and clients as MSP and she shares her own life experiences in the empowerment groups:

When I came to MSP Shelter in 1990, I had been divorced for one year. I had achieved my divorce after a two year court battle. Finally I was able to negotiate a settlement with my ex-husband. I had spent considerable time in the courts and realised that there, as well as with the police department, I was seen as less credible than my husband even when I knew he was lying. The process had been a difficult one and I was looking for some answers on how to face this hidden but occasionally blatant discrimination.

The first bridge that I constructed with group members was the obvious, the fact that I was a single mother raising 2 children, essentially alone. I spoke about my experiences that seemed appropriate. One time, I remember doing a group in which I talked of my daughter's illness with croup and the sense of being all alone with such a responsibility. A young woman who was the mother of a child with a cleft palate discussed that same feeling. There was a woman who had appeared to be unreachable who also shared her experience when her infant had croup. Quite by accident, I found that repeating my mother's and grandmother's sayings based in their religious beliefs to be another bridge to work on with the women. I remember another group in which I said to all the women, rather spontaneously, as

I looked around the table at the sad and discouraged faces, that my mother had frequently said that we all had our crosses to bear and that each person there seemed to be carrying a particularly heavy cross that day. I remember the majority of the women participating in the group. The group members began talking about the difficulty of finding housing and the difficulties being homeless imposed on them.

One of the most difficult parts of the work continues to be the suspiciousness that I face, given the fact that I am white and appear to be a 'rich suburbanite' to many of my clients (even though I face my own financial difficulties). One of the most difficult groups I have done was one in which I used the word 'ghetto'. In this instance, the women reacted to my use of the word. I suspect it would not have been received so offensively had one of the shelter residents used the word. Eventually their problem with my use of the word was processed through, but it was a difficult process. (See Lee, 1994, pp.243-245).

I find myself being very careful in how I phrase things. I am recently struck with how things have changed in regards to the way race is looked upon. As someone growing up in a suburban white community, I was taught not to distinguish people by their race or ethnic background in describing them. That was thought to be a sign of not being racist. However, since I began work in the inner city, I have been struck by how naturally African-American women will describe each other by including their skin tone. I recently watched an Oprah Winfrey show with the LA Police Department following the O.J. Simpson verdict and heard white police officers carefully describe how they did not distinguish people by their race. Oprah said, reflecting the view of many of the panel and audience, that if they did not see her colour, they did not see her. It was described as not seeing or allowing for the African-American experience in the United States. At worst, at times, I am viewed as racist. Other times, I am viewed as being condescending. It's hard to absorb all the anger that is projected on to white workers. Being seen as the enemy was particularly pronounced when I was in a position of greater authority. Yet most often using myself authentically with group members does engender trust and enables the work to deepen.

I have found that when my life has taken a difficult turn, it is helpful to look at what my rights are and further to ascertain where my power lies. Generally, first I am made to feel that I have no options or rights. The political work I have done over the years is helpful in my fighting for my rights. The worst outcome for me personally is to feel that I have been silenced. In my personal life I have learned to reach out for the help of others in dealing with my personal struggles. I have found it a great comfort to have someone to share my problems with, or to have someone write me a letter of support or to witness certain events to prove that they have occurred. In a sense, I can be that witness for our group members.

One of the difficulties that I find in the work is when I encounter a client who believes that I have the answers to a problem they are facing. What is then most disconcerting is to be seen as deliberately withholding the resources or information required. This view is often taken by someone who has bought the oppressive message that they have no power. It is difficult work to get beyond this perception to the point where I am working beside the client to try to unravel this problem into workable and understandable units.

I have found that a sometimes tense part of the groupwork is the first few moments after the group begins as I am trying to encourage the women to think about the group as their time to focus on their issues. It can be very difficult when there is a strong individual who is committed to obstructing the group process. Paradoxically, as the social worker, I find myself put in the powerful position and expected to teach the group. Helping the group to take the power and make it their own is a challenge.

As a staff member of a woman based agency, I have found it to be an organisation with many possibilities, not limited by gender. In the political spectrum of my work, I have learned that my views were more respected because I worked for an all female organisation and thus the politicians would have to listen to a woman if they were going to hear from our agency. It is also clear to me that our agency is well respected. One of the reasons for this is that it is quite an accomplishment for a female organisation to work and provide services for women in the inner city. I feel that this is particularly true when I go to the legislature as there are many men there who say they would not venture into the area in which we work.

For the clients, I have found that they see the agency as offering many role models. Many women prefer to be in a women's facility, not only due to the fact that they may have been abused by men in the past, but because they felt better understood psychologically. Many felt that there were things only other women would understand and that they would be more accepted in their present homeless condition. I have been impressed with the ability of women to have their consciousness raised while living in a woman based agency. The mutual aid part of the work is wonderful to see as it flourishes first out of necessity and then out of positive experience. I believe that change starts there as men are generally women's first choice of providers. Here women learn to take care of themselves with the support of other women. And, we all grow in the process.

WAYS TO RAISE STAFF CONSCIOUSNESS AND OFFER SUPPORT AT MSP

The use of team meetings is the primary vehicle to reflect on empowerment practice across racial lines. In order to offer service to people who have experienced oppression, staff members also need to reflect on their own experiences of discrimination and oppression as well as their experiences with clients/group members who may be quite angry and at times lash out at them and at each other. The joys and accomplishments of empowerment practice are many but the stress on the worker is grist for the mill and very important to share.

Consultants are also used to help staff in these reflections. As the primary consultant, Dr. Lee has experienced profound professional growth in working with the staff and clients of MSP. She also offers essential support and teaching in the empowerment approach. Yet at times she has felt the need to call upon African-American academicians/practitioners who can add lived experience with racism to their consultation. On one occasion, Dr. Lee invited Dr. Ruth Martin, Associate Dean of the University of Connecticut to share with a group of biracial staff members and group members who were preparing to present the empowerment group approach at the Hartford AASWG Symposium. The group was uplifted and their work was catalysed by Dr. Martin's sharing. In her reflections, we see the benefit in seeking insight and wisdom from African-American elders.

REFLECTIONS ON BEING A GRIOT-STORYTELLER/WISE ELDER FOR A DAY

I was pleased to be invited as an African-American griot to an empowerment group of staff and women at My Sister's Place. As I reflect on the experience, I can say that it was truly a momentous occasion. When I was first invited as an African 'griot,' I wondered aloud, 'Me, a griot/elder? What can I say that would sound wise and profound? And, weren't the old griots from Africa male, not female?' But then I said to myself, 'Why must men be the norm by which all wise thoughts are measured?' As I thought on what I would share, I looked within and drew on Gwedolyn Etter-Lewis' *Black Women; Life Stories: Reclaiming Self in Narrative Texts*, in which she wrote:

Oral narrative offers a unique and provocative means of gathering information central to understanding women's lives and viewpoints. When applied to women of colour, it assumes added significance as a powerful instrument for the rediscovery of womanhood so often overlooked and/or neglected in history and literature alike... (1091, p.17).

I believe, as does Etter-Lewis, and Hull, Scott and Smith (1982), that oral narrative is ideally suited to revealing the 'multilayered texture of black women's lives' (p.17). With the above statements to empower me, I felt free to allow those historical experiences from the past, including the racial degradations, the social and political situations, and family and culture to emerge. I also recognised the importance of how hearing about these experiences could empower a younger and more troubled generation. These were the forces which helped shape the history of the African-American race in this country.

I was asked to participate in a socio-political drama, a code for the group, to lead the march and to beat the drum. Group members carried huge puppets of Uncle Sam as a skeleton (symbolising death caused by US militarism), and a Mourning Woman of Colour. As I began to beat the drum, I felt a surge of emotional swelling within my chest. The feeling of marching to the beat of the drum reminded me that this was the language of my forefathers. I then shared my own story with the group:

The tin can that I used for a drum carried a picture of rice growing in a field. This picture carried me back to my early childhood and the memory of my father, for not only did we grow rice on our farm, but my father tried his hand at entrepreneurship (rice and grits mill, and a saw mill). Even though he was never a complete success, he tried and tried and tried. And always, there were the racial issues as Cornel West affirmed in *Race Matters*, the aim of which was to 'revitalise our public conversation about race,' (p.158). Years after my father refused to become a sharecropper and declared, 'my children are going to school,' race continued to matter, and education for Negroes was not considered essential. In 1941, after my father had recovered from the Great Depression, he bought a huge farm. He died a year later. Yet, the legacy of the strength to survive continues to this day. Race mattered even after we bought the farm. My perceptions were validated when I read Mays' autobiography (1987), a man born 34 years before me, and found some of the same racial issues. He wrote that the Negro who owned land 'had to be exceedingly careful not to be accused by white people of being uppity'. Further, 'the more a Negro owned, the more humble he had to act in order to keep in the good grace of the white people' (p.9). This was quite noticeable when we went away to school and returned home on vacation. My mother always insisted that we children come out to speak to Mr. So and So. I felt resentment even though these were white folks who were good to my family. In fact, one gentleman and my father were friends for years. The day of my mother's funeral, the same gentleman parked his tractor and waited with respect as the funeral procession passed. And one other gentleman encouraged me when I was in college, 'two years to go, is nothing,' he said. 'Just think that you want to live two years longer, and at my age, time flies'. Could anyone imagine that being asked to engage in a programme could bring forth such memories?

Being invited to participate in this empowerment group made me appreciate my past and helped to strengthen me for the future. Again I was reminded of the number of times, because of racial struggles, poverty, and inaccessible schooling, I was required to pick myself up, dust off and start again. I am also reminded of how badly this information is needed in the profession of social work. Racial discrimination continues to be destructive in this country, which means that social workers still need to be trained to recognise and deal with these issues early in the relationship. Stiles and Others' *Hear It Like It Is*, first published in 1972, is not outdated. They suggest that discussions of race have to become an integral part of social work process with clients/group members. Stiles and Others write that understanding the necessity for open communication about race requires an appreciation of the life experiences of blacks with whites as well as of the attitudes of many blacks toward social work (p.224).

All these years as I have worked in the profession of social work, as practitioner and college professor, I have come to understand the full meaning of the need for clear communication. I question ways to help my peers understand that the many experiences from my past have made me a solid person, sure of myself, and of my values. My mother always told us, 'you are as good as anybody'. Even though most white people have not acted that way toward me, this I know. And because of that knowledge, when in the public schools and working with a group of white women married to Navy men, I was able to help them deal with their husband's absences while on submarine duties. The women said:

> We believe you like us Dr. Martin. You never talk down to us, even though we know you are very knowledgeable and must interact with educated people. You always treat us with respect.

How do I help a group of white students in the classroom understand that the richness of my life is unique and that there is so much that they can learn? How do I help black students and social workers understand that you can do this white man's work and our own work. The depth and breadth of what you are is there. Don't give in. Don't give up. Set your sight upon a star and reach. I did it, so can you. I believe this is what it means to be a griot/elder: to help the group to grow and excel'.

CONCLUSION

Dr. Martin's lived experience, wisdom and excellent encouragement was empowering to the staff and group members of MSP, and to the members of the audience at the Symposium as well. It is an empowerment message that encourages us to relate as honestly as possible with each other. We trust that this message of stretching for the star of empowerment together, as we have done here, will reach the reader as well. We feel empowered by sharing reflections on race in the United States, groupwork and race, the MSP story, and the empowerment group approach with our colleagues abroad. We have offered theory, practice and reflections. We have noted that working together in a multiracial agency with women of colour, is not an easy process. Yet it is full of rich rewards and understanding as we learn together. We are ending with a 'Closing Thought' from a recent empowerment group meeting. We hope that this sharing of theory, practice and reflection/dialogue will promote action in the arena of transracial understanding toward the ending of racism, especially in social work practice.

Our work together has shown:

> For every difference that makes us unique,
> there is a common thread which connects us all.
> We share the need for home and community,
> for love and respect.
> May these common threads form a beautiful world
> in which all people and all cultures are honoured.

(Anon)

Note
1. Quoted from *The Empowerment Approach to Social Work Practice* (1994, New York) with kind permission of Columbia University Press.

Groupwork with Black Users with Learning Difficulties

JULIET AMOA

In this chapter I will be telling you a little about myself and the origins and development of my work. All the issues I shall be discussing are viewed primarily from a personal perspective. I will look at the needs of people with learning difficulties, focusing on the needs which are particular to black people. I will be discussing from a personal perspective how the group I facilitated for black people with learning difficulties evolved, examining the positive and negative attitudes I received both from users and professionals.

I aim to explore the processes I felt the group travelled through, discussing individuals involvement and expectations of the group. I shall also analyse the group's values and its ability to meets its aims and objectives, as well as addressing issues which arose for individual group members.

Finally I will examine the processes I went through while facilitating the group, exploring the dilemmas I faced on occasions and the feedback I received during this period.

I am a black African woman from mixed parentage. I was born in Ghana, West Africa, but have lived much of my life in Britain. I have spent my entire career in social work in one form or another. Although I have worked with many different user groups, the majority of my work has been with people with learning difficulties.

In my experience I have found generally when working with this group of people that you need the same approach as when working with any individual. You look at the person as an individual and aim to meet their needs. The only factor which sets people with learning difficulties apart is that while some aspects of the person may be underdeveloped others may not, or may have developed in quite a diverse manner. Having a learning difficulty can be a permanent state; this does not mean you are unable to learn, but that you may learn on a different scale or in a different way to the majority of the population.

During my experience I have been able to find very little material such as books or learning equipment for people with learning difficulties, especially for black people. Over the years, when discussing issues of blackness with people with learning difficulties, it became apparent that they not only felt oppressed due to their learning difficulty but also due to their blackness.

On one particular occasion a user who I was working with came and discussed an incident with me which occurred in the day centre he was attending. He was called a 'Nigger' by another user and when he informed a member of staff they asked the user who verbally assaulted him to apologise. The apology was given flippantly, yet it was felt by the white worker that this was an adequate way of dealing with the abuse - perhaps due to the serious misperception that people with learning difficulties are not affected equally profoundly by their race and gender. The victim of this assault was devastated and expressed to me that not only did he feel the apology was not meant but that further action should have been taken. He said 'being called a 'Nigger' for a black person was like being stabbed in the back for a white person'. He also felt the day centre should be a safe place where he would be protected from this kind of abuse.

This incident came as no surprise to me, but I was concerned as it seemed that when professionals came into contact with people with learning difficulties they focused on their difficulty, often ignoring their needs in regard to race or gender. It was obvious, when working with this user group, that they felt a lack of belonging to their own racial groups due to their learning difficulty, and to groups of people with learning difficulties due to their blackness. On numerous occasions users have spoken to me about the racism they have experienced, and having a learning difficulty has made them easy targets. This has ranged from name calling to physical assaults. A black user where I had previously worked had been attacked by a group of white youths, and when the incident was reported to the police he had identified two of the youths in a line up. The youths were charged, but when the case came to court it was decided that he was an unreliable witness due to his learning difficulty. It took him a long time to come to terms with this experience, and his self esteem was greatly affected.

This was one of the major reasons why a black group for people with learning difficulties was essential; especially as often - unlike a lot of black people without learning difficulties - these individuals seemed rarely, if at all, to be in environments which consisted only of black people, and very often were in situations which were majority white. Most users either lived with their families; were on an adult fostering scheme which tried to operate same race placements but where this was not always achieved; lived in residential establishments where the rest of the people in the home were often white; or lived alone.

Like most black people in Britain I feel I live in a society where often our local communities and neighbours are in majority white. As a black person I regularly seek out black groups or gatherings to be a part of, as I feel most people be they black or white, male or female, need to be in the company of people who have similar life experiences, which most definitely depend on race, gender and a whole variety of differences. For many black people with learning difficulties these experiences are limited, and they are often trapped in environments over which they have little control. This means that their views of their own blackness and of other black people are often negative and their self-esteem very low.

These work and personal experiences led me to feel that the time had come to develop an environment that would enable people to learn from each other; share positive and negative experiences; discuss issues around being black; and participate in activities which would enable them to build up their self-esteem and help them to become confident about who they were. A group would be an ideal opportunity and productive place to do this, especially as I had facilitated many groups in the past.

I had tried previously to establish a black group for people with learning difficulties, but there was strong opposition as it was felt that the users were not ready, and other staff members in the day-centre establishment where I was working would feel uncomfortable about such a group. The majority of these workers were white and had been there for many years and were opposed to any changes. Many of them felt threatened by my mere presence, and suggestions of tackling black issues were met with statements like 'we have Caribbean meals, and in self care sessions we teach people to cream their hair and skin'. Obviously, unfortunately this was not nearly enough.

At this point I thought it would have been extremely productive to facilitate a black group, but I also felt that the users may experience such negative attitudes from the other staff that it could be counter-productive. My manager also did not want it to go ahead as he was concerned that it would upset too many of the other workers. I obviously disagreed with his viewpoint, but was not in a position to over-ride his decision, so I decided to set up a group which was mixed but was still addressing black and cultural issues. This was an alternative which was acceptable to the rest of the staff group and still gave us a forum to discuss black and cultural issues. I felt it did not enable black users to feel safe enough to deal with the real issues of race and racism but it did address issues of difference.

Eighteen months later, after I had moved from the day-centre setting to a fieldwork team, I again proposed setting up a group for black people with learning difficulties. On this occasion my suggestion of a black group was not opposed so I began to take steps to create one. Time had passed and I was now in a different post with different people. I had more power to initiate this kind of group and I feel I had also personally developed and was more assertive.

When setting up this black group I had very clear ideas about how I wanted it to function, the people I wanted to be involved and the aims and objectives. I wanted it to be a relaxed atmosphere for people to grow and develop, where there would be positive images and ideas about being black, and where issues of race and racism would be addressed and positive methods for dealing with racism would be considered. Also I felt we needed to work from the premise that just being together and sharing experiences as black people would be extremely valuable.

It was most appropriate to run this group on a Saturday once a month so as not to interfere with people's day-time activities or employment. It seemed obvious to me that there should be a black co-worker and consultant for the group. People's learning needed to be aided by practical activities which would require some resources. A suitable venue near to public transport and familiar routes familiar to these particular service users was crucial as we were unable to provide transport. At that time I was employed in a social work team who worked with people with learning difficulties, and which included two black workers, including myself. I discussed the group with my team manager and colleagues, and some important issues arose.

The first issue concerned my expectation of having a black co-worker. Although I felt it was obvious for a number of reasons, primarily as this was a black group, some colleagues drew my attention to a 'black group' which was facilitated by one black worker and one white worker. My feeling was that this was an impossible situation and a group would be unable to function positively with this kind of arrangement as there would be implications for its development. The presence of a white co-worker would inevitably change the power balance in the group, and they would not be able to identify and empathise in the same way with the black group members, whose personal development may have been hindered. At that time the only comparison I could make to relay my position clearly was the inappropriateness of a man co-facilitating a women's group. My opinions regarding this were accepted and respected and were no longer an issue.

The other major concern, particularly for my team manager, was the staff time commitment. This included whether I could fit this group in with my case-load, and also finding a black co-worker with experience of people with learning difficulties and groupwork who would be prepared to work on a Saturday. My next step was to discuss this with the groupwork co-ordinator for the Borough to try to find a co-worker and group consultant. My ideas were met with a positive reaction and I was given several suggestions about how to contact the appropriate people.

The other member of my team who was black seemed an obvious person to approach but she was new to the team and I was unsure if our team leader would support both of us running this group, and whether my colleague would want to take on this commitment. I approached her and she was very keen. We then set up several meetings to plan and organise the group, and the groupwork co-ordinator gave us several names of black consultants. Eventually we contacted one who had the time to give us, although as it turned out we only needed to meet with her twice.

When meeting with my co-worker to plan the group, many further issues were raised, including the usual ones of finding an appropriate venue, creating referral systems, and deciding on the group structure and timing of reviews. In addition to these, other issues arose which were specifically due to this being a black group. The venue was important not only to provide the good transport access, but also it needed to be a building with a suitable room where we could make posters and put our work on the walls to reflect positive images of black people. We found a location which was a health authority building and we were given access to it at weekends. We had support from people who used this building as they assisted us practically, not only with giving us a key but also by giving us access to other parts of the building like the kitchen.

We wanted to create a referral system which made it clear that this would not be a drop-in group, and that members would need to establish some form of commitment to it. In the group we would be dealing with emotive issues so there needed to be consistency and trust in other members and, ultimately, safety in the group.

The referral forms which we created asked potential members to fill them in themselves and if people were unable to write we gave room for them to draw. We not only asked for people's names and addresses but also their race and interests. On these forms we also set out clearly the aims and objectives of the group and the kind of activities the members would be involved in. We both felt that primarily this group should be fun but it would also involve activities which were specific to this user group and provoke learning.

In our planning meeting we developed ideas for activities such as cooking, art work, outings, videos and discussions. However, we wanted the details of all these activities to come from the group members themselves, so even though the referral forms had a list of our ideas we decided that the first session would include 'brain-storming' as well as a chance for people to get to know each other. We felt this would be empowering to a group of people who were oppressed on two counts. We also decided to review the group every six months, with the possibility of taking new referrals at that point, but only after first discussing the idea with the original group.

At the referral stage we also discussed the term 'Black' and the fact that the political meaning was quite different to the reality of those who classed themselves as being black. We decided we would send referral forms to whoever requested them as we made it very clear on the forms that whoever was filling them in needed to see themselves as black, and as having a learning difficulty. At this point my co-worker and myself had many discussions around the term black and even though we felt that we adhered to the political meaning we also had our own interpretation of the word 'black' which was personal and a reflection of our own experiences. We found that service users took the term literally and often only called people black if they were very dark skinned, and brown if they were slightly lighter. We did a lot of work on this issue.

We also agreed to meet all potential members individually before the group started, for two reasons. One so that at least at the first session individuals would know us even if the other members were new; and secondly to ensure that people were clear about the type of group they would be joining. We decided that ten members would be a good group size, and that the first ten appropriate referrals would need to wait until the first six-monthly review date, when they could join if any old members wanted to leave at that stage.

At this referral stage it also became apparent that we needed the full support of residential establishments and carers to ensure members regular attendance at the group. Even though we would be reminding people monthly by letter and phone calls, we would need carers also to remind individuals on the morning of the group to ensure they arrived. This seemed even more important with this group as we were only able to meet once a month due to my colleague's and my own commitments and time limitations.

When referral forms were returned, those completed by potential members were very clear about why they wanted to attend, but forms which professionals had taken it upon themselves to complete were more vague. Most users had put that they would like to meet new people and participate in activities. Very few users mentioned wanting to be with other black people, but this came as no surprise as for many users at that point it was an unspoken issue.

On three separate occasions professionals had filled out the forms and in each instance this caused service users some distress. One man who was Caribbean and had mild learning difficulties had been referred, but when we met him he made it clear he felt that to run a black group was racist. When I tried to explain to him the purpose of such a group he said that it was anti-white and he was very angry, and expressed this in no uncertain terms. The second was a Chinese woman who knew nothing about the referral, and when I met her she was clear that she did not see herself as black. Recently she had been raped by a black man and was very negative about Caribbean black men. This referral was again totally inappropriate. The third was a man of mixed parentage and he considered himself brown, not black, so of course he did not want to attend a black group.

All the other responses were from black Caribbean people with mild to moderate learning difficulties who labelled themselves as black but felt negative about this label. Four women and six men were in the group and many more men than women had referred themselves (one possible explanation for this imbalance is the tendency for many black boys who exhibit 'unacceptable behaviour' to be labelled as having 'learning difficulties' at an early age). I felt that for most people the motivation for joining such a group was clear in that it was one of the first groups of its kind, and for most black users it was rare to have this opportunity, and so they grabbed it with both hands and really grew and developed from it.

On average, due to holidays and sickness, eight people attended the group each month and we ended up running for a two year period with six-monthly reviews. The group became very powerful and generated much change; group members' attitudes developed and they became enlightened about their blackness. It was a wonderful experience which I shall try to describe in the next part of this paper.

We had many discussions on many topics, but the issues of the group's race would arise regularly. The group consisted of Caribbeans except for myself. We looked at the issue of who was, and the fact that I was from mixed parentage became the topic of conversation on several occasions. Members questioned my blackness and after many discussions they began to understand this concept, but they did at times question the identity and colour of other racial groups, for example Asian people. This debate was left unresolved, not surprisingly as it is very confusing for this kind of group to get to grips with the concept of political blackness, especially as it is questioned and often rejected by the wider society.

For me personally the issue of who sees themselves as black, and the implications of this, is still an open question. The term 'political blackness' is clear, but the reality is not. In my experience, some individuals from the Asian community, and some people of mixed parentage have taken issue with being labelled black, often not seeing themselves in this category. Although this has been the exception rather than the rule, I feel it occurs for very complex reasons, but ultimately is due to society's negative view of black people. When it comes to working with an individual, who defines their blackness, society or the individual?

We watched two videos which had a great impact. These were 'Cry Freedom' and 'Lean on me'. Both of these provoked much discussion about race and racism in other countries, but people also seemed to be able to relate what they saw to their own experiences. 'Lean on me' is a film about a school in America which has a high population of black students and in which things change after the employment of a black head teacher. It looks at all the issues around racism, and in our group this provoked long discussions about members' own schooling, and we shared the positive and negative experiences people had encountered. After watching 'Cry Freedom' which is about Steve

Biko a black activist in South Africa, we discussed the police in this country. Both of these discussions were initiated by the members of the group.

We carried out a lot of work about who people identified with and why, people's origins in the broader sense, and their personal experiences. We worked on the positives of being black; we made a collage of all black people and mounted it; we went out and brought back posters of positive black images; and we had cooking sessions of Caribbean and African food.

On occasions I felt the group was not totally supported by carers and residential establishments, as members were not always reminded when to attend, and were then very disappointed when they had missed a session. In one instance a white service user was sent to the group as he was staying with a black member of the group. This was obviously totally inappropriate and we had to send him home. The importance of the group was undermined and I spoke to the carer who was white about the fact that not only had the man failed to refer himself (through no fault of his own), but that he was of course white. I pointed out that this was clearly not a drop-in centre and that as she was aware, it was most definitely a black group so unable to cater for white service users. She seemed uncomfortable about what had happened and acknowledged it was her fault, not the user's, as he would have been unable to get to the group alone or even to have been aware of its existence due to his learning difficulty.

As mentioned previously, my identity was sometimes questioned, but I felt the group had progressed considerably as when we had our six-monthly reviews, and new members joined, when they questioned my blackness I was able to sit back as other members would explain the concept of black people from mixed parentage. On one occasion a member referred to me as a half-caste and another member explained why this was an inappropriate term and should not be used.

After the group had run for a year my co-worker had to leave, and as the members were so keen we continued our meetings whilst I looked for a new co-worker. I was clear that due to the fact we had been running for a year and the group were very keen on my co-worker it would be very hard to find a new one. Not only would it have to be a black person but also someone who would be able to work at weekends and who had experience with people with learning difficulties. In the end, I was unable to find the right person so continued to facilitate it alone for one more year.

Practically, facilitating the group alone was very tiring and I really missed having a co-worker to reflect with and bounce off ideas. Even though I looked for a new worker the group made it clear they would be reluctant to accept a new person. What was interesting was that when there were two of us the group were more demanding and not only relied on us practically but also to initiate discussion etc. When I worked alone the users took more initiative: this change may have been due just to the group's natural progression, and I was left unsure whether there could have been other reasons. Overall the experience of facilitating this group was extremely positive, although the contextual issues and attitudes previously outlined did concern me.

The group as a whole seemed to develop an awareness and an understanding around racism and their blackness. Whereas some members, when initially joining, hated being referred to as black and used the term reluctantly, they left the group feeling comfortable with their blackness and proud of who they were. One very interesting factor was that even though people entered the group at different times and with different levels of awareness, through sharing experiences and maybe peer pressure they seemed to develop together and at the same pace.

I always felt concerned that this consisted only of Caribbean people except for myself. There could have been several reasons for this: one that the agencies where we advertised worked mainly with Caribbean people; two, we were in Brixton which has a high Caribbean population; three, that the term groupwork has different meanings for different racial groups; four, that other politically black groups did not see themselves as being black. The explanation could have been a combination of all four of these factors, but for me personally the question is still unanswered. As far as facilitating this group is concerned, on reflection we may be should have called it the African and Caribbean group. Even if other black people from different racial groups had referred themselves, would we have been able to meet their needs as a group? On the one hand, as black people we should all be able to come together and support each other, but on the other we need to recognise that we all have different cultural needs and also different racial experiences which do at times set up apart.

Although at times it felt like we were swimming against the tide when setting up this group we continually had positive feedback from the members, carers and other professionals who were in contact with the members. There was a change in members' attitudes and self-confidence, people's self-esteem had increased and they had developed an awareness of their own identity.

After two years the group ended due to my other commitments. I was going on maternity leave and so I have had little contact with the members, although I have had some contact with the services they use. The feedback from workers has been positive in that users have learnt a lot from the experience of the group and maintained their development and understanding. When we had to end, the members and myself were disappointed for a variety of reasons but it seemed mainly due to the point I made earlier that this was, for most members, the only forum for them that consisted of all black people, and, with the exception of myself, people with learning difficulties.

It was a situation where people could look at their own blackness openly and deal with some sensitive issues with the support of other people who were in a similar position. I feel that black groups should be common practice in services for each user group, and definitely have a valid place in all agencies.

Groupwork as a Tool in the Celebration, Resourcing and Development of Gypsy and Traveller Culture

Sarah Cemlyn

Introduction

This chapter aims to explore the contribution of groups and groupwork to the struggle of Gypsies and Travellers to achieve equal rights as a minority group, and to sustain and develop their culture. Examples of groupwork are presented, in the context of the issues and challenges facing Travellers. These groups represent a variety of origins, membership, aims, activities and agency contexts. There are also core issues with which they are all engaged. The chapter is intended as a contribution to publicising and celebrating the work of these groups, and their relationship to the survival and development of a persecuted nomadic minority.

The next section explains how the particular examples have found their way into this chapter, after which the current situation of Gypsies and Travellers is briefly outlined. In the central section, the groupwork examples are described, based broadly on a common framework. In the conclusion emerging themes are discussed, compared with existing models of empowerment oriented groupwork, and lessons for groupwork with Travellers identified.

Research for the Chapter

Information was sought about groupwork with Travellers mainly in the Midlands and South of England and Wales, through a process of networking especially with Traveller Education Groups. The initial request included both an open enquiry about any form of groupwork, and a focus on social action groups and Travellers' facilitation of groups. Several supportive and encouraging responses, and exchange of written material about group and community work, led to visits to four projects which most closely represented groupwork. Another visit was possible in North-East England somewhat serendipitously. A Dublin organisation which has published extensively was visited some years ago. Time and resource constraints inhibited the geographical range of contacts and the number of visits undertaken. The chapter is therefore only intended as an outline of possibilities and an exploration of themes.

Initial exchanges involved further definition of issues, while retaining responsiveness to the diversity of experiences. People were generous with their time, although visits were mostly single events. A combination of methods was employed including interviews, participation in group activities, and use of other materials. The issues covered included: group origins and context; and the members' use of the group for analysis, challenge and change in their situation, for individual and collective empowerment, and cultural celebration. A theme in the research of ethical and political significance has been the role of non-Travellers, including that of the researcher. The relationship between Travellers and non-Travellers in groupwork, and in supporting Travellers' rights and culture is discussed in the context of the role of workers.

GYPSIES AND TRAVELLERS

Gypsies and Travellers are a relatively small group in the UK but attract a disproportionate amount of hostility. Sometimes their presence is overexposed, at others they become invisible. The accuracy of the official caravan count in England and Wales is contested (Green, 1991), but suggests about 80,000 people. Travellers are also in housed accommodation, sometimes for want of alternative. There are various broad groupings, and many sub-groups. In England and Wales these include Romani Gypsies, who increasingly use their own name Roma; Irish Travellers, and New Travellers. Both terms are also used generically and are so employed here. The known history of different groups has been chronicled elsewhere; what needs to be restated is the exclusion and persecution which has been a predominant feature of ten or more centuries (Liegeois, 1986; Liegeois and Gheorghe, 1995). This chapter draws predominantly on work with Irish Travellers.

The situation of Travellers in England and Wales in the last 50 years reflects twin themes of enforced mobility and pressure to settle, undermining a central element of Traveller identity and culture: nomadism, the freedom to determine when to travel. The resourcing of Travellers' lifestyle on their own terms required sufficient quantity and variety of sites, and Traveller participation in their planning and management. However the 1968 Caravan Sites Act's duty to provide sites was inadequately implemented: 40 per cent of Travellers were without legal sites 25 years later, often in intolerable conditions and subject to harassment; while some site provision involves ghettoisation and forfeiture of aspects of Traveller lifestyle in exchange for security in poor conditions. Frequently allocation policies take insufficient account of sub-groupings among Travellers, resulting in difficulties on sites. Many Gypsies prefer to provide small sites for themselves, but face almost insurmountable obstacles in the planning system. Instead of enforcing appropriate provision, the government effectively criminalised travelling in the Criminal Justice and Public Order Act 1994 (Hawes and Perez, 1995).

The inadequacy of site provision underpins environmental, economic, political and social disadvantage and discrimination on an intense scale. Services which are a right such as education and health have often been unavailable or inappropriate. There have been positive changes nationally in education over recent decades, and local developments in health (Cemlyn, 1995). Provision in education, health and welfare faces complex challenges of acknowledging and meeting Travellers' needs without pathologising and marginalising them as a minority group. A similar level of complexity is encountered in relation to groupwork with Travellers. A key question is how to make groupwork available on equal terms to Travellers without imposing alien cultural norms, in a situation of unequal power relationships.

Traveller culture emphasises group connection, but these are natural family and friendship networks. In Romani and Irish Traveller culture, marriages, deaths and births are occasions for large family gatherings. The even larger social gatherings at fairs and festivals celebrate Gypsy and Traveller identity. Religion is an important focus of organising for some groups. In Ireland political protest and the Catholicism of Travellers have been combined in the establishment of a yearly solidarity pilgrimage since 1989. Across Europe the Gypsy Evangelical Movement is a self-organised movement of great cultural and religious significance for many Roma. Gypsy and Traveller self-organisation and political development has been growing since the sixties, both nationally and internationally (Acton, 1974).

However many Travellers remain disconnected, and there are numerous obstacles to self-organisation, including the dominance of settled modes of organising, the depth of oppression which inhibits analysis and collective action, the inevitable focus on physical survival for those experiencing the worst conditions and enforced mobility, paradoxically the disabling effect of some site provision putting Travellers' existing networks under strain, and the exploitation of Travellers' disadvantaged situation. While in all these situations the resilience of the culture is expressed, continuously challenging ethnocentrism and discrimination, its full development is limited in a hostile environment.

Groupwork and community development are therefore more often encountered in situations where Travellers have some stability and are in a position to explore and promote their ethnicity, culture and rights more fully, but this is not exclusively so as this account illustrates. Any such work with Gypsies and Travellers undertaken by non-Travellers involves offering an alliance to contribute to the self-organisation skills of the community, building on Travellers' own networks.

THE GROUPS

In this section an outline is given of each of the groups focusing on the following aspects: the Travellers' situation; the agency base, agenda and worker style; the origins, aims, organisation, membership and activities of the group; and perceptions of group achievements across a range of dimensions internal and external to the group.

Groups facilitated by the London Gypsy and Traveller Unit

Information was gained through two days spent with LGTU, meetings with staff, and participation in outings with the girls' and young women's groups. LGTU was in the process of an evaluation by Charities Evaluation Services and I observed a feedback session between staff and the CES evaluator (Willoughby, 1995). LGTU's own excellent annual reports on their groupwork were subsequently made available (Emmerson and Kennett, 1995; Mozzaka and Webb, 1995; Witt, 1995).

LGTU works with the Irish Travelling community in Hackney, Haringey and Camden. Some of the Traveller families live on a recently opened but isolated official site in Hackney, some on unofficial sites, and some in houses. Hackney has not had a non-harassment policy, and has only recently, under pressure, started to provide basic facilities such as water, toilets and skips, to unauthorised sites.

All families have experienced years of harassment, discrimination, lack of adequate access to services, and the instability resulting from frequent evictions (Birtill, 1995). They have a strong cultural identity as Travellers and commitment to sustaining it. However their discriminatory treatment means that their experience of their culture can be somewhat encapsulating, cut off from opportunities to exercise their rights as citizens and from interacting on safe and equal terms with other cultures.

Most of the young Travellers have had interrupted primary schooling, and few continue consistently with secondary education. They have minimal access to mainstream youth services and other educational and leisure opportunities. Within the culture of this group of Travellers young people expect to marry early and to have several children, though perhaps fewer than their parents. Gender roles are clearly defined; girls take on domestic and child care responsibilities within the family at a young age, and are closely supervised outside the family. The boys also start to work with their fathers by their teens, but the decline in the Traveller economy and resultant erosion of men's occupational role can affect both them and their fathers negatively.

The LGTU is part of Save the Children Fund. SCF has been working with Travellers throughout England, Scotland and Wales for 25 years, focusing on promoting rights and access to general services, under-fives work, inter-agency liaison and community development, although financial cuts have recently threatened to dent its strong lead in this field. During the eighties the LGTU was based in Camden, but moved to Hackney in 1994 as the work became more intensively focused in North-East London. However its work continues to have wider connections and implications, for instance the Safe Childbirth for Travellers Campaign, and the lobby about the childcare implications of the 1994 Criminal Justice and Public Order Act.

LGTU has established a clear direction and strategies for its work. There are three strategic priorities: community development; promoting the development of policy and services in North-East London boroughs; and influencing work regionally and nationally. These directions interlink, but this chapter is mainly concerned with its community development work. At the time of writing (March, 1996) LGTU had eight part-time and full time workers including job-share coordinators, and additional sessional workers for some of the groupwork. One of the workers identifies as a Gypsy.

A major vehicle for the community development strategy is groupwork with young people. LGTU has been working with girls and young women aged 10 to 18 plus since 1991. In 1993 the group's size and wide age range led to a division into one group for 10 to 14 year olds and one for those 15 and over. The boys' group for 10 to 15 year olds was set up in 1993. This direct work grew out of unsuccessful attempts to facilitate Travellers' access to mainstream youth provision. LGTU believes there should also be a young men's group but has insufficient resources. In 1994 there was also a women's group, but this was discontinued because of erratic attendance.

The experience of working with the young people's groups has led LGTU to develop and define its groupwork objectives which were revised in 1995 to include the following: develop Traveller young people's leadership, participation, responsibility, and ability to influence decisions; broaden horizons, raise expectations, present challenging ideas, and increase tolerance and respect among young Travellers for differences of culture, race, religion and lifestyle; raise young Travellers' awareness of their human and legal rights; increase social and personal skills including communication, cooperation, assertiveness and conflict resolution; promote positive self-esteem; and offer support in dealing with the challenge of growing up. The interplay of personal development, social/political goals, cultural affirmation and inter-cultural negotiation is a theme which recurs throughout the groups described in this chapter.

The LGTU groups therefore operate on similar principles. There is a strong emphasis in all three groups on what is broadly termed social education, which encompasses most of the objectives outlined above. There are also similar organisational arrangements and methods. Each group meets weekly and is facilitated by two LGTU workers. The boys' and girls' groups have additional sessional input from LGTU and/or Haringey or Hackney Youth Service, and these boroughs provide premises. There are also periodic outings. The workers summarise the negotiation around the groups' agenda as balancing fun and social education.

The groups are closed in that there is a defined membership. The boys' group has a core membership of 10. The girls' and young women's groups are limited to 15, with new recruits joining a waiting list. A key factor with the girls' and young women's groups is the number who can be accommodated in the minibus, which is used to collect and return them. Without this provision most members would not be allowed to attend. However the pick-up, which can take over two hours, is an important time for reestablishing contact and for personal conversations between members and with workers. Although not collected, the boys are returned by minibus and this is also an occasion for further discussion or group activity e.g. songs.

Outreach work with the parents of the young people is built on the long relationship of trust between LGTU and the Travelling community, and seeks to maintain regular contact and exchange. Outreach uses the opportunity of the pick-up or return, while the wider work of LGTU connects with the same families. The evaluator found the parents universally positive about the groups.

The young people are involved in negotiating a programme within each group. Similar themes occur across the groups, in particular culture and identity, cooperation and decision-making, health including sessions with a drugs peer education project, and contact with a wider range of ideas, experiences and people than would otherwise be available. Because the groups are built on the personal and cultural needs of the members, the constellation of themes and the way they are approached is different in each group. Some examples will be given to illustrate the methods of the workers and the development of the groups.

The boys' group spent some time working on identity, firstly at the individual and them at the group level. For several of the boys the stresses in their lives had led to personal difficulties manifesting themselves in emotional and behavioural ways, including conflict within the group. Previously unsettled lives due to evictions, unsatisfactory educational experiences and the pressure of being a member of a very large family all contribute to the difficulties experienced by the young people, several of whom are brothers. These issues highlight the importance of supporting the development of a positive sense of self, assertiveness and self-confidence.

The methods used in the group to work on individual identity are described as follows:

> By making life size self pictures, family shields, offering picture choices and mask-making, all accompanied by much discussion, the concept of 'the self' as a unique individual of value was allowed to germinate (Witt, 1995).

Some of the results of this work can be seen through changes in shy or quieter members: for example asserting the right to be called by his own name rather than a nickname, or asking for artwork to be displayed. The individual work laid the foundation for work on the group identity. The boys were supported to express their positive identification with the group through the collective creation of a group logo and name ('Fianna Buachailli'). This process both validated their group identity as Irish Traveller boys, and their individual identity through the production of membership cards, exemplifying the interaction of personal and group development inherent to groupwork. Also evident in this work with Travellers, whose minority group identity is under constant assault, is the central importance of cultural identity for the individual and the group.

The sessions on positive group identity led to work on problem-solving, team-building, conflict resolution and trust, in meetings at the youth centre and in outdoor activities. The developing confidence in the group as a safe and supportive environment enabled some sex education work, often very difficult to approach in Irish Traveller communities. This in turn led to work through art, drama and discussion on the uses and abuses of power, including differential access to power by men and women, and domestic violence (Witt, 1995).

Thus through the groupwork the boys develop increased personal confidence, and have gained a greater understanding of conflict and cooperation, and skills in negotiation and teamwork. The evaluative comments of both the boys and their parents recognised this. They are also enabled to clarify, celebrate and project their culture with greater confidence, and to start to examine inequality both external and internal to their culture. On this basis the young people can begin to develop leadership to contribute to the development of their community and culture.

Traveller girls share with their brothers the discrimination affecting the whole community and the denial of adequate educational opportunities, particularly at secondary level for this generation of young people. In some respects their opportunities are more restricted than their brothers', because of the protection which surrounds them due to their role in preserving the family's reputation, and their domestic reponsibilities. For the girls' group to operate with the support of the parents, the trust between the workers and the parents is particularly important. In addition to regular contact during the pick-up, written explanations about group membership and agreements about specific outings are used.

The development of skills, confidence and self-esteem has been a strong focus in the girls' group, with health and fitness as an overarching theme. Opportunities have been provided both to develop more traditional skills and to try out new ones. Activities such as sewing and cooking are gender-related, but the girls have not previously had the chance to become proficient in them. Pride in their achievements in these areas builds individual confidence about controlling their own projects and taking initiative. This is important as a support to them in trying less familiar activities such as canoeing or swimming. They have also begun to acknowledge their lack of literacy and welcome input on this as part of the programme.

The girls' group has also focused on interpersonal skills of cooperation, problem-solving, conflict resolution and leadership. The activities themselves such as games, dance and drama can promote these skills, but the process of planning and evaluating the programme each term, and making decisions within the group, is an equally important mechanism. On occasions contact is arranged between the group and a group of settled girls around a neutral activity, such as boating. (Mozzaka and Webb, 1995). This theme of groupwork facilitating contact between Travellers and settled people on equal terms is present in all the groups described in this chapter. For many of the Hackney and Haringey young Travellers, interaction with settled people is either unequal, unavailable, or to be avoided.

The CES evaluation session outlined a number of effects of the girls' growing confidence and skills and broadening horizons as identified by the girls themselves, and a great sense of pride in the group. The girls are more able to participate actively in group discussions and to initiate contact such as telephoning the workers, they are more open to new experiences and activities, and more confident about handling themselves in such situations outside the group, such as at a swimming bath. The evaluation provided a mix of comments from the girls about collective decision-making which indicated a developing dynamic between workers making decisions, members expressing individual views, airing of disagreements in the group and effective group decision-making.

Their parents commented on changes such as girls being brighter and 'more mannerly', their improved cooking and sewing skills, being more ready to do their housework, and a shy girl becoming 'bold', which implies assertiveness. This is another interesting mix indicative of the development promoted by the group, in this case of increased involvement in traditional activities and of greater willingness to challenge. The girls clearly value the broadening opportunities provided by the group. Their opportunities within the family context may also be expanded because there seems to be a degree of interaction between the girls' growing confidence and reducing parental anxiety and restriction, enabling the protective boundaries surrounding them to be extended. At the same time their increased sense of achievement may make some domestic activities more satisfying in themselves, thus pleasing their mothers. The girls also have a greater awareness of rights of access to general community facilities. The picture is indicative of growing skills in negotiation and strategising within and outside their families, and therefore of ability to influence decisions affecting themselves.

Through the group the girls both express their identity and rights as Travellers in relation to the wider community, and assert some claims to their individual rights as young people. The firm trust and respect between LGTU and Traveller families means that any intergenerational challenge in developing the culture, for instance in relation to gendered restrictions, appears integrated and remarkably non-conflictual. In Crickley's (1992) discussion of the intersection of sexism and racism in relation to Travellers, she argues that the external oppression of racism has to take priority, but this does not mean that internal gender oppression should be ignored. In the girls' group, the power issues associated with age add another dimension. Several of the LGTU objectives focus on promoting the potential and empowerment of young people growing up. In all these areas the LGTU workers are negotiating with great skill a complex route in relation to empowering and liberating practice, building on very firm relationships with group members and the Travelling community generally.

At 15 the girls become eligible to move to the young women's group. They are entering a different life phase with many engaged at 15 and married by 16 or 17, and with the age difference come other changes. In 1994 there were ten engagements, seven weddings and three young women had babies. Married women have more status in the community so there is a shifting dynamic in the group.

Most of the young women stay in the group after marriage, and several who have babies attend periodically.

Many of the methods and processes within the girls' and boys' groups apply also within the young women's group. However the level of participation and awareness is different for this older group. For instance the sharing of programme planning between the workers and members is more developed and is a key objective. Travellers' culture and identity, health, and political awareness have been three major themes. The young women actively contribute to identifying the issues of concern and interest that they wish to explore. A variety of groupwork techniques are employed including role play, video, visual aids, participatory exercises and discussion.

The young women's comments about the group and the workers indicate a very high value placed on the group, and a very trusting and resilient relationship with the workers, who are the only settled people they know well. As with the other groups, it is on this basis that the group is able to explore personal topics which could not have been approached two or three years ago, for example drugs awareness, HIV and sexual development. In the young women's group the health education theme has provided an opportunity for exploring concerns about sexual health. Such opportunities are not otherwise available within the Traveller community. Despite this shift in relation to a cultural boundary, the workers are clear that they do not move too far across it, for instance they do not discuss sexual relationships.

However assumptions about gender relationships are shifting. Marital violence no longer goes unspoken and unquestioned among the young women who have been in the group. Instead some tell their parents and the youth workers about it, and impose temporary separations on their husbands in response. These examples further illustrate the delicate negotiating role of LGTU workers, respecting Travellers' ethnicity while supporting the young women in challenging restrictions and inequalities on their own terms.

The impact of the young women's group in relation to political awareness and leadership can be seen from specific outcomes where the members have taken action. Some of these are group events, for instance challenging a leisure centre manager who denied them admittance with an affirmation of their legal rights; drafting a letter to a newspaper in response to an article stereotyping their group. This activity involved a collective process supported by the workers of questioning the assumptions in the article, clarifying the reality both of the group's purpose and of Travellers' lives in contrast to these assumptions, and deliberating the most effective way of conveying their ideas in writing.

Other actions extend further outside the group to a situation where the young women have taken political leadership in resisting eviction of a group of Travellers from an unauthorised site through organising a collective letter to the council leader, meeting with officers and joining a deputation to a council meeting. The eviction has not happened, instead basic services have been provided (Emmerson and Kennett, 1995). Traveller women have been at the forefront of developing political leadership in other geographical areas, but they tend to be older and with reducing child care responsibilities. The role of these Hackney young women therefore indicates a strong interaction between personal and political development, rooted in the groupwork.

All three groups therefore portray very positive achievements in relation to LGTU's objectives. The work provides support to young people in a similar vein to other youth work. It is based on a relationship of trust and dialogue with the Travelling community, which both respects their culture and also poses challenges to its development as a source of political strength for the community. In a different context Breton (1991b) argues that challenge is integral to support. The strand of active engagement with the culture, of dialogue and critical questioning reflects ideas of empowering practice in groupwork (Lee, 1994) and education (Freire, 1972). It is most clearly seen in the group closest to adulthood, the young women's group, for instance the newspaper letter, and the wider campaigning.

The age dimension involves a key element of the power issues in these groups. The young people are negotiating the power relationships between adults and children and the issues of growing up, in addition to the power relations between Travellers and the settled community, and for the girls especially, gender dimensions. The broad objective of promoting personal effectiveness is of particular importance for the younger groups, but firmly in the context of promoting cultural identity and confidence. This process feeds into the parallel objective of promoting political effectiveness, which comes to evident fruition in the older group. This highlights the significance of insufficient funds for a young men's group.

The relationship between Travellers and non-Traveller workers finds particular expression in LGTU's work. Its long history of direct work and campaigning, and its relationship with

Travellers in North-East London provide a foundation for the workers' involvement. However each worker has to establish their relationship with a community whose overwhelming experience of settled people is one of persecution or indifference. For many of the young people the workers are their only close contact with a settled person, and this has implications for their responsibilities as role models. In the CES evaluation some young people, while retaining pride in their culture, identified future roles for themselves outside the familiar cultural pattern, for instance as nursery or youth workers or teachers, clearly reflecting the influence of LGTU and other workers with Travellers. In North-East London there is some way to go before Travellers fully take on such roles. A different situation has developed in Dublin in the last decade, where the mobilisation of EU funds by Pavee Point (formerly Dublin Travellers Education and Development Group) has made possible a well resourced programme of political, social and occupational education based on conscientisation principles and partnership between Travellers and non-Travellers, and including the training of Travellers as youth and community workers (DTEDG, 1992, 1994a, 1994b).

For LGTU there must be a continuing strong role as a bridge between Travellers and settled people and institutions, and this is seen in all aspects of its work. With limited and threatened funding, LGTU has focused its groupwork resources on young people. It has successfully committed itself to the complex work of supporting them in building understanding, confidence and skills to assert their own and their community's rights, its cultural strengths and needs, and to begin to take leadership in the political development of their community.

Southwark Traveller Women's Group
The information about this group came from meeting the worker (a teacher), from her reports and searching deliberations, from the group's publication *Moving Stories* (Southwark Traveller Women's Group, 1992), and a brief discussion with a former member, now in Redbridge (below). The group no longer meets as such, but its achievements pointed to its inclusion.

The group began in 1989 when Irish Traveller women on an unauthorised site in Peckham, mostly related to each other, came together with community work support to campaign for improved facilities. After a fairly successful phase of action-oriented work, the momentum began to diminish, but the group took up one of the woman community worker's suggestions, of literacy work. A teachers' team member became involved, and worked with the group for the next four years. In this development process we see a different spiral to that in the LGTU young women's group, in which personal development and social education precedes community action. In this case externally oriented work led to a greater focus on the women's own lives and experiences. Hancock (1986) discusses different routes to conscientisation in community work and second chance education, and the impact of the women's movement in establishing a greater personal-political integration in community work.

The teacher's approach to literacy development was to focus on enabling the women to feel ownership of writing and literature. Rather than exercises, she and the group read together a book by an Irish woman Traveller (Joyce, 1985). This prompted the women to think about their own life stories, and the idea of writing a book emerged. This project had a creative purpose for the members and also a wider political aim of countering oppression (Laing, 1993).

Over a year and half the group of ten to nineteen women shared, discussed and, with the teacher's assistance, wrote up stories about their lives, families, culture and beliefs. In so doing they addressed 'the powerlessness of sections of our society to control the representation of their lives. The impact of these accounts is to shatter these images and false representations. ' (Laing, 1992) They express the hope that 'this book will help you look at who we really are and that at the end we will seem less like strangers to you' (Gaffey, 1992). The book won community publishing and photography prizes and was runner up in an adult learners award.

The group also developed its previous agenda of political action. Members participated in national and parliamentary campaigns about safe childbirth, travelling and accommodation rights. They became involved in education work, and gave presentations to conferences, exhibitions and professional training sessions of teachers and play workers. The focus on education work was strongly motivated by their desire for better educational chances for their own children and all Travellers. In this work they expressed similar skills and values as in their writing: personal involvement, mutual support, directness, openness, challenge, and profound commitment to the survival and development of their way of life.

Another aspect of the group's work was networking with other Traveller women's groups in Dublin, Oxford and Camden. In 1993 they used the book sales and prizes to attend a course at DTEDG, with Dublin Traveller women. This networking with other Travellers offered collective cultural strength, and a sharing of the responsibility for sustaining their minority cultural rights in a hostile environment. This enabled some release from the protection which can inhibit cultural development and enabled the women to express themselves more freely.

Over five years the group had contact with three different non-Traveller workers. The community worker represented a practical style of work focused on external goals, with less attention to individual experience. The women gained confidence in dealing with political systems which was sustained, but needed a new direction. The teacher, with a mix of creative vision and non-directive support, facilitated the group in tapping a rich vein of literary and political creativity. She had clarity about Travellers' experience of exclusion and a strong focus on individual development. In a partnership between her and the group equal participation was encouraged. The group unquestioningly accepted everyone, including new or quieter members, and undemandingly supported each other in different roles, while the teacher more persistently nurtured participation from everyone. The DTEDG community worker/ trainer, an Irish settled woman, required equal participation, and focused on the individual's responsibility towards the Traveller community. These contrasting experiences enabled members and the teacher to begin evaluating the impact of different professional styles and ethnic and class background, and to explore this together critically.

From 1992 the group was reduced by external pressures including evictions, and many members moved away. The teacher's employment with the team ceased but she continued working voluntarily with the group. They met up from all over Ireland and England in Dublin in 1993. Remaining members planned a new project in 1994 researching other Travellers' experiences of health and child-rearing, which could have increased critical analysis of their own and others' experiences; however fragmentation forced the group to disband.

Its achievements were wide-ranging, would have developed further, but are outstandingly represented by *Moving Stories,* a key resource in relation to Irish Traveller experience. Individual members have continued public education and promotion of

Travellers' rights. Their potential to encourage new initiatives drawing on the group's experience is exemplified below.

Redbridge Traveller Women's Support Group

This group provided a number of sources of information about its development: their productions of a photographic calendar, three videos and two scrapbooks, a conference speech text, in addition to a meeting with most of the group members and the worker, and supplementary discussion with the worker.

The members are Irish Travellers living on an official site outside Oxford and are all related to each other, including a mother with several adult daughters and daughters-in-law. This is the first permanent site most of them have had. It has been open for five years, and the fifteen families have undertaken numerous improvements from their own resources, as well as lobbying the council for basic facilities such as rubbish collection. One of the women had been involved in *Moving Stories*, but came to Oxford in 1992.

This was a crucial link, both for the establishment of the group, and later networking. In 1992 with this member's encouragement the women decided to set up a group, and approached the Travellers support teacher in the local school. She referred them to the community education office, where a part-time worker had just started on an outreach project, funded by central government access funds to promote opportunities for educationally disadvantaged people. The worker facilitates four other classes such as family health, and keep fit for Asian women. Despite no previous contact with Travellers, the support of the group's widening activities has become a significant element of her work. The Travellers' group is the only continuous one, but the agency pattern of providing classes has been an important resource.

The worker was a secondary teacher and recently trained in community education, whose philosophy focuses on the development of individual confidence and skills, but extends to critical participation and the development of group decision-making and control, parallelling the community work agenda (SCCD, 1992). The group illustrates the interaction in community education between access to individual learning and the development of a wider collective political agenda.

The group established itself rapidly, benefiting from members' enthusiasm, ideas and energy, their interconnections, some members' previous experience of groupwork, and the worker's support. She sought city council funding which enabled the group to start meeting in a Baptist Church, where their children joined a creche with settled children. Tutoring has been provided for successive series of classes including photography, first aid, image and make-up, cooking. Additional grants have been obtained for particular projects such as film-making, and the group has raised funds through selling *Moving Stories* and its own calendar 'Moving Pictures'.

The initial stages reflect one aspect of the group's organisation and decision-making process. Ideas arise through spontaneous discussion amongst members, and the worker's access to education resources enables them to be implemented. The group has also built in more systematic mechanisms for review and planning, including periodically setting aside sessions for writing up the scrapbook and sharing ideas for future projects. Although the group is close knit, they have adopted an outward-looking perspective and would welcome other Traveller women as members. For instance they have made efforts to involve English Gypsy women from another local site, without success as yet. There have been discussions about the group taking over more of the organisational aspects carried by the worker, and one member has trained as a creche worker. However in general the members value the current division of labour which they describe as them having the ideas and the worker the contacts, supporting them in pursuing their own agenda.

The group has an impressive history over four years. Themes in its work represent strands of activities which are purposeful in their own right, and also interrelate. One theme is access to education which for several of the women was either unavailable or negative during childhood. This theme has been interpreted broadly to develop a range of classes, and to access wider cultural experiences such as visits to museums and historic places. The scrapbooks, through which individual and group responses are discussed, illustrated and recorded, reflect the vibrancy and breadth of the group's interest in, for example, French photography, Egyptian ceramics and Roman architecture. Members stressed that they would not have had done any of this without the group. Basic educational skills are also available, for instance some women have periodic sessions with literacy and maths tutors.

A second theme is the use made of skills learnt, such as photography and film-making. These are linked to specific projects designed to portray and celebrate Travellers' lives and culture in ways which they control. Thus the calendar represents the outcome of their proficiency in all aspects of photography reflecting what is important in their own lives, and that of their minority group. Other examples include videos of Stow Fair and of paper flower-making. The latter directly expresses negotiations around cultural change: the grandmother demonstrates her skill, which she used daily for economic purposes as a young woman, while teaching her daughters for whom it is now an interest rather than a necessity. Other planned projects include writing a book about Traveller culture and health at the request of a health visitor, since there is little accurate information but considerable stereotyping in available material; supporting the health visitor in educational work with other Travellers around childcare; and writing about the differing experiences of health and childrearing of older and younger Traveller women.

A third theme extends this direction. The group has engaged with a range of professionals and undertaken direct educational work about Travellers, challenging stereotypes and prejudice. This is a major group aim. Exhibitions of their photographs have been held in Museums in Oxford and Swindon, with previews for both. Two annual exhibitions presenting their work and Traveller culture were held in the Baptist hall. They have provided training sessions in schools, colleges, priests' seminaries, conferences. They regularly invite groups of reception class children on visits to the site. The training work they undertake is well known in Oxfordshire Education Service. It tends to be undertaken by three or four women together, with some taking this on more readily, and question and answer sessions their preferred style.

As with the Southwark group, the importance of improving education for their own and other Traveller children is central. Their experience of discrimination is not only from their childhoods but very recent. When they first came to the area fourteen years before, the local Catholic school turned them away with 'we've had your sort before'. This school, hearing how well the children were doing in the school where they were finally enrolled, has since, unsuccessfully, approached the parents for them to return. Members speak of the trepidation with which some of their tutors have first approached them, and the dramatic change in attitude after the first contact with the group: 'I just didn't think you were going to be like that'.

A fourth theme is political campaigning on issues affecting all Travellers. This links with the educational work, but has also been expressed directly, particularly in relation to the passage of the Criminal Justice and Public Order Act. The group wrote to politicians including the Prime Minister, and joined a mass lobby when the Bill was going through Parliament. In their style of combining their own skill development with wider purposes, they also made a video of the action with a film company.

A fifth theme is networking with other Traveller women's groups, both nationally and internationally. This work is at the building stage, and relies heavily on their own networks. Links with other local groups have not always materialised, partly because local collective organisation among Travellers can face enormous practical obstacles (Cemlyn, 1994), and partly because of the lack of a nationally resourced coordinating structure. However the organic link with the Southwark group led to visits each way in 1993, involving much valued exchange of friendship, ideas and experiences, and other London links are now developing.

Internationally the Irish connection has provided access to networks; the National Traveller Women's Forum enables Traveller women to come together from all over Ireland. The Irish experience of development programmes prompted exploration of establishing a training centre in Oxford, and the worker and three members visited Dublin and another group in Tuam in 1993. One group member was invited to give the UK perspective on Traveller women at a transnational conference in Dublin in preparation for the Fourth UN Conference on Women in Beijing (Gaffey, 1994). The group is therefore developing an international profile, but paradoxically resources for national networks are lacking. They are in a strong position to support the development of a Traveller women's forum, if organisational resources were available.

Avon Traveller Girls' and Young Women's Group
This group is supported by the Travellers Project Development Group in the former county of Avon. Information was obtained from interviews with workers, group reports and resources, a radio interview and a video. Various reasons precluded direct participation in the group. TPDG is sponsored by the Churches' Council for Industry and Social Responsibility, and aims to promote partnership, rights, self-organisation, public awareness, to monitor services and develop resources and networks. With limited funds for development it focuses on under-fives and youth work. Irish, Romani and New Traveller groups live in the

area, which had a poor record of site provision, improving somewhat in the nineties.

The current sessional workers with girls and young women were first employed in April 1994, and had not previously worked with Travellers. They arranged an induction programme, drawing on other workers' experience and going out with Bristol Playbus to sites. They explored ideas with the young people and their families. This assessment and their own experience and skills, particularly in theatre design, drama and teaching, as well as youth work, formed the basis for planning. Their conclusions were to work with young Irish Traveller women on a recently opened site (which had a community room), and focus on projects rather than trips, which had dominated previous community and youth work initiatives. The group consisted of nine to eighteen year olds, with varying numbers but a core of about six.

During the first six months two projects developed. The workers drew on a television programme about relations between Travellers and settled people, 'Video Letters' (Forum TV, 1991). Inspired by this, and crossing agency boundaries to utilise one worker's employment at a youth centre girls' night, they worked with the two groups of Traveller and settled young women to produce 'Video Friends'; a phased exchange between the two groups through video in which self expression within the groups and dialogue between them was promoted, culminating in a joint meeting on the site. Building on this stage the workers involved the members in a Bristol-wide Festival Against Racism (Gilchrist, 1994). They developed other varied materials about themselves and their lives, and joined the workers at the group's stall in a city market to present these, and answer questions from an interested public.

These projects were multi-purpose. They provided opportunities for the workers to get to know the young women and their interests, aspirations and culture; for members to develop skills and ideas, increase their personal awareness, and gain confidence in presenting themselves and their group to the wider community; and for a group of settled young women to acquire realistic information about Travellers. Periodic trips were reintroduced once the group was established. The workers reported that these methods built up sound relationships and mutual understanding of roles and cultures, opened up dialogue which might otherwise have been difficult, and raised issues needing more in depth work ranging across personal and cultural areas.

Unfortunately TPDG was unable to renew the contracts, but the workers used limited funds to retain contact through shorter activities: a Bristol weekend, prompted by the young women's enthusiasm for new experiences during the Festival, and painting a mural in their meeting room. Renewal of funding in April 1995 enabled regular groupwork to be reestablished, which continued to draw strongly on arts work. A second video was the young women's own creation, produced from their storyline, ideas and skills. Other work explored issues around self-image and the role of women, developing into work on issues of growing up, and sexual development. In this sensitive cultural area, the workers needed to negotiate the basis of such work with parents. Again, at a point of considerable potential, external factors intervened, with several families moving away. A new basis and revised membership had to be negotiated.

These workers faced particular challenges because of their agency's limited resources. They responded by drawing imaginatively on the resources of other agencies, their personal network, including fund-raising, their existing skills, and often committing their own time to the group. They have felt rewarded in developing work which 'makes a difference'. Respect for Traveller culture underpinned the work, although cultural exploration only intermittently became a particular focus. For the young women it was an automatic part of their identity, but their interests lay in exploring topics and activities common to other young women.

The groupwork provided support in dealing with issues of growing up, a service available to settled young people in mainstream youth services. In this the workers experienced some tension between loyalty to Traveller culture and to the young women. Their plans for negotiating this balance, involving outreach work with the parents on the parameters of sex education work, but maintaining group confidentiality about particular issues, echo the longer established work of LGTU. Despite the setbacks the members gained individually in confidence and skills, and the group took on political development work through the video, Festival, and links with other groups. The personal and political elements are integrated, just as the members' identity as young women and Travellers is inseparable.

Cleveland

A brief reference is included to experience in the former county of Cleveland, in order to illustrate the potential of employing Gypsy and Traveller workers. Cleveland had a broad community development approach founded in empowerment. Over a period of years it adopted corporate policies towards Gypsies and Travellers based on equal opportunities and community development. A Gypsy woman who had been active in setting up a residents association on a site was appointed as Gypsies and Travellers Community Development Worker in June 1994, and provided with appropriate training on the job. Whereas there had previously been little effective communication between Gypsies and services, the worker has been able to promote self-organisation among Gypsies in the form of site residents associations, and enable them to begin addressing a range of problems about services and discriminatory treatment through their own action and much more effective dialogue with authorities (Lawrence, 1995a, 1995b).

CONCLUSION

In order to explore how far these groupwork experiences illustrate or extend other practice models, they will be discussed from three perspectives: divergent and common issues arising and the relationship with practice principles in other forms of work with Travellers; comparison with empowerment group models; and specific issues for developing groupwork with Travellers.

Divergent and common issues

A comparison of contextual issues affecting the groups reveals differences in agency base, worker style and professional identification and training, including community work, youth work, community education, teaching and arts work, in both statutory and voluntary sectors. This reflects the multi-disciplinary potential of groupwork. However its adoption necessitated some changes to existing practice in the discipline or agency concerned: the young people's groups created boundaries and specific objectives rather than open sessions; the Redbridge worker adapted her usual peripatetic role to the continuity of the group.

Consideration of principles of good practice in other work with Travellers exemplifies the connections between different strands of work, and the importance of negotiation and flexibility. A survey of practice in health, education and welfare found common principles (Cemlyn, 1995), and many of these are replicated here. These include cultural respect, engagement with the realities of

Travellers' lives, promotion of rights, challenge to mainstream services, community outreach, flexible agency agendas, ability to work across organisational boundaries, political advocacy and developmental work in partnership with Travellers.

Respect for cultural identity in working with a persecuted minority was central for all groups, whether or not this identity was an active focus of groupwork. One element of Travellers' ethnicity is nomadism, the legitimacy of which is constantly under assault from the dominant culture, while being paradoxically enforced through discrimination and harassment. There are challenges here in making groupwork available to Travellers on their own terms. The practice in this chapter demonstrates that facilitating access to groups through such means as provision of transport, networking and flexibility of venue is integral to the work. Resource limitations also mean that groupwork is sustained by working well beyond the agency remit and drawing on personal and inter-agency contacts, and sometimes unpaid worker time. The impact on workers is a symptom of the systematic under-resourcing of Travellers' lifestyle.

Women's greater readiness to become involved in these groups than men may reflect various factors. Traveller women, because of what Crickley (1992) calls the feminisation of racism, experience the group oppression more harshly both in terms of the effect of living conditions and harassment on their own health and well-being, and in terms of their role in seeking to minimise the stress and disruption for their families. Related to this is the readiness, already noted, of some Traveller women to take up community action roles, which may link with a similar pattern among settled women in harsh conditions (Gallagher, 1977). Another possible factor is the gender of workers.

Nearly all the workers with these groups are non-Travellers, which poses particular challenges for empowerment practice focusing on ethnicity and culture. However the practice in these groups is about more than ethnic sensitivity, an approach which can reinforce the dominant culture agenda and power by minimising external oppressive realities. Instead the composition and agenda of these groups place their base more firmly within the minority culture, while developing partnership with non-Travellers, including support, challenge and negotiation. The training and employment of Travellers is a priority. While Gypsies do hold key positions such as Gypsy Liaison Officers, this is unusual, and a coherent and resourced strategy to counteract discrimination and provide training is required, as begun in Cleveland and Dublin. Across Europe Gypsy 'mediators' are increasingly employed by authorities and Gypsy associations (Sejdinov, 1995).

Comparison with empowerment models

All the groups combined personal and political development, but the variety of routes taken indicates flexible uses of groupwork models. Two in particular will be considered. The model of self-directed groupwork (Mullender and Ward, 1991) explores the workers' role in supporting a group's analysis of oppression and development of strategies to counteract it, and the stages involved. The model's underlying focus on empowerment and collective action (as in community work) is relevant to the groups, but some of its specific features are more applicable than others. Like the model, group membership was self-determined, in some cases based on 'natural' kinship groups which could nonetheless include non-relatives. However membership was not fully open, since to some extent a natural grouping creates natural boundaries, while membership of the young people's groups was limited by practical factors like transport. 'Open planning' also characterised the groups, with members' interests crucially influencing the agenda. However particularly with the young people's groups the workers negotiated from a firm social education perspective.

None of the groups directly followed the model's core stages exploring the 'what' 'why' and 'how' of their situation; understanding of oppression was indeed a central and motivating factor, but its systematic analysis was not the primary focus. In some cases the action stage developed rapidly and was combined with creative activities. One difference may lie with Travellers' experience: the intensity and pervasiveness of anti-Traveller hostility combined with pride in Traveller identity may render some of the model's analytical stages redundant; Travellers know only too well the external source of their difficulties, and are reminded of this daily. However the picture is also more complex. Travellers require equal opportunities to increase political understanding of the operation of oppression and re-evaluate their own experience.

This theme is present in the groups, but sometimes inconsistently. The Southwark group's writing process enabled sharing, clarification and reflection on discriminatory experiences, power issues in different worker styles were compared, and its proposed project researching other Travellers' experiences would have provided further opportunities for critical comparison; LGTU's analysis of Travellers' situation is built on years of interaction with their community and enables the workers to support group members in developing their own analysis, as with the young women's newspaper letter. Redbridge group members participated in an international conference developing analysis of Traveller women's oppression and empowerment. Pavee Point, which sponsored the conference, offers a model in which an articulated political analysis, an international perspective and developed organisation and resources enable it to provide such opportunities more systematically.

The self-directed model moves between analysis and action. The political action phase of the model is well represented here, including the young women's groups; there are many actions to control representation of their culture, challenge stereotypes, promote rights and improved services, participate in campaigns, and network nationally and internationally. Networking increases mutual support for those developing leadership in their communities to promote political change. Networking and alliance building between groups is widely acknowledged in community work to be a source of strength in developing analysis of oppression and strategies for change (Gilchrist, 1995), in parallel to the collective process between individuals within groups. The extreme discrimination and marginalisation of Travellers makes this even more pertinent.

The model suggests the worker's role becoming redundant. These members take on para-professional roles, providing training alongside professionals, while the worker's role of support and resourcing may be redefined, but not eliminated. This suggests partnership rather than redundancy. An aspect to be monitored is whether some actions might meet the needs of the settled community and of statutory agencies for understanding of Travellers, more than the needs of Travellers for well resourced opportunities to reflect as well as act, and develop liberation strategies through praxis. Overall therefore the groups illustrate broad themes of the self-directed model but it is not a complete explanation. In particular it views personal change within group members as a 'secondary advantage', whereas all the groups had a strong emphasis on personal development, through social or community education.

Lee's (1994) empowerment group approach provides a

complementary perspective. It emphasises the integration of personal and political change, and building on Freire (1973) characterises the worker as a co-investigator who supports members in saying their own 'word', problematising their experiences and stimulating critical reflection. Her 'fifocal vision' is a series of lenses through which workers seek to understand the multi-layered nature of oppression and people's potentialities in overcoming it towards empowerment. Although there are many compatibilities between these two models, Lee's approach has some additional relevance.

The worker tuning in to the world of people she works with is reflected in the process of workers initially unfamiliar with Travellers acquainting themselves with their experience, taking account of historical, structural and cultural factors. The focus on co-investigation and dialogue is reflected in various ways, through the Southwark book, Avon's 'Video Friends', the Redbridge exhibitions and videos, and the ongoing process of identifying issues for the group programme. The theme of non-Traveller workers and Travellers learning together about each others' worlds, and ways of challenging myths, inequalities and injustices, and changing themselves in the process, is clearly expressed in all these groups.

The personal-political link is crucial, partly because Traveller and personal identity cannot be separated. This is particularly evident in the young people's groups in which the negotiation and development of personal identity is central. In this process being a Traveller is a constant implicit or explicit dimension of the work. The acquisition of personal skills enables more successful assertion of their rights as individuals and as Travellers. Building on collective strength, the groups facilitate contacts between Travellers and settled people on more equal terms. The groups can also support Travellers' analysis of their own culture and inequalities within it such as those based on gender. For some young people this takes place in the group itself, whereas for adults who may feel they are carrying an exposed 'representative' role on behalf of their community, a broader network of groups provides more support for this questioning and developmental process.

The personal-political dimension is also crucial because of a focus in all the groups on overcoming previous discriminations limiting personal development, for instance in relation to education and access to mainstream culture. This is not 'compensatory' experience, but a personal and political challenge to denial of opportunity. The enthusiasm and creativity with which members embrace new experiences and acquire new skills is evident in all the groups. They also create new cultural materials which simultaneously celebrate and develop the culture. This goes beyond Lee's model in that these learning experiences are not only empowerment, but also fulfilment. The strong group identity of Travellers is again pertinent here. In Lee's model the structural process of marginalisation causing group members' disempowerment impacts on isolated individuals who have to struggle to a realisation of collectivity. In contrast the stigmatisation of Travellers has a pre-existing profile as a group phenomenon.

Developing groupwork with Travellers
Varied as these groups are, they express strong common themes, linking with inter-disciplinary practice principles. Empowerment groupwork models are close to their experience without fully reflecting it. A development is needed to conceptualise groupwork with Travellers more adequately. A major element to emerge is the use of groups to support and celebrate Traveller culture, to represent it accurately, and to assist those engaged with its development, including challenging inequalities. Individual Travellers interacting with mainstream agencies, for example a child in school, have less power to name and challenge on their own terms. Groups can provide the support and safety needed to deal with the tensions and challenges of living in a hostile society, to undertake a political struggle to promote a culture under sustained attack, and to set up broader networks. The Traveller only composition of the groups is essential to their effectiveness, as with other ethnic-specific groups (Brown and Mistry, 1995). The women only composition of some of them, compared to the prominence of men in national Gypsy organisations, suggests that women's groups have a significant role to play in linking personal, cultural and political analysis and structures, and facilitating wider community empowerment.

The personal-political dimension differentially present in other empowerment models therefore requires further elaboration to include the centrality of culture as an intermediary in the interaction between these two dimensions. The denial of cultural validity is a central feature of the political persecution of Travellers. Their ethnic identity is also integral to their personal experience. All the groups demonstrate that in affirming, defending, portraying and developing their culture they are jointly challenging personal oppression and structural racism.

At the same time the strengths of existing models need to be fully available to Travellers to ensure that they have consistent opportunities for developing political understanding, critical reflection on their situation, and strategies for change that will build on this analysis and are not diverted into focusing on non-Travellers' needs. Although flexibility is essential, there seems much to learn from further sharing and evaluation of Travellers' groupwork experiences.

A Community Based Approach to the Development of Asian Women's Groups

BIJAY K. MINHAS

INTRODUCTION

I have been involved in offering a range of social and community work services within the context of 'multi-racial Britain' for over a decade.

During this time I have witnessed and been part of a process of change within the social work profession that has been undergoing a major shift in its theory and practice base from an essentially eurocentric perspective to one that is ethnically sensitive. This process continues, not only within the training and educational institutions of social work, but more fundamentally within practice itself, the very heart of the profession.

This chapter is all about Asian women and groupwork, one area of practice that has undergone fundamental changes and developments over this period. This is a subject of particular interest and value to me both as a practitioner and as an Asian woman living and experiencing the realities of 'multi-racial Britain'.

The chapter concentrates on work within the Dartford and Gravesham Area of Kent Social Services Department, where I have been practising for the last seven years. It offers a unique account of the pioneering work that has taken place in the provision of groupwork with Asian women. Whilst I have been part of this process over the recent years, the material used has drawn on not only my own personal experiences, but also that of the many Asian professionals involved in this process, and indeed the service users themselves.

I shall discuss the many fundamental issues that have been raised and tackled whilst aiming to provide, develop and establish services from an ethnically sensitive perspective for a specific client group. Apart from some descriptive detail, there is also material focusing on the processes undertaken and the trials and tribulations encountered. There are insights offered into how both service providers and funders have grappled with professional and ethical dilemmas along the way.

The aim is to provide readers with a unique insight into how one particular area in one particular county has faced, and indeed continues to face, the challenge of providing a very crucial service to Asian women.

DEMOGRAPHIC PROFILE

Dartford and Gravesham covers an area of 44.6 square miles in the north west of the county of Kent. Economically, the area displays considerable diversity and is one of the five areas served by Kent County Council Social Services Department.

The area had a population of 219,878 people at the time of the 1991 census, of whom those from non-white ethnic backgrounds comprise some 5.3 per cent of the total population. More than half of this number were born in the United Kingdom.

Dartford and Gravesham has an estimated minority ethnic population of around 15,000 people, and is home to one third of all such persons living in Kent. The largest local minority ethnic grouping by far is that described in the census as 'Indian', of which approximately 80 per cent are Sikh. The localities differ markedly in the proportion of their population which is of minority ethnic origin. At 8.4 per cent Gravesend has the highest proportion, followed by Dartford at 4.6 per cent, and Swanley at 1.6 per cent.

BACKGROUND TO SERVICE PROVISION

Historically, Kent Social Services Department has been slow to respond to the diverse needs of the ethnic minority populations it serves. Until very recently, Equal Opportunity issues had also been low on its agenda. The introduction of the Departmental Equal Opportunity Policy and Code of Practice has marked a very significant change in the way services are now designed and delivered.

The Dartford and Gravesham area has been seen as the most pioneering area within the department in showing a commitment to issues of racial equality. As the area includes a very significant ethnic minority population, that is of Sikh Punjabi origin, the Social Services Department has become increasingly conscious of the inappropriateness of its services. It has therefore been actively working for some time to offer a range of culturally appropriate and linguistically accessible services.

During 1987 -1991 the area had a team of six staff, part funded under Section 11 of the Local Government Act 1966, known as the ' Ethnic Minorities Development Unit' or EMDU. It proved to be a major catalyst for change both locally and county-wide.

Prior to the existence of EMDU, services to the local Asian community had very much been based on an 'ad hoc' approach. Often local community members who had direct experience of the Department had had this involvement through either crisis intervention or direct referrals being made through allied agencies. With the emergence of the EMDU, approaches to service design and provision changed dramatically. The most obvious difference was the impact of a team of familiar faces who could relate and communicate effectively with the local Asian community.

As EMDU developed over a period of four years it witnessed many difficulties, both in terms of its managerial support structures and in terms of how it was received by the department itself. Whilst some people accepted the need for its existence, others argued strongly against it, seeing it as a separatist provision that echoed of apartheid ! The team survived until 1991 when a decision was made to disband the unit and to encourage each social services team to take on the needs of minority ethnic communities as part of its mainstream services.

During its existence the EMDU was instrumental in pioneering services for a section of the local Asian community that had previously remained silent and unapproached. Local Asian women in particular began to develop a link with the team members, who were mostly Asian women themselves from similar cultural backgrounds, sharing their sense of normality and reality. What emerged from this relationship was to prove both challenging and innovative.

Individual Asian women became known to team members through either joint case work or through self-referral. It soon became very apparent that many of the women on the team's case-loads shared the same difficulties of isolation and depression. For some women these problems stemmed from difficult marital or family relationships that were compounded by the realities of living in a society that did not understand or accept them. For others, the stresses and strains of bringing up small children proved to be difficult without any appropriate support services or advice structures. These difficulties were particularly evident in situations where family support structures were problematic. '... stress and depression have become a part of day to day living for black and ethnic minority women' (bell hooks, 1993).

There were already two Asian women's groups in existence by 1985 which had been established through the work of two Asian female professionals working within the local Mental Health Team. Both these groups were popular and well attended providing some support services, but needed to be reviewed to explore their relevance and suitability for the women now being held on the caseloads of the EMDU. As both these groups have been long standing in the area and have encompassed a range of invaluable experiences and processes, they will be the main focus of our attention in this chapter.

NEEDS ANALYSIS AND SERVICE RESPONSE

The two longer standing Asian Women's groups have now been running for about ten years.

Shakti Group

The group based in Dartford was called 'Shakti ' meaning 'strength'. More recently its membership has been widened to encourage women of differing cultural backgrounds. It was then re-named the ' Ethnic Women's Group'. This group was developed and established, initially under the remit of the local mental health team but more precisely through the work of two Asian female professionals. It met once a week from 12.00 - 3.00 pm in a local Social Services Family Centre and was linked to the local Adult Education Centre, where a tutor in Yoga and Relaxation offered the women regular keep-fit sessions and advice.

The group emerged as a vital resource for many local women who had previously been isolated and without a forum of their own. It offered an acceptable, non-threatening and safe activity that attracted the women initially and later progressed and expanded, becoming more structured and clearer in its objectives. Essentially, the group offered local women a forum within which they could come together to share experiences, problems, religious and cultural events. It was also offering support and befriending to women who were isolated, depressed or going through personal difficulties, although this aspect of the group was not so visible. It was evident from the discussions held within the group that women were meeting informally outside the group itself within their homes or at the local Gurdwara (Sikh temple) for religious activities.

Women of all ages, from a similar cultural and religious background, sharing language and diet, were coming together with Asian female facilitators who spoke the same language and understood their realities in a way never done before. Not surprisingly therefore, these groups became well established and grew in popularity within the area: 'Culture is the air that we breath, only when we are deprived of it do we become aware of it' (Pedersen et al., 1989).

Whilst the group met regularly and members became increasingly more committed , group facilitators began to realise the real extent of need presented by some women. The facilitators were aware that a group offering solely activity based programmes each week would not be appropriate in meeting the more therapeutic needs of some of the women. It was not just about a common safe ground upon which to meet to offer each other support, it was about offering women in difficult circumstances a unique opportunity to help themselves and each other through self awareness and personal growth as Asian women.

> Counselling is a confidential service on an interpersonal level, for individuals or a group, which provides, time, attention and respect to women users to explore personal needs related to psychological, spiritual and educational well-being (Birmingham City Council. University Of Central England, 1995, p.14).

The group facilitators therefore often became involved in therapeutic counselling work, which initially took place outside the group parameters. Women were either visited at home or invited into the office for one to one work. However, this later changed when staffing allowed for individuals to be seen during group meeting times in separate rooms for more direct work involving some counselling.

Before moving on to explore the processes through which this group progressed, it is useful to look at the other Asian Women's group based in Gravesend.

Saheli Group

This group, called the 'Saheli Group ', meaning 'friendship', was first established in 1985, by an Asian female, senior social work practitioner, who was also involved in the Shakti group.

The group was based within the local Adult Education Centre and like the Shakti group offered Keep-fit classes to local Asian women. The group was later expanded, offering a range of advice and support activities that were concerned with offering information, support, advice and cultural activities alongside befriending services that aimed to empower and strengthen them as Asian women.

The Saheli group divided in 1989 to offer another group called the 'Asian Women's Group'. The reason for this split was that women expressed differing preferences. The older women wanted to concentrate on keep-fit and health advice whilst the younger women wanted to explore opportunities within Adult Education for self development and a more structured activity programme.

Both groups have had a regular attendance rate of about 25-30 women. The large size of the groups has not been too problematic as structured activities and sessions are focused on the more practical needs of the users. The Gravesend Adult Education Centre has always provided these groups with a good level of support, both managerially and administratively.

Resources

In 1989, EMDU was asked to assume the management and support of the Shakti and Saheli groups. Funding for both groups was secured on an annual basis following regular progress reports being submitted with grant applications.

The groups offered creche facilities and in the case of the Shakti group a creche worker was paid on a sessional basis to fulfil this role. The groups were solely or jointly led by facilitators from within the EMDU who were now also offering a much needed casework service to some of the women attending the groups.

The existence of the various Asian women's groups depended very much on the continued support and funding of the Department. In order for this to happen the department as a whole needed to be regularly updated on the groups progress. Periodic reports and open days were scheduled so that social workers and managers could gain some insight into the groups. The group members themselves celebrated religious and cultural festivals by inviting practitioners and managers to these events.

GROUP PROCESSES: AIMS AND METHODS

The Shakti and Saheli groups were essentially based on three main aims which evolved over time: the provision of activities; access to information and education; and the scope for some therapeutic counselling. These three aims will be discussed separately with some discussion of how group members developed within the groups.

Activities

The groups were essentially open and informal in their structure, offering two aspects of service within one forum. The first were the activity based sessions which were largely concerned with providing opportunities for women to become involved in keep-fit , relaxation, music and dance; and the second included cookery classes, health and beauty sessions.

Information and education

These were a very important and popular aspects of the groups where women gained access to information and education through open discussions and visits from various agencies to discuss services available. This was vital as it meant women were being empowered through access to information and advice. Once they were aware of their rights and the availability of a wide range of services they were able to take-up services that would help to enhance their lives and the lives of their families.

Furthermore, women were able to make choices and take more control of their lives through being better informed about what was relevant and of value to them and what was inappropriate. This can be demonstrated with an example: Asian women had often been unaware of the full range of opportunities available to adults through Adult Education. Regular visits and information provided by the workers served to help some women to take-up education programmes that in turn broadened both their experiences and opportunities within the employment market. Additionally, access to 'English as a second language' courses opened up new opportunities to those who had previously been restricted through language barriers.

Regular advice and information sessions were therefore scheduled. These proved to be invaluable as they offered women vital information that, whilst educative, was also helpful in establishing the group within the community itself as a useful forum through which women were able to access and secure other services, such as Social Security or health provision.

The groups were also informed, in an appropriate way and in terms and concepts that were familiar to them, about the roles and responsibilities of various agencies, Social Services being just one. This again was useful in allowing women access to information and knowledge that served to enlighten and empower them.

Therapeutic counselling

This aspect of the groups provided the women with a safe, protected and acceptable forum through which more vulnerable members were able to gain strength, support and more therapeutic counselling and assistance.

It was inevitable that over time the groups would take on a more therapeutic and counselling role. Often women would only attend the groups to look for the opportunity to talk to group members or facilitators about their feelings and emotions following difficult personal events. Meanwhile the relaxation and keep-fit sessions which complemented this aspect of the group were also seen as important for those attending, and needed to be built into the structure of the groups.

Initially, the need for one to one counselling proved to be difficult. The group setting was not an appropriate forum within which personal issues could be discussed. However, some women were willing to share their problems in the groups arguing that their circumstances were already known to other group members. The issue of confidentiality in these cases was difficult to tackle, particularly for those women who did not want private and personal issues discussed in this way.

In order for the group to offer everyone a safe and non-threatening environment vital issues of group confidentiality and establishing group boundaries had to be considered and worked through within the group.

Women members taking leadership

The group sessions were very much led by the women themselves. Often it was important to use group sessions to establish exactly what the women themselves wanted to do. Women were therefore actively encouraged to take responsibility in defining their own needs and interests. This allowed some of them to become confident and to develop themselves personally, enhancing their self esteem whilst allowing them to develop and discover leadership qualities otherwise untapped.

Group facilitators would delegate certain tasks to these women, such as the arranging of guest speakers, children's holiday activities, outings, rotas for refreshments, fund raising events and book-keeping. Some women over time were able to move out of the group membership role to become either volunteers within the groups or creche workers. This transition took some time in being accepted by other group members who struggled with changing roles and relationships. This process at times led to disagreements and challenges to the worker's power that needed to be resolved within the group by the facilitators who helped define new roles, responsibilities and boundaries.

The groups and the community: issues and dilemmas
With the emergence of any new service come the many trials and tribulations of recognition, growth and acceptance. At that time the social work profession as a whole was being challenged and this was just one area of service involved in this process.

The problems and dilemmas experienced by the various groups became particular features of these groups. We will now explore these and the ways in which attempts were made to overcome problems and dilemmas within practice.

Links with the Sikh community
The close geographic area served by these groups was very important and could not be ignored. In the area most Asian, Sikh families knew each other well. It was therefore imperative that workers were aware of the 'insular' nature of the community and the real practical problems of dealing with well established and often threatening 'grapevine' channels. Some women already knew a lot about each other before attending the group. Each woman was therefore made aware of the need to maintain confidentiality, as a breach of this would have huge implications within the wider Asian community.

The image of the groups both within the Department and the Asian community was also important. The groups had to be understood and seen as valuable resources by social workers and other referring agencies, otherwise referrals may either not be made or made inappropriately. The Asian community also had to understand and value the groups. This applied in particular to men within the community, be they 'religious or community leaders', husbands/ partners, fathers or sons, etc., of the women attending the groups. The local Sikh community from which most of the group members came, was not very familiar with the Social Services Department. It also at that time had very limited information and awareness of the roles and responsibilities held by 'social/community workers'. Historically, the Department had had minimal contact with the local Sikh community so needs were undefined and were therefore unmet.

The EMDU was instrumental in developing a dialogue and good rapport with local religious and community leaders. The community work undertaken to develop this relationship was detached from the casework that some workers were also involved in. It was a difficult task to accomplish and reconcile where tensions prevailed in community work and social work roles and responsibilities. The statutory nature of some casework dictated a more legally binding role, whilst the community development aspects necessitated a very different approach which involved gaining the trust of the community.

The many problems faced by group facilitators arose from this background and from obvious tensions that existed in offering any kind of service to Asian women that may result in them discussing issues or taking actions that were deemed to be unacceptable to the community or that could be interpreted as threatening to traditional and cultural values.

Some women were actually involved in taking legal advice which may have resulted in them taking legal action against abusive partners. This led to considerations of women either leaving or evicting such partners from their homes. Whilst it is important to note that these women were in a minority within the groups, the reality was that only one such case had to become known within the community before the groups were threatened in their existence and challenged in their aims and objectives by the community itself.

There were also clear tensions and conflicts within the group about issues of male power. This was particularly evident where men used physical and emotional power within situations of domestic violence and/or issues involving child protection. Some women felt that these issues were not addressed by the Asian community and were often ignored, whilst others felt that these issues should be isolated away from the community as a whole. These latter women tended not to see male power itself as problematic. It was the mis-use of this power by certain individuals that was at issue.

Some of the women in the groups believed that empowerment of women was empowerment of the community. This process has been very evident within the groups in the way women began to realistically reflect on their lives and situations, emerging in time with a broader world view that re-defined them whilst retaining them within their community. This was a unique feature of these groups as it occurred at a pace regulated by the women themselves. It was also very important as it involved them in a process of thinking that led them from the individual level to the group level.

Confidentiality

Crisis involvement in case work situations meant that any involvement with local families may not have been positive. It was also likely that given the communities well established 'grapevines' , details of individual cases could be known within the wider community. This had serious implications for client confidentiality. The community, as a whole, was not trusting of the department and therefore had a reluctance to become involved with it.

On occasions women would actively encourage more vulnerable members to share personal information, whilst remaining secretive about their own situation. It was clear particularly in the early existence of the groups, that group members were teasing out and checking the group's boundaries. This led, at times, to frustration and anger within the group which was divisive but nevertheless a vital stage in the group processes of building trust and confidence.

Issues of confidentiality became central within the groups as workers struggled initially, to balance the more therapeutic aspects with the more activity based focus. Group facilitators were faced with the difficult and challenging task of offering a group based service to women who were asking for the groups to be both a vehicle for support through which they as women could gain strength and awareness, whilst at the same time being a vital avenue of escape for those who were suffering traumatic and often intense problems in their lives.

This process took time to be resolved but once set in motion it helped to establish important ground rules, and to develop a feeling of commonality amongst the women. Trust was therefore established and respect for each other was nurtured. Women soon realised their strength and potential as women as they had not done before. Equally of value was the supportive environment they created which began to penetrate every aspect of their lives as Asian women, wives and mothers.

Group image and referrals

These women were essentially new to the concept of groupwork. They had over the years been meeting , but the real focus of attention had been on the keep-fit and relaxation. This had been very comfortable and non-threatening. Once some women began to use this forum for support and therapeutic purposes the group encountered some difficulties.

The image of these groups was of great importance as they existed and functioned within the community. Community links therefore inevitably played a vital role in them being accepted and seen as worthwhile. The groups could not be seen as a platform from which local Asian women gained support and assistance in destroying the community and the family unit. Women attending the groups did not themselves endorse this and saw the groups as having a vital role in promoting the Sikh culture and religion as well as the value of the family. Even those women in irreconcilable circumstances that led to families being separated, recognised the value of community support. These women did not wish to severe ties with the community, even if domestic problems led them to end difficult relationships. Women were more likely to gain support from other women in these situations, despite divorce or separation from partners and other family members.

The groups became a catalyst for change for those women who wanted them to be. For others they were useful forums through which they became better informed and more aware. Commitment and ownership in the groups was demonstrated through regular attendance and growing membership. Once group members had gelled together the next task was to ensure their existence through Departmental support and funding.

It became very apparent that the growing number of women attending the group were doing so through a very well developed system of networking that existed within the Asian community. The networking was done, not by group facilitators, but more importantly by the women themselves. This served to illustrate the value of the groups for Asian women locally. It was by the groups strength and understanding, not always recognised, that these women actually understood their own oppression and that of other women.

Networking amongst the women was beneficial as it meant that often more vulnerable women were eased into the groups through existing members who already knew them and were aware of their circumstances. The primary source of referral to the groups was often the women themselves.

Ethnic minorities development unit issues: staff resources, training, supervision

The team members in the EMDU also faced real ethical dilemmas about supporting local Asian women in situations of intense emotional and at times physical trauma that led to them taking legal or police action. The local Asian community to whom it also offered community development services would not permit this to happen without reprisals.

This dilemma was tackled through the very distinctive approach adopted by the group facilitators. This approach rested on the fundamental belief that women did not exist in isolation of their communities or families. Therefore the important role of the community and the family within the Asian culture had to be acknowledged and respected. The professional dilemmas facing group facilitators were concerned with responding immediately to the needs of these women by providing relevant and ethnically sensitive services. However the range of services available from the Social Services Department were catering for the majority white clients in the area:

> British therapists working with ethnic minority families may be handicapped by a number of factors. They will not possess the same world view as their client families; they will not be aware of how normality and pathology are culturally defined; how the prevailing belief system organises the perception and behaviour of the group, what is idiosyncratic, and what would be accepted by the group as being deviant and what is culturally sanctioned behaviour. They will not be familiar with culturally prescribed rules for sex roles and family roles, and how they are different from rules deriving from Western European cultural context' (Annie Lau, 1988).

The EMDU was also struggling for agency recognition and acceptance. The demand from the women for services grew as too did the problem of convincing service planners and funding managers that a very real gap existed, compared to the mainstream services on offer. Historically, the Department had failed to recognise or respond appropriately to the needs of the local minority ethnic communities. In 1987 the EMDU was established to face this challenge and to tackle the presenting issues.

The EMDU were the focal point in dealing with all manner of referrals from the local Asian community. This situation led to any case that did not fit the system's criteria being referred onto the team. The team became widely known within the community and within the Department, both at local and county level. Team members roles ranged from offering direct service responses to clients to being seen as advisors on cultural, linguistic and religious matters.

Meanwhile one fundamental factor had emerged. Local Asian women had through a system of networking begun to approach the team workers for support, advice and casework input. This role was fulfilled initially, but before long it was evident that the services being requested were far more than one social worker's remit would allow. What was very apparent was the huge deficit that existed from local agencies such as women's refuge services, police, housing, education and social services departments, in addition to legal services and domestic violence support services. Team members could at best alert these agencies to these gaps.

Group facilitators and the agency

The groups were reliant on the existence in the area of a few Asian female practitioners who came from Sikh, Hindu and Muslim backgrounds. This was not problematic because all the facilitators spoke Punjabi and had a sound understanding of the local Sikh community. Women users were more conscious of the 'client-worker ' relationship, which was new to them, than the religious or cultural differences that existed. Furthermore, whilst group members were predominantly Sikh there were other users from Hindu and Muslim faiths. The religious differences were therefore respected and celebrated in the various group functions that were held throughout the year.

It is also important to mention that geographically some of the groupworkers were living locally in the area. This was advantageous as they had a distinct understanding of local community dynamics, but there were also many disadvantages. Difficulties were presented as women, particularly when in distress, would locate workers at their home addresses and would expect to be seen outside office times. This was a problem that required sensitive handling as it was evident that the boundaries and professional issues governing worker - client relationships within the profession as a whole, were new and meaningless concepts to women who saw these workers as 'family'. The reality was often that women needed time to understand the client-worker relationship and to accept that this relationship had to be respected and honoured if it was to be beneficial to them. This was difficult to do when women would refer to facilitators as 'sisters' or 'daughters' amongst other relationships. Such issues and dilemmas faced by group facilitators were difficult and placed on them extra stress and pressure to balance what was already a difficult task.

The staff responsible for the running and overseeing of these groups were not always qualified social workers. In the previous decade there have only been two qualified social workers attached to these groups. This in itself led to mounting difficulties of unqualified workers being marginalised and isolated in providing essential and innovative services for the local Asian community. The situation was compounded by a lack of awareness and understanding of issues from within the Department itself. The failure to provide any real formal structure of managerial support became a feature of the groups as too did the expectation that the workers themselves would resolve professional and ethical dilemmas in practice.

Group facilitators were sometimes themselves new to the arena of groupwork, let alone groupwork with Asian women, an area that was markedly different and largely undocumented. Experience had served to demonstrate that a more directive approach had to be adopted when establishing group rules and boundaries. The roles and responsibilities that group facilitators had were crucial. However for group facilitators to be effective they needed to be able to establish themselves through developing trust, respect and understanding within the group parameters. Women involved in case work relationships with social workers outside the group were particularly strong in reinforcing and supporting the group facilitators role. This was another area through which the role of the facilitators, regardless of their background, became strengthened.

Group facilitators were also sometimes unfamiliar with counselling processes and the therapeutic aspects of groupwork. Whilst some general training was available, training on cross-cultural patterns of working and providing services was not. Workers were therefore often left to their own devices to gain information and understanding of working in an ethnically appropriate manner.

The Asian women professionals who facilitated the groups were also having to undergo a process of self awareness and analysis. It was essential that they themselves, as Asian women, had an opportunity to work through issues of feminism and the empowerment of Black women as a whole, prior to becoming involved within the group situation where these issues would inevitably arise. How group facilitators felt and then responded to certain issues would have an impact on the group dynamics that could not be ignored.

Group facilitators became aware of the lack of literature and documented research, on the subject area of groupwork with

Asian women and Black feminist perspectives as a whole, for example Ackers (1993), Rice (1990), Davies (1981), Hill-Collins (1986). There were therefore many issues that arose that needed to be worked through by both group facilitators and group members.

I feel it is important to mention here the experiences of these and other social work professionals committed to the struggles of developing good anti-racist and anti-oppressive practices based on ethnically sensitive theories. There remains an immense amount of pressure on these practitioners to respond positively to the needs of oppressed groups. Unfortunately the pressure to respond is compounded by the reality that resources, training and funding were often lacking and awareness of racial issues limited (Northern Curriculum Development Project, CCETSW, Leeds, 1992, *Improving Practice with Children and Families*).

For those committed to achieving positive changes, there are the problems of being marginalised and isolated, whilst at the same time being seen as 'specialists or experts' and facing unrealistically high expectations from clients, colleagues and employers. These where the very reasons that Section 11 funded posts and initiatives were criticised.

A recent research project conducted in Birmingham to explore local counselling services for Black and ethnic minority women with mental health problems revealed some of the difficulties experienced by black and ethnic minority workers. These included clients having different often high expectations of service; pressure to collude with oppressive practices as you are expected to understand the cultural significance of the oppression; distrust and testing out behaviour to ascertain where your loyalties lie. - Birmingham City Council, University of Central England (March, 1995).

It is important to acknowledge that whilst there were advantages in workers from within EMDU being seen as 'specialists', as services were now far more accessible and relevant to the Asian community, disadvantages were also prevalent. During this period workers struggled to become accepted within the mainstream; training and professional development opportunities were restricted; as too was understanding of their roles and responsibilities. Boundaries and remits were undefined as workers faced huge challenges in the context of traditional frameworks of practice and Departmental structures that had been ill prepared for the teams existence.

These were all daily realities for the workers in the EMDU.

The task of identifying service gaps and then responding with plausible solutions within the constraints of budgets and resources was a real one. The Department itself also needed to be informed and made aware of the dynamics underway. Programmes of racial awareness training and workshops designed to offer some insight and understanding of the local community were initiated, designed and led by workers within EMDU.

The unit itself became an important catalyst for change and Asian staff were instrumental in developing pioneering and innovative services for the local Asian community. New models and frameworks of practice were being introduced within the Department that were ethnically sensitive and proved in the long term to be indispensable to the success of various projects.

CURRENT CHANGES AND DEVELOPMENTS

Through continued funding and support the groups have flourished over the years. In recent times, however, the groups have undergone considerable changes.

The Shakti group now known as the ' Ethnic Women's Group' is maintained through a service level agreement between the Social Service Department and the local Racial Equality Council. It has achieved more substantial and regular funding which has enabled a sessional worker to facilitate the group. It is now open to women from differing cultural and ethnic backgrounds. These changes occurred in 1993 and have meant that the group continues to exist and remains mainly Asian in its membership. The keep-fit sessions are no longer a feature of this group.

The Gravesend groups are now run through Adult Education and are facilitated by two Asian women as outreach workers employed by Adult Education, with part funding from Section 11. These groups are also now open to women from differing ethnic backgrounds but still remain mostly Asian. The groups, whilst offering some therapeutic input, concentrate on raising understanding, awareness and accessibility of Adult Education opportunities within the local Asian community As this increased diversity has been relatively new to the group it is difficult to assess any impact on the group itself. It continues to function with a majority of Asian members, and because most women can speak some English, non-Asian members are not isolated in terms of communication.

More recently, in 1994 some research conducted by the

Department within the local minority ethnic population, indicated a significant number of minority ethnic children defined as ' in need' by the 1989 Children Act. In response to this the Denton Family Centre offering multi-cultural services and Pre-school provision has been established in Gravesend by the Social Services Department. The centre offers a variety of services to all members of the local community, including a number of groups for women.

Some of these groups have been newly developed and are essentially multi-cultural, also offering their services to white members of the local community. Despite this most groups remain predominantly Asian. It has therefore been difficult to comment on any changing dynamics within the groups. The department has now chosen to adopt a 'multi-cultural' approach in its groupwork service provision for Asian women locally. This approach has meant that groups that had previously catered for very distinct needs of Asian women are now open to women from all ethnic and cultural backgrounds, which in itself raises issues.

This has introduced an ethos of 'integration' within the groups which does not take into account the very unique history of the groups and the reasons why they were established. The groups evolved over time to meet the specific needs of Asian women. Why the need to 'integrate' the groups arose and with what rationale is not clear. It is difficult therefore to determine how the needs of Asian women will still be met. The impact on the users and the groups themselves is also hard to fully evaluate. What can be seen is that the groups still remain predominantly Asian.

The outcome of this change shall be interesting, both in terms of the group dynamics and the role of the facilitators in the groups.

There are a range of groups available to women locally including the following: an ante-natal/post-natal group , a women's personal development group, parenting group, drop-in mornings, health and fitness groups, and women's support groups (see diagram). The groups are relatively new and are still in the process of becoming established. However it is apparent that the many differing processes and dynamics discussed above are currently underway at different stages within each of these groups.

Additionally, it is important to mention that a group for Muslim women has also been established since 1989 by women from the Muslim community itself, and it is supported through grant funding by the Social Services Department.

Another significant and more recent development has been the establishment of two elderly Asian person's day centres based within Dartford and Gravesham. These centres, known as the Guru Nanak and Milan Day Centres, provide valuable day care services to the local Asian community. Some of the 120 women attending also attend the various women's groups. The centres are extremely popular as they offer a range of services that are appropriate to the needs of older women.

GROUP ACHIEVEMENTS AND SUCCESSES

Over the last decade the groups have been vitally important in providing many local Asian women with a much needed service. Women have developed in themselves, becoming better informed, more aware and able to make choices about their lives. There have also been marked improvements in how women empower themselves and each other.

The groups have developed some degree of unity and solidarity, allowing the women to channel their energies into becoming more confident and assertive. The groups are led by the women themselves. The group members play a crucial role in defining the direction of the groups through their own needs as service users. Women are therefore encouraged to take control and initiative within the groupwork setting.

Group members are also involved in promoting themselves as Asian women. For example, in the early years the groups produced an Asian cookbook and a tape of traditional Punjabi folk singing. Both these initiatives were marketed and promoted widely. Some group members have moved on to completing Adult Education courses leading them to better career opportunities. Others have become involved in facilitating the groups and securing careers within the caring professions. The groups have been and continue to be a platform for women who would otherwise have limited or no access to the services provided within the area.

CONCLUSION

The key role played by the Ethnic Minorities Development Unit in its relatively short existence cannot be ignored or understated. The Unit was crucial in opening the Department's doors to a section of the local Asian community previously unaccounted for. Staff worked to offer services that were culturally appropriate and linguistically accessible, built on trust and understanding.

The team was unique because it was offering services not only to the community but to the Department itself. The unit became a major catalyst for change at a time when issues of race and ethnicity were beginning to surface for the Department.

The work done with local Asian women through groupwork involved the introduction of new and innovative models of practice. As the groups evolved therefore, they began to challenge traditional groupwork theories and practice. The needs of local Asian women are now being met through a variety of group initiatives in the area. The groups co-exist to provide a range of services, some concerned with learning new skills, whilst others empower women through information and access to services or therapeutic counselling.

Many lessons have been learnt, initially through the inevitable trial and error practices that occurred. These lessons have been invaluable and have served to help both service providers and service users in developing more appropriate provision. An example of this can be seen in the need for these groups to be recognised and respected within the local Asian Sikh community. Initially women were reluctant to attend groups because the concept of groupwork itself was new. Once links with the local community based organisations and the local Sikh Gurdwara's were established the groups gained credibility and acceptance. This feature of the earlier groups was particularly important in developing positive working relationships with the community as a whole.

The role of women members using the groups in gaining community support and acknowledgment has been crucial. The group members generally retain very close contacts with the local Gurdwara's where not only do the groups hold religious celebrations but where they are involved in supporting each other outside the group in family and community events. This has served to strengthen relations and has offered the groups a raised profile.

The groups held at the Denton Family Centre are no longer seen as 'separate' from mainstream services and are therefore part of the Department's overall role. Departmental commitment and support to these groups continues to grow with heightened awareness and understanding of the many issues. However, the role of the local Sikh Community in relation to some of the groups held at the Denton Family Centre is still being developed and tends to be restricted. This is partly due to issues of client confidentiality and the statutory roles and responsibilities of the department, which restrict the level of community involvement.

It is also about the Department needing to outreach and extend itself more to the community.

Over the years however there have been significant developments both in terms of service design and provision and staffing.

The Department has established the Black Worker's Forum to offer Black and Asian staff support, whilst professional development opportunities are offered through a secondment scheme available to Black and Asian staff wishing to gain professional social work qualifications. The number of Black and Asian staff employed within the Department's mainstream services has also increased and has been particularly encouraged within the Dartford and Gravesham area.

This process has been enhanced since 1994 by a major Departmental Equalities Programme of training. This programme is involving managers and 40 project groups in working together to effect positive changes within Social Services policy and practice county-wide.

Despite these many developments, the challenge for the Department to respond appropriately and effectively is a very real one and continues to be met with commitment and heightened understanding and awareness.

Many social workers construe black families as fragmented structures. They often are unable to see these families in their true historical context. Whenever they are able to do this, they will see continuity, certainty, patterns of predictability and strength (ABSWAP, 1983, p.71).

The Department acknowledges that the process is an on-going one and that there is much more work to be done in developing links and an effective dialogue with the local community. The establishment of some services, however innovative, has served to highlight the deficits that still remain within the planning and provision of services.

Acknowledgements

Acknowledgement is made in particular to the following who have supported the development of Asian Women's groups in the Dartford and Gravesham area: *Social Services* - Indu Abbi, Farzana Ahmed, Bill Anderson, Surinder Bhachu, Mike Cosgrove, Eamonn Dillon Kulwant Drury, Dil Khan, Rashmi Maru, Santosh Masonde, Arun Pilkington, Surjit Rakkhar, Mike Robinson, Gwyneth Williams, Keith Wyncoll. *Adult Education* - Marinette Bazin, Julie Quick, Carol Goshal, Kusumam Musatan, Raj Purit, Dot Riley. *Racial Equality Council* - Dev Sharma, Sarabjit Walaia

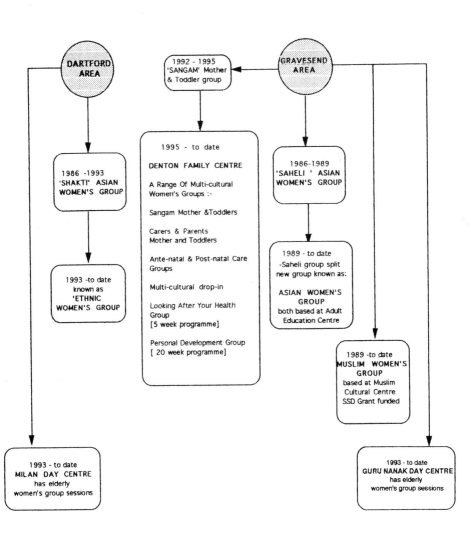

EVOLUTION OF
DARTFORD AND GRAVESHAM AREA
MULTI-CULTURAL WOMEN'S GROUPS
1986 - 1996

DARTFORD AREA

GRAVESEND AREA

1992 - 1995
'SANGAM' Mother
& Toddler group

1986 -1993
'SHAKTI' ASIAN
WOMEN'S GROUP

1995 - to date

DENTON FAMILY CENTRE

A Range Of Multi-cultural
Women's Groups :-

Sangam Mother &Toddlers

Carers & Parents
Mother and Toddlers

Ante-natal & Post-natal Care
Groups

Multi-cultural drop-in

Looking After Your Health
Group
[5 week programme]

Personal Development Group
[20 week programme]

1986-1989
'SAHELI ' ASIAN
WOMEN'S GROUP

1989 - to date
-Saheli group split
new group known as:

ASIAN WOMEN'S
GROUP
both based at Adult
Education Centre

1993 -to date
known as
'ETHNIC
WOMEN'S GROUP

1989 -to date
MUSLIM WOMEN'S
GROUP
based at Muslim
Cultural Centre
SSD Grant funded

1993 - to date
MILAN DAY CENTRE
has elderly
women's group sessions

1993 - to date
GURU NANAK DAY CENTRE
has elderly
women's group sessions

Communities in Struggle: Bengali and Refugee Groupwork in London

GITA PATEL

Black in the context of this work will mean young people who because of the colour of their skin experience racism. The use of the word Black refers to an historical experience of economic, social and political power relationship, and the history of colonialism and slavery. Within this definition of Black there are many varied communities living in different contexts in our society, ranging from the British born Black person to the recently arrived refugee. There are however certain issues that affect all these communities, and ways of working which can be used to address the needs of different communities. The work is examined in the context of racism and sexism and the shared experiences of these types of oppression.

This paper will aim to explore the issues of race and culture and the impact on the dynamics of the group processes. The approach to each group incorporates our view that the groups of young people are living within a racist society i.e. one that perpetuates a set of ideas, beliefs and attitudes which vary throughout time and place and social location but which are based on the belief that Black people are inherently inferior to white people (Marshment, 1978). Within this definition of racism the group leaders, being Black are seen by society as inherently inferior to White people. I hope to show how the workers experiences of racism had a significant impact on the dynamics of each group.

In addition to the clear definitions of Black and White there are the further complexities of culture and its effect on the young people. Culture is defined as an accumulation of knowledge amongst a social group that determines the total reality of the life that people live (Fernando, 1991). It is also defined as a set of knowledge, beliefs and attitudes which are acquired by a person as a member of society (Rack, 1982). The society in which an individual lives determines the culture that they accumulate, and indicates an experience that is constantly changing and growing.

One of the key aspects of all these groups is the exploration of culture. There is a simplistic idea amongst the caring professions that the needs of a community can be met by employing a worker of the same 'culture' to work with the client. This assumes that culture is homogenous and the young people and the workers have formed their own cultural identity within this society. The groupwork relating to culture is the acknowledgement that young people are living within two very different sets of values and our role as workers is not to tell them what their culture should be, but to allow them to negotiate for themselves a culture that they are happy with, and that reduces their internal conflicts.

I will be giving a brief outline of three different groups, some of the issues that arose and the methods of groupwork that were used. The first was a group for young Bengali women, which was run by two female Asian workers in an inner London Family Services Unit. The second group was concerned with working with young Bengali men, initially in response to racial and police harassment in the area, and the third was a short term counselling group for young refugees, run in a local school,

All of the groups described were started after a period of time working in the relevant communities, involving, community work outreach work, and making links with community representatives This was an important aspect of the work and enabled us to provide an appropriate service to the young people. Often a person's expectations of being in a group comes from their experience in their family (Klein, 1970). The work in the community helped us to establish some of the cultural and family expectations. Brown (1992) describes a boundary between the overlap of groupwork and community work. In our experience, particularly in the work with the Bengali community, this boundary was complicated and sometimes difficult to distinguish.

There are assumptions that Black and minority communities can be classed as having one experience and one culture Black and minority communities are not monolithic entities (Perelberg, 1992) and the outreach work was invaluable in providing an appropriate type of group. The methods used and the way the groups were run were very different because of the nature of each community in which the work was carried out. For example, after assessing the expectations and culture of the Bengali families in contrast to the expectations and culture of some other Asian families, different methods were used for work with the Bengali girls than those for other Asian girls and young women.

For each group there were particular distinct and unique

issues relating to the culture and social position of the group members. In addition there were three main aims relating directly to race and racism.

EXPLORING CULTURE AND DIFFERENCE

The groups were not homogenous in terms of race and I believe that one of the essential starting points for all the work was being able to acknowledge and openly discuss the similarities and differences between our experiences of our race and culture. I believe as Kadushin (1972) states that the "colour blind' approach or the assumption that everyone is the same is a problem when working cross-culturally in a group.

IDENTITY AND SELF ESTEEM

A common issue with all the groups was working with the young people on their identity and self esteem . Often the young people in the groups were unsure of their identity. Of course adolescence is an age where all young people are trying to form an identity, some can go through a smooth process, but for others there may be circumstances in their lives or internal issues which lead to a confusion of their role and identity in society (Erickson, 1968).

For Black young people, growing up in a White society or arriving in a totally different country as in the case of the young refugees, can lead to this confusion. The experience of racism erodes self esteem and confidence, and a young person can internalise the racism, and believe they are inferior to white society (Thomas, 1995).

PROVIDING ROLE MODELS

Part of the aims of all these groups was to provide role models for the young people. Most of those participating in the groups had parents or other elders in their community experiencing powerlessness, through unemployment, poverty, racism, and war. The young people did not want to be like their parents who seemed only to suffer hardship. The messages that the young people could see from their parent's lives were that being Bengali or being a refugee was a negative experience. They found it difficult to see how they could ever negotiate a good life as a member of their community. Seeing other Asian people and Black people who had somehow managed to become 'successful' in their eyes provided them with some alternatives and some options for their own future.

The two groups for Bengali young people were held in the same community. The area in which this group was run is made up of mainly estate- based public housing, occupied by Bengali and white working class families. Information about the successes and failures of the Asian community in the UK tends to see 'Asian' as a homogenous group. As the most recent Asian group to settle in Britain, the Bengali community in London has historically been faced with poor housing, poverty, unemployment and low educational achievement, much lower than any other Asian community or other minority community.

The area where this work was carried out is well known for racist attacks and has a history of organised fascist activity on some of the predominantly white estates. Earlier the Bengali community in the area consisted mainly of older men who arrived in London in the 1950s and 60s. A large percentage of this community came from the rural area of Sylet in Bangladesh, they worked mainly in the restaurant and hotel trade. In the 1970s and 80s they began to bring their families to England and the process of migration became established. With this increased visible presence of Asian people in the area i.e. women in the streets and children in the local schools, the racist attacks began to rapidly escalate. Attacks on women and children were frequent and common and at one stage in the early 80s Bengali children were being escorted to school in order to protect them and their mothers from being attacked.

The Bengali families in the area were mainly homeless at that time, and in the early 80s after a Bengali person was killed by a fire in one of the temporary bed and breakfast accommodations, there was an occupation of the Town Hall to highlight the terrible housing conditions of the families. This occupation brought to light some of the other issues concerning Bengali families such as low educational achievement, high unemployment and racist attacks. The Bengali community is considered one of the most disadvantaged of Britain's ethnic minorities (HMSO, 1986). These issues are important in looking at the work with the Bengali young people as they represent their childhood experiences, of poverty and bad housing, whilst being in a powerless position in the face of racist attacks towards themselves their parents and their community.

The Bengali Young Women's group was co-led by a female Asian groupworker from a local Family Centre and myself.

Previous work in the local area showed that there were several groups of young Bengali women, including those who had:

1. recently arrived in England, with hardly any fluency in English, and experiencing displacement and disorientation;
2. lived here for five years or more, and were beginning to make choices about cultural and social identity; and
3. been born or resident here since an early age.

Within these groups, there were differences in the values and expectations of the families and the community. We decided to target Bengali girls, aged between fourteen to sixteen years, who had been resident in this country for over five years and were fairly fluent in spoken English. We felt that these young women would be at the stage of negotiating the two cultures and would benefit from some support and exploration of their position.

CO-WORKING

As two people from different agencies co-working a group we had many areas - both personal and professional - which we talked through and negotiated to establish an effective way of working together. These discussions formed quite a substantial and very important part of our preparation work, (Mistry, 1989) and were continued during the life of the group.

One example of how these negotiations were useful related to an event that happened even before the group began. We sent a letter to parents offering to visit them at home to talk about the group. Two young women used this letter to tell their parents that the group had already started, and that they had attended one session when in fact they were out with a group of friends. One of the girls then rang us to request that we back up their story to their parents. We told them that we would not directly initiate contact with parents to inform them of this, but if the parents contacted us we would tell them the truth.

The fact we were both Asian (one of us Gujerati and the other Bengali) was in a way not enough to enable us to run an effective group where the young women could explore their feelings around their culture. If one of us had had very fixed ideas about young women and did not accept their rights to explore and question their own lifestyles then the group would not have been useful for any of us. On the other hand if there had been no understanding of the parents position then again the girls could have simply been made to suppress their feelings of understanding and pain that they had on behalf of their parents.

Apart from these issues, we spent a period of time talking about our own personal identity, family, cultural issues and attitudes about being Asian women living in this country. We particularly discussed our past experiences as young women growing up in England and the impact it made on our lives and values. Again this was important in establishing a working relationship because of the nature of the issues to be covered during the groupwork sessions. The introductory meetings proved to be of immense value in the running of the group.

FAMILY AND COMMUNITY CONCERNS

The young women were keen to discuss issues of racism in society but saw it as a matter outside their control. Many of them lived in families that were subject to routine racial harassment but they tended to see this as a problem for the men in the family. They were the ones who tried to protect their sisters and their daughters. The young women were fearful and angry but did not want to get involved, or were not allowed to become involved in any resistance to racism.

The primary concern for most of the young women was around issues of gender and being female in a traditional Bengali community. The Bengali community in the area is varied and some families are much more lenient towards their daughters than others. All the young women in our group came from families that were quite traditional in their attitudes to the girls. Traditional refers in this case to the clearly demarcated roles of girls in the Bengali family, in addition there are the cultural expectations and constraints of the girls regarding their behaviour in society. In the Muslim tradition, each individual in the family has a duty to uphold the family honour. Their family culture may be the reason why the girls chose to attend a group such as ours. Other girls in families with more relaxed rules may prefer to go out with their friends rather than be part of a formal group, or may prefer to mix with boys and girls in their leisure time. The girls in our group were often not allowed to go out at all expect to go to school unless accompanied by their family.

Most of these restrictions can be explained by the fears and concerns expressed by some of the parents regarding the safety of their daughters. This related to the possibility of racist attacks, but more importantly to social contact with local Bengali boys which might possibly develop into romantic or sexual relationships. The families were keen to preserve certain traditions which prevented this type of relationship forming.

Some parents had gone to the lengths of accompanying their daughters to and from school to limit or stop such contact. They justified this by saying that although they could not influence the behaviour of other people's children, they could take these precautionary measures to safeguard their own children. The young women felt that often parents were most concerned about how the community would respond, as opposed to considering the feelings of their daughters. They felt hurt and upset that their parents did not trust them.

Talking to the parents was an equally important part of the preparatory work, as it enabled them to see us face to face, seek information about the group and share any views or concerns they had about the group.

It is our opinion that, in working with this group of Asian young women meeting with parents to establish familiarity and trust between them and workers is an essential ingredient in the success or failure of a group. We found that one key factor in deciding whether or not to allow their daughters to attend the group was related to whether or not they perceived us as being 'respectable' Asian women. Making home visits where they could ask us questions helped to establish this trust.

As Asian workers we thought we had a clear idea of what the parents would expect from us. One of the first issues was how we would dress when visiting the families, clearly we would be judged from the moment we entered the household. Whether the girls were allowed to attend the group was to a large extent dependent on what the parents thought of us as Asian women influencing their daughters. Our communication with the parents was constructed around their expectations for their daughters, which was slightly different to the expectations of the girls themselves. For example the parents asked whether we would be having discussions on Bengali culture, (e.g. history), as they felt that their daughters did not get an opportunity to do this at school. We of course would be discussing Bengali culture but perhaps more in terms of the Bengali culture of the young women in Britain rather than the historical culture of their countries of origin. The girls felt they could learn this from home and wanted the group for other things. The information presented to the parents and to the young women had slightly different emphasis which related to our understanding of their own particular experiences of their community and society in general. As Asian workers our own experiences contributed greatly to these sometimes delicate negotiations between parents and their daughters.

The parents were particularly questioning as to whether or not there were going to be any males in the group and were happy to let their daughters attend only when we assured them the group was for females only and was going to be run by two women. These parental expectations of the group were in sharp contrast to those of the young women who were happy to use the group as a space to discuss various issues, share their feelings and do fun things like eating in restaurants which they had not previously done, as opposed to just wanting to discuss issues related to school.

CONTACTING SCHOOL

The girls we worked with all attended a local school and one of our first contacts was to was to meet with the relevant Head of Year at the school.

The teacher's reservations about the group were interesting, and gave us an insight into the ways the young women were perceived by the school. The worry was that by attending the group the young women would suddenly become assertive and start challenging the school system and their parents. The school were worried about being unable to contain the assertive young women, and indeed made it clear that they would not support the young women in family problems. We wondered whether the same reservations would be present when considering a group for white young women. Being assertive and being able to challenge and make demands are seen as positive for white young women, but caused serious concerns about the Bengali women. The stereotype of the passive Asian woman was easier to deal with.

The white teacher had clear images of the Bengali women, their families and their communities, which seemed to us to be negative. The role of authority that the teacher has, would clearly affect the young women's image of themselves. One of the reasons for the group was to address the negative influences of racism on their lives.

The girls were picked up after school, and then dropped home in our own transport after each session. This was an important factor in parents giving permission for their daughters to attend the group, as safety was one of their primary concerns. The group was held once a week after school for 2 hours, some sessions were held at the local Family Centre and some were conducted in other locations linked to activities i.e. in the park or at a restaurant. They combined theme-led discussions and activities. The young women were concerned about confidentiality particularly regarding what the groupworkers would or would not share with parents. We assured them that matters discussed in the group would not be discussed with parents unless the girls specifically asked us to.

Role of the groupworkers

As Asian women our views on family and our position with regards to the Asian communities were very relevant to how comfortable the young women felt about talking to us. With this group, we as workers had to adapt to the expectations of the parents and of the young women of us as Asian women. Of course our own experiences, personal and professional, meant we were well aware of these, and our initial meetings prepared us for our roles in the professional work.

The group leader has authority, the real authority of their position as well as the power and authority which the members projective fantasies invest in them (McCullough and Ely, 1968). In some ways we were the ideal parent, the ideal friend or the ideal future model of themselves. For the parents we were perhaps the ideal daughter, who their own daughters could model themselves on. In this group we not only had the expectations of the group members but also of the parents. The authority we were given was based on the cultural frameworks of the young women and their parents, which were sometimes in direct conflict.

Relationships with boys was a big issue for the young women, and all their friendships with boys had to be carried out without any of the family knowing, and also during school time. This obviously involved complicated organisation and a lot of time and energy, and was one of the fundamental culture conflicts that the young women faced. As workers we had to be sensitive to their own exploration of this. Although the young women said that relationship with boys was a big issue for them, they still judged other Asian girls by the standards of their parents. For example if they knew of a girl who had a boyfriend she would immediately be classed as different to them. This proved interesting in the group as the workers were inevitably judged on the traditional standards of relationships between men and women, not just by the parents but by the girls as well. Although the girls thought they could talk to us about boys they did not want to see us as too different from their parents. They all thought they were much more 'modern' than their parents but in fact their values reflected the parental values, albeit to a lesser degree.

All the girls seemed to have clear views and strong identities in relation to their culture. However, their image of themselves as women was a source of internal conflict. For instance, they could talk about how they liked themselves and the way they looked, but in practice they found it difficult to feel confident about their bodies. We attempted to redress these ambivalent feelings by giving positive praise and also space to express such feelings.

The Bengali girls group then served to highlight the issues of conflict for the young women and for us as Asian workers. The issues of constantly negotiating the boundaries and culture in which they live, caused anxiety amongst the group. The young women did not feel they were in abusive or unbearably oppressive family relationships, hence in our opinion they were not at risk. They were relatively happy at home and none of them expressed any desire to leave. Our role then was to support them to stay in the family and learn to negotiate their position as girls, within their own family and community, and also to provide them with some positive feelings about their future lives as women in their community. The girls were somehow pleasantly surprised to work with us as Asian women in a different way to other women in their community.

As Asian women workers we formed a bridge between the young women and their parents and elders in their communities. We were adult Asian women who were clearly approved of by the parents, which was confirmed through our home visits and our conversations with them. Yet they were able to discuss issues which they could not think of talking about with any other Asian adults. This contact with us could support the young women in seeing themselves as Bengali and also, provided them with a different view of what being Bengali means for them and for us as workers.

Conflict was also caused by the fact that we were Asian as in the example mentioned earlier of the young women who tried to use the group as an excuse to be elsewhere; perhaps they would not have asked that of a White worker. They thought as we were Asian we would understand and agree to their requests. We however remained firm to our agreement not to lie for them but also not to approach the parents directly ourselves. The girls who had requested our collusive support did not attend any of the group sessions, and would probably not have made use of the group. For these girls the group would not have offered a solution to their conflicts of wanting to see friends (male and female) in opposition to their parents. Unlike the girls who did use the group they may have felt their families to be unbearably oppressive and were unable to even consider any negotiation with them, hence their solution to tell lies and carry on with their lives.

After the start of the group we had little contact with the parents, and did not perceive any visible change from the reports of the young women. The changes in the parent's views could only really come from the skills that the girls had learnt in negotiating their own needs. In our experience workers trying to negotiate on behalf of the young women could lead to more conflict and problems for the young person. The young women in our group did have good relationships with their parents and would be able to approach them more effectively than we could.

BENGALI YOUNG MEN

The groupwork with young Bengali men could be described in several ways, for example as an unstructured group with goals of empowerment and social action. It also raises the political consciousness of oppressed and disadvantaged people.

This groupwork took place over a number of years and involved many different aspects of campaigning, political activities, individual and groupwork and community work. Some of the people involved in the work have changed over the years, and today the work continues with the running of a club specifically for the Asian youth in the area. It is not possible within the scope of this paper to outline the details of all the different aspects of the work, so I am going to concentrate on some of the key issues in the group and how the work supported the development of the young men and perhaps the development of the community

In the course of my work as a community worker I organised a meeting following the racist murder of a local Bengali restaurant worker. Many young people, mainly men attended this meeting. They were concerned about the issue of racist attacks and wanted to do something about it as a matter of urgency. The meeting was extremely emotive, there was a lot of fear amongst the older Bengali people and the young men wanted to set up a helpline so that the Bengali restaurant workers who were walking home late at night could call somewhere for help if they were in trouble. Some of the older workers and members of the community agreed to stay behind and talk with the young men about setting up some form of regular support and activity around racist attacks. Straight after the meeting many people stayed at the Community Centre till the early hours of the morning discussing how to set up a 24 hour helpline, and we organised a rota for the work.

The group ran for a number of years and the period that I describe began with the above incident and was initially focused around providing a service to a community under attack. The distinction between groupworkers and group members was not clear cut, in terms of decision making and leadership. All the professionals involved agreed that the young people themselves should be party to all decisions that were taken.

The composition of the group can best be described as having three layers, the first being made up of professional workers and adult individuals who lived outside the area but had an interest in supporting the community. This core group consisted of about six Asian women (some Bengali, others not), two Asian men and two White English men. The second layer consisted of about eight young Bengali men ranging in age form 18 to 22 who regularly attended meetings and made decisions with the workers. This core group of around 17 people co-ordinated all the work that took place through regular meetings and discussions. The third layer was the largest, about a hundred Bengali young men who took part in the organised activities and attended the group for support, advice and information. Very few local Bengali women attended or became interested in the group, perhaps for some of the reasons described in the section on the Bengali girls group (the young women in the group were from the same community as these young men). There were one or two notable exceptions of young women who made a powerful impact on the group. These young women were particularly clear and assertive about their position in the community and were happy to speak at meetings and demonstrations, but did not want to take part in the core group.

The campaigning aspect of the group received widespread publicity and became quite well known as the group raising the issue of racist attacks. As a result many workers and politicians showed interest in the group and would become involved for short periods of time. The core group operated together consistently for about three years.

Several key issues were identified in this group.

RACIST ATTACKS AND RELATIONSHIP WITH THE POLICE

When the group started the young men were very sad and angered by the death of one of their community. They were increasingly witnessing racist attacks and felt powerless and disempowered by their situation. In addition to the racist attacks the young men were consistently picked up and arrested by the police in the streets where they lived. They were under attack from all sides and had no way of dealing with their state of helplessness. Dealing with both the racist attacks and the treatment by the police was the main focus of the work at the beginning and still remains the central aim of most of the work in the area.

RELATIONSHIPS WITH PARENTS AND ELDERS IN THE COMMUNITY

The young men felt responsible for their parents safety, the man who was killed was an older man, and this attack made the young people see how vulnerable their parents were in a society where they were constantly experiencing racism.

Traditionally the whole of the Asian community has been seen as very passive. The majority of older people would be very anxious about even questioning the way they were treated in all areas of life, their advice was usually to keep quiet and not cause problems. They had anxieties about 'being allowed to stay in England' if they dared to question the Authorities. Many of the Bengali families were living in a constant state of fear. In my opinion this state of passive behaviour and powerlessness is created by racism, part of this is the feeling that most of the older Asian have that they do not have any rights as citizens in this country, because racism constantly bombards us with the notion that we are outsiders in British society, and that somehow our rights to live in Britain are granted by the mercy of the British, and can be taken away at any moment. The Asian communities are certainly not universally passive, as a glimpse at South Asian politics will show. Fernando (1991) says that racism can cause a 'learned helplessness', which can lead to depression in Black communities.

The young people, and particularly the young men are much more assertive than their elders about their rights in this country; most of them have been born here or came here at a young age, and attended school here. Many of them are British and were not prepared to accept the racism and discrimination that they were subject to. As children they had seen the treatment that their families received and felt powerless. Many of them had felt anger and determination to tackle racism when they were older.

The focus of the work was how to challenge and question what they saw as injustice against them, using methods of organising effectively. The Bengali young men like any other group of young men were often very angry and wanted to act in ways which would inevitably get them into trouble. Our ways of working were an attempt to use alternative methods rather than the adventurist ways of most young men, which would have exposed young Bengalis to more racist attacks and police harassment, because of their race. White young men could possibly carry out the same activities without putting themselves at risk.) Some of these ways were: organising meetings, marches, and demonstrations; making formal police complaints; monitoring racist attacks, and learning to deal with the judicial system, the council and local councillors. They also learnt how to use the media to highlight their circumstances.

Littlewood and Lipsedge (1989) describe some reasons why young Black men resort to violence which has caused many racial disturbances in Britain and America. They say that the young men feel they are unable to achieve their aspirations, and believe that the legitimate channels for bringing about change were blocked to them. In our experience the young men saw the discrimination and harassment they received from the police and the judicial system as violence in the same way as the racist attacks they were experiencing.

Our role was to offer ways of using the legitimate channels. This was at times difficult as I do not necessarily believe that those channels can achieve real changes for Black youngsters, Black leaders in the past have thought that changes cannot take place through these channels (Malcolm X, 1965). The alternatives for them were using violence which would only further criminalise their community. I can also accept the view that violence could have a positive mental health function (Littlewood and Lipsedge,

1989); however the use of marches, demonstrations and pickets allowed the young people to verbalise their anger in a safe way. Many Black people may have found anti racist marches to be therapeutic, and channelling anger in this way has been used historically in Black struggles (Davis, 1975).

The kinds of pressures that were put on the young men were enormous; we as workers witnessed police trying to provoke them. If the young man responded he would immediately be arrested for a public order offence. The men were witnessing their communities being attacked, denigrated and subjected to violence, and were being arrested and provoked by police on a daily basis,

The group discussed ways of dealing with these incidents, and for us as workers achieving a balance of real empathy and anger, and learning how to remain safe was difficult. Some of us Black workers were having the same experiences on the street as the young people and had to be conscious of our position in the group.

If one of the workers was at risk, the fact that we were professionals could sometimes help. In one incident of a racist attack, four young men and two workers were all taken to the police station. The white worker (a local teacher) was allowed home within the hour, one of the Black workers was allowed home after several hours, and the young Bengali men were all kept overnight.

The issue of Black and White workers in this group were very complex and changed throughout the work. As I mentioned earlier our group received considerable media attention and publicity and as a result attracted some political parties as well as individual men who wanted to gain power over the group. Perhaps what they saw was a group of mainly Asian women, and up to a hundred young Bengali men, and felt that somehow it would be easy to gain control of us and receive publicity for themselves.

In one particular incident a White male politician showed interest in the group and began talking to the boys on the street using what Brown and Mistry (1994) describe as 'macho' ethos and 'male' language to sell the image of violence to the young men. Of course many adolescents are attracted by this way of dealing with racism. The reality was that if there was any violence it would be the young Black people who would be the most likely to be arrested and locked up; they had to learn to fight back in a safe way. These men that used the 'macho' tactics could not accept us as Asian women working with a large group of young Bengali men and taking a leading role in the work. The man concerned had not even talked to us women or in fact to any of the Bengali men in the core organising group, instead he had chosen the younger and more vulnerable Bengali boys. As a White man he had assumed control over a small group of boys who saw us as ineffective, because we would rather organise a picket or demonstration than encourage direct violence. Our core group was challenged by this incident and spent long hours negotiating with some of the younger Bengali boys. It did cause tension within the group as the boys could not identify a strong male leader in our collective core group. Eventually we did manage to overcome this difficulty through many prolonged discussions and debates, and the male politician did lose interest once he discovered he would not be able to assume control.

This pattern was repeated on several occasions by other men, White and Asian. The fact that our core group consisted of mainly young men and Asian women, and the fact that we operated collectively rather than have one strong leader or spokesperson made the group vulnerable to this type of take over by people seeking power.

There were of course several men and white people who worked effectively in the group and consequently the issues of racism and sexism were highlighted through many incidents. The relationships between Black and White in such an anti racism group are highlighted well by Mistry and Brown (1991), and several assumptions were made by group members about the power of the white members or of the men in the group. The fact that the Asian women were in the majority played a large part in tackling some of those assumptions.

Out of the work with the young people many other issues about their personal lives were discussed in groups. For example the issue of family responsibility, was on all the young men's minds. Often the families were quite poor, with unemployed or low paid jobs, and their future depended on the sons. Traditionally the son has to care for the parents when they are older. Many of the men were going back to Bangladesh to have arranged marriages, and becoming fathers at quite a young age.

Throughout the work with these young men the aim was to help them to control and make decisions about their own community. Part of that work was teaching them about their rights and giving factual information and support on legal issues and the working of Local Government. The main barrier to them carrying out the work themselves was related to low self confidence and feeling powerless to deal with Authority figures.

Of the young men who were involved in the work from the start, two have gone on to study Law and several have become workers, with youngsters in their own community. Many of them were and still are on the steering groups and Management Committees of local organisations, and play a major role in the work in the area.

REFUGEE GROUP

This group was set up as part of the work of the Nafsiyat Intercultural Therapy Centre based in London. When offering therapeutic support to young refugees, we recognised the need to develop work in the local community with this client group. Offering support in schools and colleges was one of the ways of reaching those who may not otherwise gain access to counselling support. The main aim of this group was to offer counselling to refugees between the ages of 16 and 20. The group members were from several countries; Eritrea, Ethiopia, Sri Lanka and Somalia. Several of the young people had been involved in or witnessed acts of extreme violence before fleeing. Some of them had come here with their family after fleeing from war in their country. Others had left their families and come to England alone, not knowing where their parents were or indeed whether they were still alive. Some believed their fathers were in prison in their country.

The first stage in setting up this group for young refugees was several months of outreach work which identified various issues that had to be considered in setting up the group. Some examples of these were:

1. Culturally the concept of counselling would usually involve talking to an elder in the community or a member of the family. Talking about their private and family lives to a stranger, was a strange and unusual idea to many young people.
2. Young refugees may have had many negative experiences with people in Authority both in their own country and on arrival in the UK. They would be cautious about trusting anyone enough to be able to use counselling.
3. The young people in the refugee communities are experiencing an enormous amount of stress in trying to cope with their social circumstances. Some of the social factors we

identified in the community were: homelessness or poor and temporary accommodation; language difficulties in accessing education; and poverty and unemployment which led to a loss of status. Many in the refugee communities are asylum seekers and the stress of Immigration procedures and awaiting Home Office decisions was evident.

The outreach work showed there were a range of needs in the refugee communities. The two ends of the scale were:

1. Young people who needed psychotherapy for quite disturbed behaviour, which was possibly related to the traumatic experiences that they had witnessed or been subjected to. These refugees were being referred to our therapy service.
2. Young people who coped well in their lives, but who may be under a great deal of stress, because of their refugee experiences, and having to cope in this alien and often hostile country.

It was this second category of young people we hoped to reach in setting up this group. They were unlikely to look for support from professionals, and would probably only come to the attention of the mainstream services once they were in crisis. In order to work with them, we had to go out to where they are; schools, colleges, youth clubs and Community Centres.

The outreach work involved visits to several schools and colleges and a meeting with two counsellors in one of the colleges led to the formation of the group. The counsellors spoke to several young people and invited them to attend a first meeting with me to discuss setting up a group.

We held all our group sessions in one of the counsellor's room. Having worked in schools before, one of the biggest problems encountered is finding a safe and appropriate room each week, to provide the counselling support. This is such a basic issue but one which can make a big difference to whether the young people feel safe, comfortable and able to talk about confidential issues.

The first meeting was attended by several young women. The group had been advertised in the same way to men and women, but no young men came. We thought it may be because the worker was female, but boys were not told about my gender before the first meeting.

I was the only worker in this group and as an Indian woman, my position as a worker from an Intercultural Therapy Centre was made clear. My race and background was discussed in the first meeting along with the race and backgrounds of the young people. I believe that when working cross culturally the issue of race and ethnicity needs to be addressed by the group leader in order to allow exploration of similarities and differences for the young people. Some of those in the group were from differing cultures, and maybe sharing differences allowed a relationship to develop amongst the various communities. As a worker I became another representative of a country in the group's exploration of culture. The refugee experience was something I did not share, and this was acknowledged in the group. Many traditional counselling or therapy groups do not allow space for the leader to express their own race or cultural identity. I believe when working cross culturally workers should share information with group members about their own race and cultural experiences.

The reasons for having the group had to be made clear from the start, and presented in a way that did not label the young people. When setting up a group for young refugees it is important not to let them feel they are a problem; often the problem is the attitudes of society rather than in the young people themselves. If the clients feel they are in a group because they are different they may see their difference as failure and introject the rejecting attitudes that others display (Heap, 1979).

The women were told that the group was not an activities group, but a talking group where they could talk about their feelings relating to their refugee experience and to their lives in this country. The issue of confidentiality was discussed in detail, and as a result the first meeting became relaxed very quickly and the young women started talking about their personal circumstances. The relative ease of the group in relaxing was one of the advantages of working in the college setting (Dwivedi, 1993)

Some examples of issues that were discussed in the group sessions were:

Language
The fluency in English was different for different members of the group. Some who spoke good English would translate for others who were struggling with the language. One young woman whose English was not as good as the others insisted on speaking in English, one of her main aims for attending the group was for her to be able to practice and try out her English in a safe place where she would not feel embarrassed or put down.

Culture

The young women spent time explaining their backgrounds and cultures to the other members, which was a very valuable exercise and allowed them to have an individual identity in the group. This was the advantage of having a group that consisted of people from different races.

Education

The young people were very ambitious in their career prospects, wanting to train as professionals, doctors, lawyers etc. and return to their country once they completed their education. The discussions about education indicated the transient state in which may of the young people exist, and how their expectations of British life are related to that transient state.

Family

Family was a major issue for all of them. Some young women were unaccompanied and looked after younger siblings. Several of them had fathers and mothers back in their own country who were in prison or who they could not contact. This created anxiety for all of them and the issues of loss and separation from family were present in all their lives.

The other striking thing for all the young women was the huge sense of responsibility; suddenly having to grow up and look after other members of the family. One young woman had never really been anywhere without her parents, then all of a sudden she was in a strange country having to care for herself and her siblings.

Housing

All of the young women had lived in many places, in their countries, on the journey here and since arriving in this country. One had lived in three bed and breakfast hotels in nine months. They all felt insecure in their present accommodation and hoped one day to return to their country and live in a comfortable house. They could not imagine feeling secure in England.

Isolation

The young women found it difficult to make friends, and felt they did not know how to do so. Often in their own country if they sat next to someone in school that person was their friend. Here things seemed much more complicated and they could not really understand what they were expected to do. The social and cultural expectations and responsibilities of friendship in a British school society were alien to them.

Past traumatic experiences

The discussions in the group touched on the young people's past experiences before arriving in this country. One woman listed about seven countries that she had been through in the process of fleeing her country and arriving in Britain. We also discussed the fear that some of them still have relating to their past experiences. When they were asked to describe their ideal house the issues of safety came up i.e. one woman wanted a house that was all open with only one floor. She said 'There are no doors in the house and no stairs so that if there was a fire we could escape easily and run out of the house'. Another wanted a house with a very high wall surrounding the whole area. The issue of a safe house raised many traumatic experiences that the young women had in their country when they were living in the midst of war. They thought they had forgotten about it but realised how those experiences were affecting their everyday lives.

The group concentrated on the present and the issues of living in England, but the past events inevitably came up in the process of the discussions. The young women were not pushed to talk about the past, but were offered the choice. The group was not intended to be a long term therapeutic group, and raising material which could not be worked through in the life of the group, could have been more traumatic for the young women. What the group did offer was a sharing of the experience of trauma. The members knew there were other young people who had parents in prison, and who had lived through wars and conflict in their countries. One young woman was pleasantly surprised to be able to talk about her journey to England, she felt she would not talk to anyone else in the college, but once she knew the others were refugees she felt happy to talk.

This group was a therapeutic group but the facilitation was more directive than other groups because of the low levels of confidence and the lack of self esteem amongst the young women. We agree with Douglas who says that high anxiety levels and long silences in a group can increase a young person's feelings of worthlessness, and pushing them to take responsibility for the group too soon can undermine their confidence (Douglas, 1976).

The group clearly provided a much needed service for the young women. Most of them were extremely isolated and did not have anyone to talk to or anyone who was interested in them. The group provided that support and interest which helped their self confidence and self esteem. The young women gained an understanding of how talking can support them and of what counselling and therapy is for. This will be a helpful resource to use in their future lives, and possibly empower them to deal with the future.

One of the important aspects of this group was that the young people were from different countries and communities, yet the shared refugee experience provided a focus for the group. The common experiences seemed to be more important than the differences in race, language and cultures.

The methods used need to be discussed in relation to work with young men refugees, either by running a group specifically for them or by targeting young men in the preparation stage of the group. It may be that a different approach is needed.

MODELS OF WORK

All three groups were working with Black and minority communities, but the ways of working were quite different in each case. In assessing the methods of working, it is important to note that time was spent carrying out developmental and outreach work in each community to establish what issues were present for the group. For example when offering groupwork to the Bengali girls, parental visits and transport home were essential for the girls to be allowed to attend the group.

For the group offering counselling to the refugee young women, it was appropriate to offer the service in the college rather than in a Centre. The issue of trust is very important for all refugee communities, and offering the support in the safe environment of college was important.

With the Bengali young men the model of groupwork was completely different, the group was focused around activity, and defending their community. The young men would have found it very difficult to attend a group set up for them to talk about themselves.

The work with young men and young women in these examples is quite different. The refugee group was open to both sexes, but only young women turned up. The group around racial harassment was open to everyone, but with one or two striking exceptions it was attended mainly by young men. The formal type of referrals and structured groups did attract young women. The young men were more interested in a group which was about taking action and focusing around a particular external problem such as racism. The work carried out with the young men was only recognised and talked about in the context of activities i.e. football, fighting racism, youth activities, political issues. The young women could easily identify the main reason for the group as being 'to talk about ourselves and our problems'. Douglas (1976) thought that mixed gender groups in adolescence were not appropriate, as young people had to face their sexual identities prematurely. For the refugees and the Bengali young people the issue of sexual identity is closely linked to the cultural views on male- female relationships. Culturally the mixing of sexes in the Muslim community and in some of the refugee communities was not acceptable. Several young men in the Bengali group thought themselves to be very modern but seemed to find relationships with women of their own age uncomfortable. Brown and Mistry (1994) also say that there is widespread evidence to suggest that same sex groups are often more effective for women and this seemed to be the case for both of the young women's groups.

The communities that we work with as professionals are constantly changing, and we could find ourselves working with people from any part of the world. In the case of refugee communities, we could be working with a totally new community within the space of days or weeks, depending on world events. The ways of working need to be geared to working with all the different minority communities, which means that even if initially we do not know anything about their language or culture, we should be able to provide a service that can assess needs and offer flexible services to all clients. The issue is not as simple as offering groupwork to communities by workers from the same communities: obviously in some cases this is needed, but it can lead to Black and minority communities struggling for resources to provide their own services whilst other organisations do not take responsibility for carrying out the work. This is seen clearly in the amount of work and the lack of resources for the newer refugee communities.

In some ways all the work described here was across cultures, even with the Asian young people. ' Asian' consists of many cultures, and my Gujerati culture is very different to the Bengali culture, in terms of country, language, religion, and gender. When as an Indian worker I am working with the refugee group the complexities increase, in terms of culture and understanding. In the refugee group everyone came from different countries, members and worker. One of the positive points about this was that each individual felt they could start with a 'blank sheet' in terms of who they were culturally. They could tell us exactly what they wanted, thinking that we had no idea of their country or culture, although as I have stated earlier the worker has to initiate this openness about race and culture. For example when working in the Asian community the group members and the worker would already have made assumptions about the other Asian person which could lead to negative stereotyping. In the case of the parents of the Bengali girls they would make a judgement about our 'respectability' on spoken or unspoken messages such as the way we dress. In the Refugee group my role as the worker was to provide an environment where each member could be an individual and express their own identity. For some of the members, having to explain to someone who was understanding about their cultural background proved to be therapeutic in itself and helped them to identify themselves as a separate individual.

Too many professionals see the solution as a simplistic one of providing a worker of the same 'culture' for a client of that culture i.e. provide a 'Black' worker for a 'Black client and a Refugee worker for a refugee client. A cultural match of workers can be useful for many clients but the cross cultural issues are still present and have to be acknowledged and addressed.

In addition to and quite distinct from the cultural issues, all three groups had the common experience of race and racism. Again providing a same race worker is not the simple answer. Thomas (1995) says the Black therapist may have been trained in the same way as a white therapist and may be ill equipped to deal with the race issue in a therapy session. The same could apply to Black groupworkers, a Black worker could be perpetuating the same ideas of race and racism as a White worker if neither of them has addressed their own ideas and views on race and racism. Many people in this country, Black and White have strong prejudices towards refugees, and so in providing an appropriate service we would rely on the Black or white persons' attitudes towards refugee communities, rather than solely on their race. In working with young people a worker from the same culture can offer support but can also inhibit the young person particularly from talking about certain culturally taboo subjects such as sex and sexuality, gender or religion. Many young refugee clients at Nafsiyat specifically request a counsellor who is not from the same culture as themselves. There are many reasons for this, some of which are issues of confidentiality in small communities, political positions in conflicts in their country, and the cultural conflicts that exist between all adults and adolescents from the same community.

A model of work which can be used in working with all communities has to consider the specific realities that exist in our society for Black people. These include some of the issues that were raised by the young people in the groups, including the realities of racism, sexism discrimination, cultural conflicts, unemployment, and housing conditions, which can all affect a young person's ability to use a group. If the groupwork approach allows acknowledgement and discussion around these issues, it can be tailored to work with all communities. Being open about similarities and differences in cultural backgrounds can support people from any community. This involves the people who run the group being prepared to be open about their own culture, language and lack of understanding or knowledge of a group members culture. In our experience most young people enjoy explaining their culture in a safe environment and it can be a valuable exercise for them to express their individuality.

Some of the groupwork described involved long periods of planning and preparation, and the ability to be flexible in the ways of working to be responsive to young people. The work with the Bengali young men could never have happened if individuals were not prepared to volunteer their time to stay up at nights and work on rotas to operate the telephone helplines.

IDENTITY AND RACISM

In this discussion I shall again use Black as a general term to describe an individual's social, political and racial experience and position in this society. I believe the cultural issue is distinct from the issue of racism in terms of Black and White. The Black and White division is more of a political and social definition of communities in Britain. The individual however defines themselves according to their own needs and personal experiences; some young people define themselves in more than one way, for example a young person who is born here may say I am African but I am also Black British. Young Asian people may define themselves as Black British and Bengali or Indian.

Most of the young people discussed in this chapter did not define themselves as Black, but used terms that had personal meanings for them. However our discussions around racism centred on the use of the words Black and White and perhaps the position of other ethnic minority people who experience discrimination. Most of the refugee young people described themselves as Eritrean or Somali, by their country of origin. The Bengali people did not describe themselves as Black or Asian but Bengali, but they all identified with the concept of Black and the struggle of Black people in general.

There has been very little work on identity issues for young Asian people, due to the myth that they do not have problems around identity because our communities are so close and give our children large doses of traditional cultural values which help Asian children to form strong identities. This of course may be true in many cases, but the strict values and strong cultural values could in some cases actually cause more anxiety in terms of identity amongst Asian young people. If the gap between home life and life outside the home is very wide, the young person will find it even harder to negotiate between the two and it could lead to a total confusion of identity. They may find it hard to fit into society and at the same time be accepted by their families. These internal conflicts have been suggested for the high rates of eating problems (Mumford et al., 1991) amongst Asian women and perhaps the high rates of suicide amongst Asian women in Britain.

The groups described here had identities that were accessible to them i.e. they were not being brought up by White carers. The Bengali young people lived in the midst of their communities, and the young refugees had been brought up in their own communities. For these three groups the issue of identity was about recovery and acceptance.

In my opinion all identity work should be about exploration rather than indoctrination or glorification of any culture. The young people should be allowed to explore and make their own choices about identity in an environment which can see and accept a Black identity as a positive one. In my experience many workers will try to impose identities on young people, particularly when they are of mixed race. The definition of Black is used as a political statement to indicate a position in a society which is racist, but when it is a discussion around identity, which is a deeply personal issue there must be room for exploration. All workers need to be clear and confident about their own identity in order to work effectively. The role of the worker is to enable a young person to make their own informed choices and decisions about who they are. Workers who try to impose identities on Black young people can only make them feel less able and inadequate about themselves, rather than promoting a positive identity.

What difference did it make that Black workers led all of these groups? Some workers believe that the race of the worker is not crucial as long as they are competent, and that the cross cultural difficulties are exaggerated. (Kadushin, 1972) (King, 1982) (O'Shea, 1972).

Others (Brown and Mistry, 1994) believe that the sex and race of the groupworkers has a profound effect on the group behaviour and process. I feel that in all of these groups the workers being Black and having the authority of our position was critical in many ways. We are seen as being powerful in a society from which the group members may feel excluded. The aspect of seeing a Black worker who fits into society can support a young Black person's search for a place in society; this may particularly apply to newly arrived refugees.

Heap (1979) says that as a basic principle authority, is a difficult aspect of the groupworker-group member relationship, but for Black workers with Black clients it can be used positively as a role model of Black people that they can integrate into their own ambitions and image. Kadushin (1972) says that a client can identify with a Black worker by assuming a 'common racial experience'. This is a clear advantage for a Black professional and allows the client to identify with a positive image of Black. For young Black people seeing Black adults in authority can have a powerful effect on their own self esteem, and be ego supportive (Heap, 1979)

SUMMARY

In this paper I have attempted to look at some of the key elements in working with Black and minority adolescents in the context of our present society, where social, economic, and political factors come together to form unique and separate individuals and groups of young Black people.

Each Black community in Britain forms its own culture in terms of accumulating a set of beliefs in the context of their situation. Some of the factors that influence this culture are patterns of migration, class, religion, language skills, education, social status and position in the whole community. These are the cultural factors which I believe need to be explored and discussed in order to provide an appropriate service to a particular Black community.

Understanding of the culture alone however is inadequate in serving any section of the Black community. There also has to be an acceptance and understanding of our political position in a white society, and the issues of power in terms of race and gender. Many workers see cultural issues as the only issue. I believe that anyone can find out about culture, but the workers or the institutions attitude towards other cultures is what is often a barrier to working with Black people.

For example an agency can possess detailed knowledge of a culture or country e.g. Ethiopia, but can still inherently believe that refugees from Ethiopia are poor victims (perpetuated by constant images of African refugees in the media) and need to be helped by powerful White professionals. Full cultural knowledge cannot support a young person if they and the country they come from is seen as inferior.

Cross-Cultural issues exist in all groups. The groupworkers whether they are Black or White have an impact on the dynamics of race and culture in any group. An all White, or single culture group exists in a country which is made up of many different races and cultures, and as such has to address their relationships to people from other cultures. The openness and discussion about race, identity, gender and class can take place in all groups as long as the worker takes responsibility to allow this exploration. In cross cultural work I do not believe there are any clear cut answers in relation to Race, except the historical fact that racism exists. All other issues are often extremely complicated in the group dynamics, as I hope some of my examples have shown. An effective groupworker should aim to explore the rigid categories of race, gender and class and allow individual expressions of what each category represents for each member.

All workers, Black and White, need to examine their personal views on power issues, race, sex and class. We are all influenced by the institutionalised issues of power in our daily lives as well as in our professional workplaces and training. We have to acknowledge our own powerful position as workers and how this can be used positively to enable young Black people to develop their position in this society.

Towards a Developmental Framework: Empowering Youthwork with Young Asian Women

SAKINNA DICKINSON

For a long time you have profited by my shyness and modesty
Traded so well on my motherhood and fidelity,
Now the season for flowers to bloom in our laps and minds is
here.

Kishwar Naheed (*Who am I*, 1990)

The context of the ideas, models and practice discussed within
this paper is work with
Asian women and girls. Broadly, we are referring to South Asian
young women, from diverse nationalities, religions and cultures,
between the ages of 14-25 years This age range has been set by
youth policy in Tameside, Greater Manchester and may be
different in other areas. In practice the work often includes
younger and older females.

The broad age range means that we have to deliver activities
which correlate with the personal experiences of young women
who may be at school, in further education, in employment or
unemployed, in relationships, married and/or with children. It is
important to emphasise this variety of situations because it
relates directly to the social standing and identity of young
women, and has direct bearing on the types of groupwork we
offer. The physical setting of the work is in multi-racial and
multi-ethnic neighbourhoods. The context is crucial in
understanding the developmental strategies framing this work.

To date, we have a set of aims which are informed by youth
policy and relate specifically to the needs of the young women.
These aims also reflect analysis of good practice in other areas
and the views and opinions expressed by young women who have
been a part, or are still a part, of the project. These specific aims
are also formulated in response to a critical analysis of the ways
in which multi-cultural and anti-racist models have failed to
respond to the needs of young Asian women. The fog created by

these policies at the grass-roots level has led to practice which often attempts to meet so many agendas that they fail not only to respond to the needs of young women themselves but serve also to perpetuate the racist pathologising of their lives. In attempting to challenge this pathologising, our practice has had to find ways of working that recognise the oppressions of the young women but which also enable them to place them in context and find individual, group or community strategies that will deliver change.

All young people are critical of the seeming restrictions and constraints in their lives. All young people engage in behaviours that will be considered 'rebellious.' In my view, an important facet of our work ,is to reclaim this phase for Asian young women as a normal feature of their development. The aims of the work can then be summarised as enabling them to:

1. gain an informed understanding of issues in their lives;
2. explore the possibilities in their lives;
3. adopt a positive and informed approach to realising these possibilities;
4. gain an understanding of power and oppression;
5. create friendships and positive support networks for themselves and others;
6. be active in their communities;
7. celebrate a positive' Asian' identity.

Our methodology is dependent on the issue that we are dealing with. The project offers opportunities for young women to access both traditional and non-traditional activities. Specifically these methods are:

1. creative tools such as drama, video, photography, writing to explore and record the lives of Asian women;
2. sport, outdoor pursuits and other recreational activities to promote sense of self, health and well-being;
3. opportunities to learn new skills through formal and informal courses and training;
4. debate and informed commentary to explore issues of race, gender, culture and religion.

We use a community development model of practice that seeks to engage with the personal, social and political dimensions of young women's lives. This developmental model is based on working in an incremental strategic manner to deal with dual issues of race and of gender. Thus we actively engage with the process of empowerment in a way that is culturally aware and sensitive to the specific context of Asian women. I think it would be useful to explain this a little further. Within Asian cultures there are very strong traditions of women challenging and subverting the sexism which they experienced. There are folk traditions and folk narratives which illustrate this dimension of women's roles. These traditions lie in the discourses produced by women for women to correct some of the injustices and imbalances in their lives. Whilst these traditions remain on the whole undocumented there are now:

> ...attempts to re-interpret myths, epics and folktales : to critique mainstream religions and cultural practices and search for alternative texts or practices and to discover historical or particular method's of women's resistance in India (*The History of Doing*, Rahda Kumar, p.45)

Women have always been questioning and changing traditions in response to the prevailing social conditions. These changes have not been dramatic or instant, they have been paced within the natural cycles of generations. These changes are not obvious or visible; often their power and potential is found in this invisibility. There are many discourses in relation to women. These may be framed within economic, political, psychological debates. All of these seek to explain the condition of women today and offer some clues as to the position of women tomorrow. In these gradual movements the position and roles of all women are changing. It is these subtle shifts that Padma Perera is alluding to in her short story:

> On her fifth birthday at the turn of the century, she is given her grandmother's ear ornaments. Forty-eight uncut rubies to the pair : set in hammered gold that curls close as petals around each glowing centre, with a row of pearls trembling in a crescent below to complete the pattern and cover the whole ear. Maybe it is a part of her dowry. Only eighty two years later I do not know. She in turn gives me one of the pair. When I am married - what happened to the other, I do not know either. But in my generation, given the shifting cruelties of ornamentation, we don't have all the requisite holes in our ears since the cartilage is left alone and only the holes are pierced. So we turn the jewel into a pendant for a necklace: involving links and chains .
> Everyone says the new craft is not like the old, the rubies not as deep. But I think of her, my grandfather's sister.

And when I am done with marriage and have dispensed with a lot of paraphernalia, this one thing stays with me. I carry it across continents, sometimes in a brown paper bag on crowded streets; keep it in a filing cabinet under 'F' (to Fool burglars); and wear it, a shared symptom at my throat (Padma Perera, 1974).

There has been much debate about these changes and what this means for individuals, communities and societies. Developmental work is an exploration of these changes but more importantly it is part of the drives for these changes. As women in a multi-racial society, it is clear that we have a history together and also a history apart; both of these are critical in 'a feminist re-appraisal' of the world in this context.

Youth work refers to a variety of statutory and voluntary provision which seeks to promote the personal and social development of young people. These services include social, recreational and leisure facilities. Traditionally, the youth service has been staffed by and served the needs of white young men. To date the needs of other groups are acknowledged at policy level, but there is wide variation as to how these needs are being met at a practical level. The youth service has also faced dramatic cuts and reorganisation over the past ten years. This has had a significant impact on the implementation of policy which seeks to meet the needs of these other groups; including young women, disabled young people, Black young people.

It would be safe to say that the needs of Black young people as a specific group were largely ignored by the youth service until the rebellons of the 1980s. These rebellions forced the youth service and other agencies dealing with young people to look at strategies to identify and then meet the specific social and personal needs of Black young people. These strategies resulted in a mixture of anti-racist practices, multi-cultural policies and equal opportunities statements. There was also a rise in short term projects through central government initiatives which sought to address the social , economic and political disadvantage faced by Black young people. Inevitably, these services were directed mainly at Black young men as they were the most visible group. The short term funding created a number of fundamental problems. The root of these problems lay in the unrealistic timescales afforded to 'developmental' work.

Where projects were set up to meet the specific needs of young women they were very much a measure to balance the equal opportunities equation. Generally, the view persisted that Asian young women would be unable to participate in youth services. This was rationalised in different ways; lack of interest, too much parental control and the patriarchal structure of their communities. These issues deflected the responsibility of service providers to explore pro-active models and practices which would enable young women to participate.

Different groups have different needs, and barriers to their effective participation will also be specific to their personal contexts. At a service level personal and social education for young people needs to incorporate opportunities for learning, accessing support, developing skills, validating experiences and exploring feelings. This enables them to understand their individual potential and their position as young people in society. In developing a youthwork perspective for Asian young women this service integrity has to be maintained. So far, in practice this has been problematic for a number of reasons. These are better understood if we explore the position of this group within the larger debates that have taken place and are taking place in relation to Black young people.

It is clear that race policy within Britain has shifted visibly on paper in relation to Black young people with the greatest emphasis on exploring issues of race and culture. Historically policy initiatives were directed by the goal of assimilation with its inherent ideology of inferiority in relation to other cultures, family and community structures and life styles. In practice, it was assumed that Asians as other Black groups would begin to use existing provision, fit into existing curriculums and begin to see themselves as white young people. Their lack of participation was not seen to be institutional failure, but rather the problematic nature of the culture of Asian young people. The issue then was not of structural changes or more appropriate responses, not a delineation of needs based on evidence but an assumption of needs based on race and culture. With the inception of multi-culturalism this emphasis was further entrenched. The consequence of this was to make race and culture visible and problematic. Difference in this context then was not to be respected but to be defined and to be actioned or ignored. The benchmark of 'good' practice was the mainstream service.

In addition, with more attention being paid to responses for the containment of African Caribbean young people there began to emerge an agenda of division and difference. Asian young people were viewed on the whole as part of a 'supportive' culture with a strong tradition and legacy, thus their personal, political and social needs would be met within this arena. At a service level a remedial curriculum aimed at improving language (English) deficiency began to be adopted as a general pattern for circumscribing and meeting needs. This, it was assumed was sufficient to meet the political, economic and social oppressions faced by Asian young people.

Asian young women were afforded a different and peculiar reality as young people within these debates. The specific image of them as passive, subordinated and subjugated to an Asian male identity afforded few if any opportunities for the development of service responses that would enable this group to participate. Conceptualised as submissive, economically, socially and spiritually dependent she became by extension intellectually illiterate and an unchallenging upholder of tradition and culture.

Since the 60s and 70s there has been a gradual tightening up of immigration laws. Politically then there has been a desire to have a 'fixed' black population that is measurable and that behaves in predictable ways. Institutions have recognised the need for anti-racist policies to protect this fixed population from overt and hidden discrimination, however, little has been done to remove the misconceptions of particular groups. In delivering appropriate personal and social education, intervention has to begin with this as a fundamental step. This will reveal the complexities of race, gender, political motivation and negative stereotyping. Each of these will need to be actioned specifically in order to create frameworks that can be deemed 'developmental' for specific groups.

APPROACHES

Living in Britain creates a fundamental problem. On the one hand Asian women realise that they have the potential to access many different opportunities. On the other hand, the racist and sexist stereotypes persist. Any changes in the accepted pattern of behaviour or any serious questions as to their shifting and changing roles within the context of their lives here will often be seen as disloyal to their culture, religion and identity. In this context then we need to create discourses where the stakes are not a loss of identity or moral decline but rather an affirmation of the positive value and worth of our identity, morality and spirituality.

There has been an ongoing dialogue between policy makers and the adult community about what is and what is not appropriate provision for Asian girls and young women. The needs, expectations and desires of the young women themselves have been regarded as secondary. The task for the youth worker who is often presented with models of work and practice from a variety of contexts is to be aware of this dynamic. This means an inherent understanding of the principles of youth work but also an ability to relate this to processes that are achievable and feasible for any given group. A failure to understand this relevance is inherently disempowering not only for the group but also for the worker.

There is now a strong awareness that feminism or rather a female perspective has its own context for Asian women. It is wise to investigate this when developing appropriate intervention and locating philosophical alliances . In effect, most developing cultures have acknowledged the rights of women. The historical journeys that women have made in their own contexts is the language and base of future development. Workers working with this group need to be aware of this context and how it is cross-fertilised with other contexts. In terms of Asian women this has been a movement spanning centuries where they have moved from needs to rights, from parity in particular contexts to larger debates of self-determination and all that this involves, intellectually and politically. There is broad agreement on most issues in relation to freedom and self expression. In practice, however, most women have found that the social, political and economic structures to deliver these rights are not in place. Personal and social development is a direct engagement with processes which will bring this about.

As a youthworker with a specific group it would be easy to deliver programmes of work which in essence are a youthwork construct. Working within a white institution, operating within a service which is based on the perceived needs of white young men, and which despite its best intentions, will continue to be driven by these concerns it is easy to see how these constructs become benchmarks for practice and how these are then the limitations within which we begin to operate.

The issues that we have to deal with lie in the inherent dilemmas of being young, being female and being Asian. As a group we can only begin to unpack these dilemmas by using appropriate tools and approaches. The net result of these experiences has to be an enhanced ability to be critical of oneself, one's community and society in general. This perspective then enables young women to make positive choices in the context of their own lives in terms of harm and good.

This dynamic presents a fundamental problem in terms of setting a curriculum. Some issues are easier to deal with than others. Thus, typically this groupwork with Asian young women has been fraught with difficulties as we have struggled to find frameworks which are responding to the complexities of young women's agendas but also within the limits that have been set by external debates around race, sex and gender issues.

We are clearly on dangerous ground here, for in giving credence to the current voices of young women we are challenging not only racial and gender stereotypes, but also historical perspectives. For in recognising that there is an interchange of ideas and values and importation of these values into particular contexts, we are in fact recognising that young women have access to many discourses which previously they did not have or did not recognise in explaining their lives and their relationships.

In addition, as workers, if we are to maintain our integrity we also have to find ways in which these debates can be lifted from the personal to the public arenas in order that these insights can feed the ongoing debates on race and gender. As a worker there is an inherent dilemma here. Recognising that developmental work elicits information which will inform future practice, clear decisions need to be made about how this is to happen. Obviously, the relationship between a youthworker and a group is bound by a set of ethics that have been set to by the group. In deciding to operate as a closed or open group young women are making clear decisions about the relationship they wish to have with the rest of the world. Thus, as workers we have to have a very clear framework for resolving this issue.

At an institutional level we recognise that our groups are a part of a larger service, and that often there is a blurring of agendas when this is presented to the wider world. Thus, we have to find ways of being a part of this wider forum and being private and safe in our own contexts. We recognise that often our groups are the only opportunity that young women have to reveal their internal selves. At face value these selves may run counter to the prevailing public norms, traditions or moralities. Ethically then, in order to maintain this safety we need to be fully aware of this duality in our work, and organise our public agendas within these limits.

In essence this is a debate about process and product. There is a general trend within mainstream youthwork which i s involved in making young people more visible. This is to satisfy a variety of agendas. In relation to our particular context we cannot escape this visibility. However, we can to some degree control this visibility. Thus, our practice must have sincere debates about the quality and value of this visibility and also the potential that this debate on visibility can deliver. We also have to recognise that this debate is fundamental to any empowerment process and, that in beginning to resolve issues of personal (invisible) and social (visible) identity women are engaging with the act of becoming 'citizens' and thus moving their agendas into the political sphere. In so doing women (and workers) are therefore able to compete for resources, recognition and rights in a more strategic manner and thus shape their community spaces in ways that reflect their needs and their lives.

What this approach is bringing to this discourse is a level of awareness of women's own history, their reliance on the family and their community and the wider black community as a source of support. Through its progression it will naturally encounter profound difficulties. Despite this, and despite the differing appraisals individual women make, there will always be a central cohesion and unity around specific gender issues relating to their subordination and their actions to bring about change. More crucially, it will change the ways that women are able to access resources - social, economic and political - in order to assert their identity and define their potential.

Therefore, developmental groupwork needs to offer a framework that gives us opportunities to create ourselves, make choices as to our private and public selves, recognise our personal identity and the identity of our audience. It also needs to give us opportunities to create languages to operate within both arenas. Groupwork needs to engage with the process of empowerment in a meaningful way that is culturally aware and sensitive to the specific context of Asian women's lives. It is clear in delivering groupwork one has to operate within the mores and accepted behaviours of a given community. Our work has to recognise that young women have rights, for this is the essence of youthwork, but in defining and exercising these rights they also have to make choices that will keep them safe in their own particular contexts.

DEVELOPMENTAL GROUP PROCESS

An analysis of the development cycle of any of our groups would be useful here. I think within youthwork the term group is used interchangeably to describe formal and informal collections of people. In addition it is also used as a convenient label that assumes a degree of commonality around certain issues or identities. For our purposes the term group means lots of different things. The definition of what this is dependent upon the developmental stage of our intervention.

In the first stage our groups are open to all Asian young women who feel they may benefit. This means as workers we have to adopt a number of concurrent strategies. These strategies will include raising awareness within the community of the group's existence by means of written publicity, face to face contact, and networking with other agencies, schools, organisations and professionals who may have contact with young women. At this initial stage of contact expectations are already beginning to be raised with all of these people as to the what the group should be.

In the second stage those young women who are interested in the idea of the group (or whose parents, other adults or peers feel they will benefit), will begin to attend the group or will register their interest in other ways. Again, as workers at this stage we need to be clear that young women have made no formal commitment to the 'group' and are acting on their own behalf. In this stage young women are normally checking out the potential of the group, checking out the workers, checking out the other young women who are attending. We as workers are being given some very clear messages as to the common spaces in these young women's lives, for example they will discuss issues related to college or school, bullying, racism, family, relationships, careers, health issues, or interests in fashion, music or films.

In the third stage we normally begin to offer some activities that individuals have requested, and also begin to build up a working relationship with the young women, and often with their families. This may be a skill based course for example photography or drama, or it may be a series of workshops to explore specific areas related to health, or to personal safety.

By maintaining a constant evaluation with respect to issues and ideas by observation, soliciting opinions and sometimes doing more formal, structured evaluations we begin to form an accurate picture of the context of their specific lives. Agendas remain open where possible and remain (on the whole) with the young women. Constant and constructive feedback is essential in maintaining this integrity.

It is at this stage through our individual interactions that we begin to mark up the issues that young women have started to explore for themselves and with others. So for instance young women may wish to explore relationships, traditions, feeling unhappy, pressures at school, at home or from peers. We also begin to get a clearer picture of the level of commitment from individual young women to the 'youthwork' process. We also have to address the dynamic of new women joining the group and how we ensure that they feel some sense of ownership of the group.

Intervention at this stage is kept to a minimum in order to ensure that the power relationship between the women and our roles as paid workers is not abused. It is easy at this stage to begin to promote propaganda or assume an identity or set of values which is based on our own understanding of what these women should be like or what these young women should believe. We will intervene, however, if individuals are being affected by particular behaviours such as gossip, personal comments or bullying but this again is not based on a particular set of rules. At this point, the group has in affect already started the process of setting boundaries and appropriate behaviours . Issues that appear to have been resolved outside of the group are those which relate to personal identity as opposed to social identity. The timescale for each of these stages varies, as operating with inappropriate timescales effectively closes down dialogues.

During the next stage we will begin the process of structuring the group (or formalising the structure, as often it happens naturally). This means that we involve the women in setting the boundaries for the group, taking on commitments around confidentiality, commitment to attend and anything else that is considered to be important in making the group 'safe' for everybody. This movement is from being a public arena to being a private arena. At this stage we can begin to deal with specific issues. We also begin to assess whether it is possible to continue as an open group or w hether we become a closed group. This decision depends on the issue or the activity that the group is engaged in. This movement can also produce a variety of reactions and accusations- from being elitist to being reactionary. If we do become a closed group then this is explained to any potential new members, and, as we operate a variety of different groups in the area which are all at different stages in their development, we are also able to suggest alternatives.

In working with young women we have to deal honestly in deconstructing racist and sexist stereotypes. The most difficult task in doing this is to find ways that are free of value judgements or ways that will not alienate or pathologise the roles and lives of women. It is hoped this approach will allow for the growth of new sets of relationships for women across age, religion and culture.

Complex issues such as sexuality for instance have particular taboos. However, by maintaining the integrity of public and private and using appropriate resources this model can be used as a positive method for deconstruction. The key is to place them into an appropriate race and gender perspective. By focusing on women's skills and strengths we begin to form an analysis of the way in which these women are using the spaces accorded to them to negotiate their personal, family and community relationships - and enable them to adapt these spaces in constructive ways. The key in this model seems to be pragmatism, not idealism.

Clearly the legacy of anti-racist movements has created a number of discourses. It is possible and appropriate to argue for specific anti- discriminatory practice and thus a step towards equality. Firstly, by understanding the position of the group within the communities in which they live and secondly, in delivering services such as this groupwork with appropriate resources, information and interactions which will begin to unpack the inherent structural inequalities in their lives. Theory, policy and practice are all subject to the prevailing social, economic and political context of the work, and ideas are subject to fashions and trends thus, debates about equality are comforting but meaningless unless they are followed through by planned and sustained action, and effectively monitored.

As an example of this we could cite the following. The process described here spanned four years and the specific issue based work is ongoing.

In stage one the youthworkers organised a group for young women. Most of the women attending this group were married with young children.

In stage two the group began to mark up their common ground. Although there were a number of different definitions that women were using it was clear that all of these revolved around issues related to their own health and the health of their families. Women described their frustration over a whole range of issues including lack of information, lack of practical advice, problems when dealing with health professionals.

In the third stage, we offered women the opportunity to begin to explore these issues in depth. In this groupwork we began to deconstruct the concept of health by encouraging the group to begin an exploration of the issue at a personal level. In this way the group began to form personal definitions of health and well - being. This method allowed the women to be open about their values, their attitudes, their strengths and their perceived weaknesses. Ongoing evaluation revealed that all the women valued this opportunity to talk about and share their experiences in this safe environment. We continued with this personal and social development by offering women opportunities for:

1. Building assertiveness skills and their confidence.
2. Practical skills such as first aid.
3. Offering advice and information on specific illnesses and conditions.
4. Collating information on local support networks.
5 Organising workshops in alternative health approaches such as massage, stress management, relaxation and aromatherapy.

Through this groupwork women were able to recognise the ways in which their personal definitions were often superseded or compromised by health professionals. So for example women's general feelings of ill-health were often explained away in terms of their life styles, family pressures or culture and no solutions offered, or women were offered medication without a proper investigation of their physical symptoms.

As a result of this groupwork we were able to analyse women's health issues in terms of:

1. The personal and political context.
2. Related issues and contexts.
3. Solutions available.
4. Solutions that needed to be available.

We as workers then began to explore ways in which we could feed this information back in order that we could begin a dialogue with health professionals and health services providers. Initially we approached fieldworkers for example health visitors and equality officers within the local authority. As a consequence we were encouraged to meet with strategic personnel within the Health Authority. The outcome was the creation of a community based project dedicated to the health needs of the Asian community in which these women live. The agenda of this project was to look at pro-active measures to deal with specific health issues that women had raised within the group and to look at the health issues of their families and the wider community.

Developmental work is not static and by definition cannot have fixed curriculums. However, the principle of creating change through processes which empower and processes which challenge the rationale for power points within a given community or society enable there to be a constant ebb and flow of ideas and expectations of change. Empowerment within any context is a daunting task as it involves the identification and analysis of a vast array of different relationships. This analysis illustrates the complex and often conflicting forces that operate together to shape and determine individual, group and social interaction. Any process of empowerment has to be gender specific. Asian women's lives in Britain are mediated by racism. They are also mediated by the patriarchal structure of their own and the wider communities. Therefore, any discourse attempting to empower Asian women has to address both of these issues in a constructive and meaningful way.

A service which is concerned with rights, justice and meeting needs has to be built on systems that provide material evidence, quantitative objectives and measured practices. To date one of the major factors that has impeded the development of appropriate intervention for this group is the lack of a clear conceptual framework. Women, obviously, have been amongst their communities resisting in the roles assigned to them the oppressions of race. This support has been physical and moral. Similarly, women have organised and operated in Black alliances to support the struggles of other oppressed groups whether at home or abroad. In the specific context of youth and community work we necessarily need to become increasingly gender specific in defining rights, responsibilities and oppression. This applies equally to work with young men and young women.

To sum up these issues then it is clear that a positive, pro-active framework for developmental work has to be acutely aware of the following:

1. That multi-cultural policies and anti-racist strategies are based primarily on the needs of the institution.

2.   That structures and frameworks created by these policies intrinsically limit consultation and representation of Asian women.

3.   That the institution has to be clear about the aims and objectives of intervention.

It has to be recognised that to bring women centre stage requires changes not only conceptually but also in challenging the stereotypes that persist at all levels .The initial steps towards this have already been achieved. Women's roles in relation to their communities have already been marked up in different arenas such as education, health , personal and social welfare, as being fundamental to the life stage of given communities. What has not yet altered, however, are the structures for participation, and as a result at a visible level women remain hidden. Thus, they are not able to act as equal partners in any relationship whether this be social, economic, political or personal. More specifically, developmental work without this specific gender context has negated women's contributions by denying them access to decision making. All too often consultation has been limited and tokenistic or with those who are already visible. Thus, assumptions have been made that women's needs ' will be those prescribed by these other individuals, or similar to the male groups around them.

It is clear that this does not and cannot follow. Women have to be active partners. Only in this way are women able to locate themselves in their roles as mothers, wives, workers or autonomous beings. 'Active' in this sense means that asking women to produce lists of needs is not enough ,women are socialised into the existing status quo. Their sense of powerlessness will always impede them from putting what are seen to be personal and private demands on the agenda. The first step to rectifying this situation is to create conditions in which these demands can be imagined, and then to offer them tools in order that they can be expressed. Appropriate service delivery is one step towards this goal. In essence this means an adoption of key concepts:

1.   That young women play vital roles in the well being and development of their communities, and service delivery needs to maximise these roles by providing appropriate support services.

2.   That structures need to be created which facilitate ongoing and increased participation of women in the service in order

that it becomes representative.
3. That access to services which support young women will
   have positive long-term effects for individual women and the
   community as a whole.

In conclusion, I would suggest that there are many positive
visions of the future that women hold within their hearts and
their minds. Removing blocks that prevent women from
articulating these visions through practical measures as we have
discussed goes some way to giving the future back to women, and
undoing some of the havoc that has been caused by racism and
negative stereotyping.

Black and White Issues in Training Groups: A Psychodynamic Approach

AILEEN ALLEYNE

Over the past ten years, there has been great demand for Equal Opportunities training. As an independent trainer I have received requests from Social Services Departments, the Probation Service, alcohol, drugs and HIV agencies, counselling courses taught at all levels, and from all disciplines within the National Health Service.

In contrast to the early eighties when in many organisations, Racism Awareness Training as it was known then, was mandatory and generally problematic, training now appears to be more voluntarily pursued, less openly resisted, but nevertheless still fraught with political and personal difficulties.

The aim of this chapter is to set out and review a model of training that I have been using successfully in Equal Opportunities and Race work, using a psychodynamic analysis to aid the discussion of some of the group processes involved.

The chapter will also highlight some critical issues and crucial concerns in understanding black/white relations as part of the Equal Opportunities framework.

It is of immense importance to state at this point the great influence of 'macro' processes on this work I am about to describe. The ever present and ever shifting structural and socio-economic-political influences as is demonstrated in institutional racism and other forms of prejudice, clearly impact on the way Equal Opportunities and Race issues are embraced. It would be very tempting to focus on this aspect of the subject as no one is spared from the effects of our political environment, but my intention for this chapter is to shift to an area we rarely give as much credence, and concentrate on training which is geared to including and understanding the 'micro' processes of Equal Opportunities and Race, that is, the internal and interpersonal dynamics operating in its midst.

I need to explain what I mean by the term training.

Training in the context of the work I offer means facilitation of the needs of the organisation in the agreed area of Equal

Opportunity. This is different from the very familiar didactic teaching methods used in other kinds of training. Change therefore takes place in an atmosphere of learning directly from each other. The teaching mode is facilitated through exercises which are experienced in couples, triads, small group and large group work.

Facilitation includes timely tutorial inputs given by me the facilitator which address the need to discuss and understand ideas conceptually. Frameworks are offered for closer examination of complex processes in black/white relations and video taped programmes relevant to the topic will sometimes be included.

UNDERSTANDING DYNAMICS AT THE REQUEST STAGE

Pre-transference issues

A working relationship with any group generally starts at the request stage, or in some cases even earlier. A trainer's reputation (good, bad or indifferent), may precede her, thereby creating a pre-relationship even before any meeting takes place.

The organisation may as a result have pre-expectations about the quality, approach and style of the work on offer. In my experience, training in Equal Opportunities and particularly black/white dynamics, appears to carry with it unusually high expectations of the trainer and of its possible outcomes.

In counteracting this situation, I am very keen to know *exactly* what the team wants, in what form they want it, what are they hoping to achieve by having the training *now*, and how they intend maintaining any changes brought about as a direct result of the training. I am careful to stress to those who hire my services *my choice* to focus on the particular area of interpersonal and intrapsychic processes relating to difference, but by no means excluding the wider parameters of politics, economics and social inequalities.

Up to date, no one has turned down this service, but rather, have jumped at the chance of using it to get at the nub of team work with issues of difference, prejudice and oppression.

It is my belief that all conscious and unconscious interactions occurring before groups meet and training takes place, contribute to the pre-relationship dynamics or pre-transference relationship. As a result, I take careful note of the language used to describe training needs, the time and money allocated and all early observations which inevitably form the pre-transference relationship.

To demonstrate how important this pre-transference relationship is for groupwork training, I will elaborate on a few of the examples given.

Blurring the focus

Often groups which request training under the broad heading of Equal Opportunities, present these requests in a very confused manner. The person making contact may say, 'We are trying to address Equal Opportunities issues by trying to find out why black clients are not using our service'. This request would also include concerns about whether the agency needs to focus on particular groups or cast its nets wider to embrace all groups in the community it serves. Within this very same request the aims would extend to the needs of the team to examine staff working relationships in a racially mixed staff team. Sometimes the remit will be even further stretched to encompass transcultural issues in counselling. And all of this in half a day's training!

Within this particular mishmash there are three distinct needs being raised. The first appears to be Equal Opportunities Training which covers policy making, service delivery, monitoring, funding and recruitment issues. The second request would be addressing mixed staff relations which could come under the heading of 'Working with Issues of Difference in the Workplace'. The last need is for training in Transcultural Counselling. These three very different training needs should be tackled separately with more than half a day for each training session.

At this point my task is to try to understand what is going on for the organisation in the midst of all this confusion and even defensive muddle.

First of all, despite fierce denial by some, it is still politically shrewd and culturally fashionable to be seen to be pursuing Equal Opportunities Issues. The immediate pay-offs for the organisation are creating an acceptable face to the external world and a sense of security within. Guilt, shame and blame are temporarily absolved from the organisation's conscience, and everyone can sit back with an ease of mind that they have done the right thing.

Secondly, Equal Opportunities, Anti-discriminatory Practices and Racism Awareness, are merged to mean one and the same. The tendency to homogenise different parts of this complex area of work ('macro' and 'micro' aspects), suggests to me an unconscious fear of not allowing difference or separateness to exist even at this level. The parallels here with race inequality are several. For example: 'blacks are all the same'; black people being seen only as victims and 'special' cases, and not allowing for differentness within same race groups (which incidentally, is a real internalised issue for members themselves within same race groups).

The pressure to focus means one will have eventually to see and face what is truly there, and we know that certain kinds of truths unearth primitive fears and anxieties leaving us feeling exposed and vulnerable.

I am suggesting that groups unconsciously attempt to manage this fear and prevent this exposure by lumping different Equal Opportunity needs together, creating a blur and an easy avoidance of the painful work of recognising and accepting difference within this complex sphere.

We might remember ex-Prime Minister Thatcher's comment about 'being swamped' by difference in the form of immigrants from developing countries seeking residence in England. The implied threat of dilution to British culture, and even of annihilation are evident in her words. Could black/white issues in training create similar feelings?

Killing time

Most organisations find it difficult to confront inequality and the specific concern of black and white issues. A hierarchy of needs within 'other important training areas', is frequently created as a defence against taking on board the importance of race prejudice, oppression and racism.

Training groups seem to think that one half day is sufficient to deal with issues of equality of opportunity and there is a sincere belief that all that is needed is to understand the language of Equal Opportunity and master, what I have come to believe is, people's notion of there being specific skills to acquire and clear recipes to follow. Inherent in this approach is an ignorance and arrogance that this area can be learnt quickly in a prescriptive way and at an intellectual (cognitive) level.

Denying the complexity of race and cultural issues and minimising the time necessary to attend to them, are effective ways of 'killing' off their importance and the challenge to the self.

We can further understand this defence in developmental terms. A person's or an organisation's attitude towards time can be equated with the attitude towards authority figures or feelings of being taken over and controlled. If the person or organisation has experienced excessively critical authority figures, or been made to feel powerless, a dismissive attitude towards time may result. Most organisations seeking training have either experienced pressures from the outside (political), or from their members within, usually black (personal).

Both kinds of pressures to meet what is difficult and challenging, have often led to feelings of powerlessness and therefore a grudging lending of time to training.

The discussion so far offers some explanation for the resistance, ambivalence, fear, and the tendency to put other areas of training above and in competition with the race component of Equal Opportunities training.

TRAINING - THE PSYCHODYNAMIC APPROACH

Since beliefs in racial difference are among the most irrational that men and women hold, it seems that the science of the irrational, psychoanalysis (that is to say, the science which seeks to understand the sources of the irrational in the human mind), is one science to which we ought to look for their explanation (Rustin, 1991, p.61).

Psychodynamic analysis with its many theoretical influences can offer us the opportunity to understand human behaviours and interactions at a deeper level. The approach focuses more on mental forces operating within the psyche of individuals, groups and organisations, and is concerned with those processes contributing to growth, psychic development and stability.

The advantages therefore are that what we see in, and experience with others (and here I would like to stay with black/white relations) are influenced by a number of factors such as, our histories, traditions, positions in society, value and belief systems, and the way these influences are incorporated into our entire makeup as individuals and our different racial and cultural groups.

The psychodynamic approach which is used by a handful of trainers who are already familiar with psychodynamic and psychoanalytic concepts, offers a rare and refreshing approach to understanding human interactions and the irrational within the area of meeting and working with issues of race difference.

I have found the concepts within Object relations theory to be the most valuable and realistically appropriate amongst the various psychodynamic models. This theory is primarily concerned with interactional relationships between ourselves and others with whom we must learn to relate productively (Faibairn, 1963), as well as the interactional relationship between the ego and internal different parts of ourselves (Klein, 1952a; 1952b). Both aspects of the theory contend that there are attributes of 'goodness' and 'badness' *in* us, and *out* there with which we must learn to integrate and deal with maturely.

What is helpful for me as a trainer/facilitator in using this theory is that it enables participants to understand the hidden and complex process of putting onto others (projection) those unwanted bits - the badness - which cannot be tolerated in the self. In black/white relationships this is an ever present phenomena.

The psychodynamic intention is then geared towards deepening participants' understanding of powerful unconscious processes which operate when meeting the unknown and unfamiliar. In black/white relationships there is a lot of the unknown and unfamiliar which we manage in several ways to handle through, stereotyping, scapegoating, denigrating, idealising and so on.

An understanding of these processes enables participants to tune into their own functioning and begin to meet the 'shadow' side of their psyche which reacts to difference with ignorance, hostility, curiosity, fear, revulsion, indifference and even annihilation.

The core elements of this training model are:

1. participants thinking about and sharing their own values and beliefs systems;
2. discussing openly their responses to working with people different from themselves;
3. highlighting the difficulties therein;
4. identifying responses in relation to the defences we employ to protect and shield ourselves from the unfamiliar;
5. exploring how these processes hinder and enhance various therapeutic encounters in the workplace.

The more time that is allocated to work on these issues, the more sustaining and truly challenging are the effects on group participants. For a start, individual move on to having a better understanding of how the different Other - the black person for example, is a figure constructed to be of service to groups of people who have historically held power and dominance over others.

Black participants begin to have a deeper understanding of how the black Other must remain part of and party to the self-celebratory opinions of the dominant group. No real exchange of views and feelings can be permitted to intervene by the black Other, lest the precarious power of the dominant group is threatened.

When participants begin to hear this reality in an atmosphere of safety and respect, they soon see parts of themselves in this process; and as with the effect of a true mirror reflection, there is a slow move towards accepting elements of this reality as part of their upbringing and present world.

A psychodynamic approach to Equalities Training is challenging, requiring a particular flexibility from the trainer. This involves developing a working rhythm with the group whilst being able to hover sensitively over difficult and resistant areas.

Coupled with my choice of model and theoretical approach, is a need to understand groups and group dynamics. Several models inform this understanding such as the works of Argyle (1969), Yalom (1975), Tuckman (1965) and Bion (1961). The training that I offer in Equal Opportunities and Race issues is run loosely along the lines of a task performance group using experiential modes of learning. The dynamic interaction between group members and their tasks, functions and roles creates a rich matrix in which group and individual learning take place simultaneously.

There is no intention on my part to create a therapy or psychoanalytic group atmosphere in these trainings. This would clearly be inappropriate. The task therefore is set out by the employer who, after consulting with employees is then able to negotiate with me the trainer. I am particularly interested in requests being made this way and not those imposed as mandates from on high.

CONTRACT MAKING

Training contracts with organisations vary from half a day to three consecutive days of groupwork with teams of either the same discipline and rank, e.g. probation officers, or drug workers; or whole agencies comprising of managers, management committee members and workers at all levels.

I will usually request that the employer set out in writing what their collective needs are for Equal Opportunities training. I also request information on how many staff are attending, their status, racial, gender, and age characteristics. In my experience, there is little or no way of creating balanced ratios between these differences and therefore, I mostly work with predominantly white group and others with a handful of black and Asian members. It is rare to have the experience of facilitating a racially 'balanced' group or a predominantly black group. I also find it relevant to know if any members are openly gay or lesbian as a way of including them *more directly* in the programme. This is not to say that if there were no openly gay or lesbian members, this area of difference would not be addressed.

I usually work with groups I am given, and plan the training programmes accordingly. The choice of agenda with the different mixes of group participants will be discussed a little later.

Other aspects of training contracts sometimes include homework requesting participants personally to bring along 'live' case material where race and cultural conflicts are present. This material is utilised in the training to full effect, thereby giving participants a real (as opposed to an intellectual) opportunity to work on their own material.

I will sometimes request situational themes relevant to the organisation or vignettes to be sent along for me to study beforehand; the idea being to try to find a way of incorporating these themes into the training programme.

Generally, I study training requests very carefully to ascertain whether I want to take up the offer. My answer is partly dependant on such practicalities as the distance from home, cost and fees. I also consider whether the time allocated is adequate for the amount of work requested. Does the training feel like the team's need or management's need, and is it clearly stated? Am I personally motivated to accept this particular request?

Contracts with employers (including a 'cancellation' clause) are agreed formally with me offering in writing, clear objectives and intended learning outcomes of the training. A brief professional work profile accompanies the programme which is flexible, and a pre-reading list also follows. I usually state any requests I may have, for example, a maximum of say, 14 participants. I also request suitable semi-circular seating arrangements, and audio-visual equipment to be in good working order. I emphasise the importance of good time-keeping.

Local authorities in Britain have adopted different approaches to Equal Opportunity. London boroughs, for example, dealt with what was then a new subject in the late 70s and early 80s under the heading of Race or Racism Awareness Training. This was changed to Anti-Racism Training in the late 80s, and now Equal Opportunities, Anti-Discriminatory Practices, Working with

Issues of Difference, and Equalities Training for the 90s. These changes were due in part to increasing understanding of the 'macro' structural context, and the need to bring about change structurally as well as intra- and interpersonally. Throughout the earlier period, the main approach to Equal Opportunity training appeared to be one of stamping out racism by modified cognitive behavioural approaches. This technique, which seemed like 'guilt-tripping', became a way of employing guilt induced responses in white people and focused mainly on the imperialist past and black people's oppression.

There was an obsessive pre-occupation and focus on definitions of words like, race, racism, racialism, institutional racism, culture, black, and ethnicity. It was sadly interpreted by white participants that if they became fully conversant with the terminology, then there would be an acceptance and an automatic exemption from the 'terrible' label of being a racist. Overall, black people attending these courses received little in the way of understanding their own difficulties in working with issues of race and culture.

On reflection, the intent of these training sessions was mainly to educate white workers on the issues of race. Racism Awareness, Anti-Racism and Equal Opportunity or Equalities training, all became synonymous with black and white relations and black/ white dynamics, ignoring the rest of the human racism, namely, anti-Irish racism, anti-Semitism, internalised racism and so on.

Whilst the pioneering and experimental nature of earlier race training should be acknowledged as a natural part of its growth process, these highly charged sessions fraught with hostility, ambivalence and resistance, were taken on at a time when black trainers themselves were learning how to deal with their own cultural wounds.

The behavioural approach encouraged an atmosphere of confession and shaming. Trainers felt they needed to be tough to get their anti-racist/anti-discriminatory messages across, and the majority of participants who dreaded these mandatory sessions felt attacked and demoralised.

PROCESS AND DYNAMICS IN TRAINING GROUPS

Beginnings

The dynamics and group processes within any work group are largely determined by the focus of the training agenda. A two day workshop for example, with an agenda which is clear and unambiguous such as, 'Understanding Black/White Dynamics in the Workplace' has, in my experience helped prepare participants for a specific focus on understanding relationships between black people and white people in the work setting. This focus has helped to avoid the usual competitive tendency to bring in other cultural issues and minority groups as a way of creating a hierarchy of oppression.

Conversely, an agenda with a wider brief, for example, 'Working with Issues of Difference' or 'Anti-discriminatory Practices in the Workplace', can create anxieties about which group/s will get more attention and which group/s will be included and excluded. As a trainer working with both agendas, I have often noticed more confusion, anxiety and competition in groups with wider briefs. The many ways in which participants deal with these feelings are expressed by the following dynamics:

> Participants arriving late
> Comments like, 'this is only an excuse to talk about racism'
> An immediate focus on, and pre-occupation with black peoples' plight with accompanying expressions of guilt
> Food, e.g. sweets being passed around during the session
> Repeated requests for clarification of words used by trainer and of the group tasks
> Use of phrases like, 'I treat everybody the same, regardless', 'I see everyone as human beings regardless', 'I don't see colour; people are people'
> Reluctance to engage in small group work
> Creating a hierarchy of oppression by discussing who is worse off
> Questions raised 'and what about the Irish?'
> Retorts like, 'and black people can be racist too'
> Participants rescuing each other from discomfort
> Participants having to leave early
> Not being able to attend both days because of an important meeting
> The trainer ends up doing a lot of talking

The above dynamics are not uncommon and therefore have created a need for me, the trainer, to set the scene fairly early on into the programme.

A useful way forward is in the negotiation of the group contract and the group's aims. A contract which is agreed to give equal time to the groups addressed can be helpful. Clarification of the group's aim can be reiterated after say, an opening round where individuals identify their personal needs. As the trainer, I would acknowledge what people have asked for, and state clearly what can be realistically achieved in the time allocated for the training.

An example of this can be seen in a situation where the request from a drugs agency was to provide a one day workshop on 'Anti-discriminatory Practices in the Workplace'. The staff was interested in exploring cultural and racial prejudice amongst its team members and work with clients. In the opening round, requests for what people wanted from the day were very varied. Some white members wanted to know how to work with black members who automatically saw them as racist and as a result every difficult interaction with them or black clients was labelled racist. Some black members wanted to get clear guidance on how the manager and team as a whole would handle situations where white clients refused to see black members of staff. A lone Greek member wanted to concentrate on the needs of Greek Cypriot drug users, and another member wanted to address the needs of Gypsies.

I reiterated that it was impossible to allocate adequate time to all the needs of the team, and I enabled them to create a realistic agenda for the day. They unanimously agreed to work on staff relations in the morning, and to address the needs of their diverse clientele in the afternoon. The use of role plays highlighting racial conflict between black and white staff was a useful training tool enabling staff to get to the heart of the matter without personalising individual staff difficulties. The role plays also helped to distinguish racial prejudice and racism and to understand that the refusal of white clients to see black staff is a form of 'political resistance', otherwise translated 'racism' by the act of racial discrimination. The act of black staff on the other hand automatically labelling all white staff as racists becomes 'racial prejudice', because it creates a *generalised* unfavourable view of white staff which causes offence.

A clear rule of thumb with the above diverse needs being expressed in a workshop, is if they are not addressed, it would certainly lead to acting out behaviour such as, people leaving or sabotaging by being brutal in their personal attacks or choosing to opt out of certain parts of the training programme.

A workshop type of training can survive the flexible nature of negotiation of the group's agenda. In my experience, some contracts which are made in a more careful and elaborate way can make for an easier task of creating a set programme and working fairly closely to that plan.

As a black, female trainer, there are particular dynamics affecting how groups respond to me, and in turn, the consequences of these dynamics and how I might deal with them. On the one hand, there is much evidence to indicate that groups meet me with an element of caution and even suspicion. Questions such as what is she going to be like, might be no different to the expectations of any other trainer, but I have frequently felt that the legacy of past Racism Awareness Training approaches precedes me. This is the legacy of 'the aggressive, confrontative, guilt inducing, and shaming approach', (quote from participants), which has left its indelible mark.

My approach in these situations is to prevent participants' fears from growing by acknowledging that they are quite common and understandable for the reasons just explained; and that in recognising the group's feelings, I have met them in their psychic place. My experience is that this simple act of meeting participants in *their* place is all that is needed initially to keep things under control.

On the other hand, I can experience the group's idealisation of me because of my understanding approach to their fears and anxieties. I can be perceived as the good black caring female who is not like those other autocratic, aggressive trainers.

This idealisation can be 'held' by the trainer and worked with in the training programme with no negative effects. There are times however, when this dynamic can become all pervasive and stagnate any healthy interaction of challenge and change within the group. In this situation, idealisation has become a defence against feelings of any possible discomfort.

My role in this situation has been to articulate what is happening in the group without condemning or criticising. Enabling participants to move on has been aided by a quick lesson on how to give feedback constructively, and how to challenge sensitively. Participants have unfailingly warmed to the idea that feedback *must* give value to the receiver not release for the giver.

Another example of handling early dynamics in my role as black female trainer, is concerned with an overzealous and guilt ridden stance white participants take up as they focus on the black participants oppression. In my experience of facilitating training groups, this position is usually adopted by white members who have labelled themselves the awful, horrible oppressors. They carry the responsibilities of a colonial and imperialist past like a heavy burden and bear their wounds and shame for all to see.

As a black trainer, I have come to expect this position being taken up by a few, and in some instances, a large majority of white participants. An interesting observation over the years, is the tendency for inner city whites who are more exposed to different races and cultures and therefore more challenged about their white awareness, to be more expressive and more open with their guilt. The opposite can also be said of this same group when they have moved through to a stage of identity development where there is no need to hang onto this legacy in a restrictive way. The attitude of suburban whites will invariably present as more entrenched in their racist and prejudicial beliefs because of the lack of exposure and challenge to their status quo.

It is very difficult in my role as trainer to handle the range of responses relating to white guilt. It has felt necessary to allow for some expression of this guilt, for to deny it has meant a pre-occupation with the accompanying shame. A shame culture that is allowed to persist in a training group induces confessions and a need for absolution to be made. This means that the black trainer and black participants alike, will be expected, or made to feel the need to offer forgiveness. This is unhelpful.

A positive way of handling these responses is to first of all acknowledge that these feelings are real and present in the group. It is useful to encourage participants to talk about how they have come to have these feelings, thus providing a shared experience of human responses to cultural guilt and shame.

Guilt, and shame in particular, are 'Cinderella' emotions of which we have little understanding. It is of major importance to black/white relations and can be viewed thus: shame guards the boundary of privacy and intimacy, guilt limits expansion of power. Shame covers up weakness, guilt limits strength. Shame protects an integral image of the self; guilt protects the self against hurt. We can see therefore the enormous investment in these feelings which overarches every aspect of black/white dynamics.

Acknowledging participants' feelings is important, but it is necessary to move the group forward. Remaining in this place of guilt and shame can be become emotionally constipating and debilitating. It has therefore been important for me to stress the need for *active* and responsible ways of combating racial prejudice and bigotry.

Identifying and working with dynamics at the middle stage
The study of groups and groups dynamics show that a group negotiates five important stages during its life cycle. These stages are, *Forming, Storming, Norming, Performing, Mourning,* (Tuckman, 1965). These are not necessarily experienced in the order listed, but can fluctuate, hover or become stuck at any one point.

Groups addressing race and culture may be in any of the first four stages during the middle period. The earlier sections of this chapter have focused on the difficulties at the beginning stage of training groups and how these might be handled by the trainer. It is important to note that in some cases these difficulties can continue into the middle period, hence, creating identifiable problems with the group 'forming'. To examine more closely what can emerge at the middle period, the following two situations are discussed in some detail.

In the first example, a group of *primary health care workers* comprising the white female manager and white (English, Scottish, Welsh, Irish, Jewish) staff, and other black (African, Black British, African-Caribbean, Asian, Mixed parentage or Bi-racial) members, came together with a brief of 'Working with Issues of Difference in the Workplace'. Dissatisfactions within this diverse multidisciplinary team - its storming - started to run very high after the lunch break on the first of a planned two day training.

The morning sessions started very slowly with the group sharing what they wanted to achieve over the two days and any accompanying anxieties. An exercise enabled members to examine their different values and beliefs systems and its influence on staff interactions and work with clients. I sensed that there was some major dissatisfaction with the new manager who was experienced as changing things too quickly. There was also a sense of the group fearing the power of two of its members who were union representatives and who seemed more at ease and confident in talking about equal opportunity issues.

In a 30 minutes exercise, this team was asked to split up into triads to discuss a time, or those times when they felt powerful and powerless in their multi-racial/cultural team. The brief was that they teamed up with two others members who were culturally different from themselves and who were not of the same status.

After ten minutes, I realised that several of the triads who were all in separate rooms were not engaging in the exercise. One white male who left his group on the pretext of using the toilet and who bumped into me in the corridor stated that I 'had come at the wrong time', and that I was, 'sitting on a powder keg'. He also confided that 'it did not feel safe working with such small numbers', and that 'it would be better to work in larger groups'.

It soon became clear to me that the other triad groups had become stuck, not because they didn't understand the exercise, but because they felt very unsafe. I interpreted this as the group's 'held in' murderous rage towards its manager and those members, e.g. the union representatives, who held power in one way or another.

After some deep thinking accompanied by a moment of mild panic, I decided to let the half hour run its course so we could discuss what did nor did not transpire in the various small groups.

There was a shuffling of feet back to the large meeting room and lots of uncomfortable silences, broken only after some gentle prompting on my part. The black members had adopted a stance right from the start which read, 'lets *just* observe what is going down here... lets spot the one who is going to make an ass of themselves'. A few black participants appeared cautious of me in my role of black trainer and who, as one member confessed towards the end of the day, could have turned out to be her worst nightmare; an 'Uncle Tom', 'Aunt Jemima', or a radical separatist embracing Afrocentric, even Farakhanite views on race.

As members explored why this exercise on 'power and powerlessness' was difficult and didn't work, a number of complaints were heard. The Asian female staff felt left out and unhappy with the 'black' label. The Jewish staff felt displaced as a white person not fitting into 'in' groups. The Irish members were vehement in staking out their patch on race and anti-Irish racism, and the lone individual who was open about his gay sexuality insisted on sexuality issues being 'just as important as race' and demanded to know why we were avoiding it. The white male who had earlier bumped into me, commented on being working class and needing not to forget his roots despite his efforts to work his way up the ladder to becoming a professional.

On reflection, what was a simple exercise had become a catalyst for the group to hear its individual voices. These voices it would seem were being silenced in the agency by those who held power. The hierarchy of power and 'difference' was very clearly felt in this agency. People held resentments towards those who carried it more overtly and the group's resentments were being acted out by the paralysis experienced by the exercise. This agency also experienced a high level of staff sickness.

Being confronted with one another and their mistrust and unresolved anger, proved difficult initially, but as they had to stay (the half hour) with the discomfort of unexpressed feelings, they eventually were able to communicate with each other their dissatisfactions in an atmosphere of relative safety provided by the training.

Working on my own on this occasion with the above dynamics proved extremely difficult to manage with everyone desperately trying to stake our their claim. People's fear of being left out and feeling powerless raised intense feelings of inclusion and exclusion causing this group to split along racial and cultural lines.

This staff group experienced its storming through its dissatisfactions which were present at the forming stage. Groups intent on sabotaging may unconsciously storm as a defence for maintaining the stuck status quo. The trainer must be aware of this dynamic and address it head on.

With this particular inner-city group, I chose to end the first day of the two day training on 'Working with Issues of Difference in the Workplace', by arranging a short exercise for its members to celebrate what they felt they had in common as a racially and culturally diverse team. The work on day two was geared to enabling them to build bridges in order to work effectively as a team, and I also suggested that they strongly considered regular fortnightly staff meetings with an outside consultant who could enable them to continue what they had started to achieve in the training.

My second example raises issues at the middle and ending stages of group processes and is concerned with a group of *twenty student social workers* in their final six months of training. This group had a fairly balanced ratio of black and white, male and female members. My brief was to provide a two day training on 'Race and Culture in Counselling Practice'.

I was told briefly by the tutors that two previous attempts at Anti-discriminatory Practices training were unsuccessful, with devastating consequences of splitting the group racially and culturally, leaving members with an air of suspicion and mistrus.

I realised from the beginning that I was taking on a difficult task, but was not prepared for the amount, and indeed, the intensity of negative feelings bordering on murderous rage (similar but more powerful than that of the first case example) which this group had been carrying for some time. On reflection I had taken on an anti-group, a 'sick' group. There was a sad realisation for me and no doubt the students alike, that they were leaving a social work diploma course in six months time to pursue responsibilities in a multi-racial, multi-cultural society, but not having resolved cultural and racial conflicts in their own 'backyard'.

I personally found the dynamics and learning atmosphere on this course extremely disturbing and wondered how its members could successfully mature with an adequate degree of cultural competence by the end of the diploma programme.

Right from the beginning, this Transcultural Counselling Training programme indirectly stirred up the group's old wounds leading to overt signs of storming.

There were several late arrivals for the training due to their apparent confusion with the starting time. There were long and drawn out discussions about breaks and ending times. The pre-planned programme was disrupted in a major way and it became frustrating trying to get participants to move away from superficial issues and engage with the important task.

White members focused on what was left over for them from the last two Race trainings. The main themes were that people were left more confused than ever. They hated the aggressive and autocratic style of the previous black external consultants who they felt disregarded their feelings and just wanted to get their agenda delivered. The black and other minority members didn't feel they were getting much and opted to stay silent, watching and observing with a clear message of, 'we've been here before and nothing is every going to change or be any different'.

The focus of Transcultural Counselling had to be deferred in order to address the 'real' agenda. Reparative work was ethically necessary at this stage. We achieved this by focusing on what was enabling about the previous two trainings. The idea of getting them to think symbolically about what they were bringing into this training was also to prove helpful in encouraging more creative expression of difficult feelings without the fear of saying things literally and acting out.

This group seemed unable to deal with a new lease of life after the earlier exercises enabled a positive shift and grudgingly slipped back into its invested raging state. Attempts at successful role play failed. One role play presented a challenge for the counsellor to work with a young 22 year old man who presented with internal conflicts arising from his situation of being gay and a Christian.

The second role play created a heated exchange on the issue of racism. A group of black members insisted that there was no such thing as white on white racism, and to bring anti-Irish racism and anti-Semitism into the discussion was a devious ploy on the part of whites to 'dilute' the discussion about 'true' racism - white on black racism.

What transpired from this point excluded any focus or attention to counselling skills, counselling approach, or counselling knowledge. The plenary session degenerated into a full blown circular argument on homophobia and those whose oppression had the rightful entitlement to racism.

The salvaging task was a difficult one made via a tutorial input in which the group's 'stuckness' was confronted and made clear. Other group dynamics were challenged and clarified, with me offering different ways of understanding and working with the issues raised. Some members clearly did not agree with what I had offered, but I decided I had to be strict with this wayward and disillusioned group. The group struggled from here on, with five members leaving in the afternoon and being reduced to half its membership by the second day. At the end of the training there were eight students left.

Reporting the days' events to the resident tutors produced a lost and helpless response. Aborting this training was a real option, but the remaining members who labelled themselves the 'marathon braves' acknowledged that ironically some learning had taken place in an atmosphere where a group of originally twenty social work students were never able to resolve their cultural and racial conflicts.

Many areas of learning were identified on reflection. I was angry with the tutors for inviting me to facilitate this training, and also with myself for taking on this inappropriate request. This group was hurt and let down by the 'abuse' of its tutors and had unconsciously held onto the hurt by way of punishing them. The investment in this dynamic sadly backfired on the group itself. I was brought in to do a clean up job; fix a major haemorrhage, which strangely was one of the reasons given by a member who left the course. The request for this training in effect was for *reparative work* and as a result was clearly an abuse of the trainer - and participants alike. I felt I should have been given more detailed information about the state of the group, and equally should have elicited more explanations to the many questions raised for me in this invitation. I felt satisfied however that I had used my skills and knowledge of group processes appropriately to deal with some of the confusion, splits, displacement of anger, and acting out in the group. My regrets are not stating quite as clearly to the tutors what I have expressed here and not letting them know they needed to accept blame on this occasion.

Groups would be seen to be in the norming stage when differences like those revealed in the social work students' group are resolved and a real learning process arises out of the resolution process. Only at this stage can meaningful exchange and the celebration of differences be sustained for the production of the group task. From this, participants are able to engage in self-reflection, self-mirroring (finding oneself in others), and self-monitoring (tracking oneself).

Identifying dynamics and evaluating outcomes at the ending stage

The intended learning outcomes for training in working with race and cultural differences and particularly black/white issues are, that participants are able to identify personal blocks in relating to the other, and understand the mechanisms operating in keeping these blocks alive. Training is geared towards deepening participants' awareness of unconscious processes and their influence on resistant attitudes. Another important outcome is recognising areas of commonality and being able to celebrate differences rather than fear and react to them. The examples described earlier show variations in learning outcome.

It is important to evaluate whether or not training goals are being achieved. As the trainer, I have evaluated my own, and the group's success by using a number of indicators, e.g. whether members have kept their attention and are able to stay the full course of the training; whether skills learnt and awareness gained can be translated into the reality of their work setting. I am privileged to get feedback from participants and groups alike who have made real shifts and major changes. These have varied from black support groups being set up by black workers for black workers; a rolling programme of transcultural training being funded in a few agencies; more emphasis on non-discriminatory language being used in pre-sentencing reports (Probation Services); plans made to ensure magistrates themselves are trained in anti-discriminatory practices; and changes made to work policies with regard to clinical transcultural work with clients.

Further positive evaluation is indicated by a strong interest in the bibliography given on courses and requests made for specific reading material. Other good signs are measured by participants using 'live' case examples to work on and feeling safe in taking risks to challenge and be challenged. My own sense of my effectiveness is measured by: members openly acknowledging and appreciating good facilitation; being clear and flexible; maintaining a stimulating atmosphere and a level of expertise that is not hackneyed and benign. At a more intuitive level, I go by what I see and that is the deep levels at which participants are able to show the capacity for involvement, empathy, reciprocity and exchange.

These dynamics along with the written evaluations from the participants can offer very useful feedback to the trainer who is then able to assert her training methods, approaches and effectiveness.

The following is a sample of actual comments taken from participants' evaluation of psychodynamically orientated training courses.

> Excellent clarity of thought - feel it allowed tremendous space for exploration + would like to see more of this approach (Jackie, black female from London).

> The balance between 'introspective' work and external (practice-based) work was good. It seems really important to get in touch with what we bring with us before we try to work on the issues involved. Practice sessions essential even if painful at times (Di, white female from Shropshire).

> Whether the course increased my skills or not I'm not sure. But it gave me the confidence to utilise what I know and do with a real sense of purpose and direction (John, white male from Birmingham).

> Stimulating two days which explored deeper issues relating to prejudice and oppression. I am more aware of how I may offend and oppress others and because of this, want to explore further unconscious processes. I wish there was more time to look at ways of effectively challenging institutional prejudice (Luca, bi-racial male from London).

Feedback generally highlights a number of points. Participants seem to prefer and benefit from a training approach which manages a creative synthesis between introspective work, that is, work on exploring one's own values and beliefs systems and one's own blocks, and linking this with practice based exercises which address the reality of their work. Participants have generally reflected positively on increased levels of awareness of themselves as cultural individuals. There has been an overwhelming appreciation from those who have found their voice which was lost through guilt and fear of being labelled in one way or another. And there are those who have regained confidence to challenge positively. Many have commented on regaining a sense of direction which was lost in the struggle to combat institutional racism and oppression. A majority of participants have found real value in the psychodynamic approach which has a focus on exploring the unconscious realm of human interactions and its connection with cultural and racial differences.

Issues for trainers

Equal Opportunities training can be very rewarding and even more exciting and challenging using a psychodynamic approach. Consistent positive feedback and evaluations have led me to devise a personal approach with techniques which are simple yet powerfully effective. The following points highlight this approach:

1. Be fully briefed about the nature and appropriateness of the request and contract to be established.
2. Analyse and work with pre-transference issues, i.e. being cognisant on pre-training dynamics and their influence on the course.
3. Deal with anxieties and 'baggage' at the onset of all training by allowing its actual or symbolic expression in an opening circle round.
4. Acknowledge and support the lone black member's position in a predominantly white group, by highlighting and deflecting those inevitable tendencies to dump (project), scapegoat, create as 'spokesperson' for black issues, and use as abdicator of white shame and guilt.
5. Emphasise early 'introspective' work which is covered by exercises examining values and beliefs systems, and trust exercises highlighting complex dynamics in black/white relations.
6. Use of visual aids after 'introspective' work can create a supportive break from what is painful, yet allowing for reflection on ways forward. Helpful videos on issues of differences can be rented from Social Services, Probation Services and Counselling bodies.
7. Set clear strategies for role plays of 'live' or appropriately constructed scenarios. This teaching tool is best used and timed before and after lunch, thereby allowing time to

process. Constructive challenge is best made at this stage of the work where difficult and even painful realisations can be taken on board in an atmosphere of established trust and safety.

8. Trainer's input is necessary after each block of work allowing for teaching which uses timely introductions of relevant texts, appropriate self disclosure, anecdotes and statistics if necessary. The inclusion of the group's here and now dynamics can be worked with to provide 'real' material to illuminate the workings of conscious and unconscious dynamics in intercultural situations.

9. Organise endings well to create adequate time to work out ways forward and clearly identify what was learnt. Encourage members to share what was being taken away, future learning needs, and any other learning for work and life generally.

The above approach is embraced by ingredients which include warmth, clarity of ideas and speech, non-gratuitous humour and diminishing the emphasis on terminology. Other ingredients include not encouraging an atmosphere of overzealous 'political correctness', not colluding with black group members and not blaming white group members.

Because the psychodynamic approach has the effect of creating a state of deep arousal and agitation, I feel I often become the container for the group's fragmentation and projections. It is imperative that these are analysed and understood. Support and holding is maintained in regular supervision. Meeting fortnightly with two other independent trainers and using other colleagues for consultation on difficult and problematic training issues is invaluable. Supervision whether it is individual, group or ad hoc consultation, is the necessary stabiliser and forum for the trainer to debrief. Failure to maintain this support system can easily result in emotional and mental exhaustion and consequently clinical burnout.

As Hawkins and Shohet (1989) confirm, the professional carer 'can survive the negative attacks of the client through the strength of being held within and by the supervisory relationship' (p.3).

This concept of supervision is taken from Donal Winnicott's (1965) theory of the 'good-enough mother' needing to withstand the frustrations of the child by being supported in her role either by the child's father or other supportive adult.

As a black trainer who also works as a psychotherapist and clinical supervisor, I choose to work on my own for selfish reasons. I find it is less stressful overall, but it brings with it a loneliness and isolation. This is however counteracted by my other work as part-time tutor and as a psychotherapist within a local collective.

The advantages of working with someone who is an equal (your equal) can prove richly rewarding, less burdensome and immensely supportive. In my experience, this kind of partnership is rare and not easily sustainable.

Trainers who work consistently in partnerships can provide each other with immediate support and feedback, and can offer training groups the benefits of a rich dynamic experience of complementary trainer styles. However, there can be problems of working from different standpoints which may not necessarily fit well together. A trainer who believes in racial integration will not be able to work therapeutically with a colleague who supports separatism. In a partnership where one partner holds firm on say, an Afrocentric approach to counselling, and the other sees Afrocentricity as meaningless terminology (as opposed to a clear conceptual framework for counselling others), they will not be able to work effectively together.

Training in black and white issues and other areas of Equalities Training generally will need continued monitoring, critiquing and evaluation. As race relations undergo changes within our society, the backlash will be felt in many ways and places, including the workplace. The changing political climate will dictate organisations' professional focus and in turn, the demands for continued training in intercultural issues.

Prison Groupwork for Foreign Nationals

LIZ HALES

BACKGROUND

As the level of international crime has grown, particularly in the field of ;drugs importation, the number of prisoners arrested outside their own country has also increased. This means that in some European countries, 30 per cent of the prison population is made up of inmates who are foreign nationals. Within England and Wales as a whole, the numbers recorded at the time of writing were around 8 per cent. The picture is however different in those prisons that cover arrests at the main ports of entry or regularly take transfers on from such prisons.

HMP Wormwood Scrubs in London is one such prison, holding in 1995 approximately eight hundred male prisoners aged 21 or over. It takes prisoners from the courts that deal with all arrests at Heathrow Airport as well as courts that cover a catchment area of Middlesex in London, where there is a high percentage of residents from other countries such as Somalia and Sri Lanka. Such refugees have been granted residency in the country but have not been granted UK nationality.

As a result of this one, half of the remand (unconvicted) population consists of inmates who are categorised legally as Foreign Nationals, over whom the Immigration Department has powers of removal and deportation. The reasons for the high remand population are the difficulties that prisoners face in getting bail where they have no links in this country and the court fears that they will abscond. Immigration Service Detainees are also held on the prison remand wing awaiting Removal or Deportation at the end of their sentence. The percentage of foreign nationals on the convicted wing remains at approximately 30 per cent and this high percentage is maintained at other prisons that receive a regular flow of transfer of prisoners from Wormwood Scrubs. These long term prisoners are mostly serving time for drugs importation charges. Indeed, the current sentencing policy, with 75 per cent of drug importers receiving sentences of four years and over (Abernethy and Hammond, 1992), means that a large group of those serving long sentences in many prisons is made up of those involved in the international drugs trade. This impact on the Prison Service, which has been developed with the focus on British prisoners, is therefore one that can no longer be ignored, a point clearly made in the report *A Prison Within a Prison* (Tarzi and Hedges, 1991).

Since joining the probation team at Wormwood Scrubs four years ago, one of the main thrusts of my work has been to look at how imprisonment presents particular problems for this group of inmates and what adaptations and solutions can be offered. An important part of my work within the prison has been through running groups for these men and in this article I would like to discuss some of the issues that have emerged.

When I joined the prison probation team there was a group being run for African prisoners and discussions about these inmates took place within the context of race relations, as is the normal practice within the Prison Service. As a result of this, discussions focused on the racial dimension and combating racial prejudice within the prison. Work with these prisoners, however, soon revealed that the issues were far more complex and that prejudice and ignorance in relation to language and culture were equally dominant factors. What was also revealed was that recent positive developments within the Prison Service in relation to access to phones, family visits and the concept of a 'Local Prison' to handle arrests from the local courts and by inference the local community, provided no support to those arrested in transit from another country. We needed to explore what adaptations and additional facilities could be provided for these men (see Hales and Connolly, 1995).

Discussions within the prison resulted in the setting up of a Foreign Nationals Liaison Committee, which was to feed back to the Race Relations Management Team and within the Probation Team I was allocated special responsibility for issues relating to prisoners who did not have UK nationality. In moving away from the racial to the nationality dimension we were, however, not free of criticism and were accused of being prejudicial in using the term 'Foreign National' when we might well be referring to inmates for whom the UK was their home and who had lived here for many years. Our argument in keeping to this term was to focus on those for whom the court could recommend deportation and who were vulnerable to decisions made by the Immigration Department. The Foreign Nationals Group thus became a regular part of the prison regime.

The next issue thrown up was that of how best to group these prisoners for work together. Language was one of the dominating factors and the type of groups varied over time as did the prison population. However, as the majority of prisoners had been arrested on drugs importation charges, the two major groups were from South America and West Africa. The majority of African prisoners were sufficiently fluent in English, whereas many from South America rarely spoke more than a few words in English and the provision of a group run in Spanish became the only solution. The pattern emerged of weekly groups held in the evening, lasting one and a half hours, on alternative weeks for African prisoners and for Spanish speaking prisoners. The African group was a dominantly black group although it sometimes included white South Africans. The Spanish group was dominantly white although black Africans from Spanish and Portuguese speaking countries usually opted to attend this group. Numbers of prisoners attending were often around 20 and I was always aware that the work done in these groups only helped to meet some of the demands.

GOALS OF GROUPWORK

Having given a very brief summary of the background, I will now go on and explore our goals within the groups. One of the issues, which was obvious to any worker in the prison who was in contact with foreign prisoners, was the terrible sense of isolation and powerlessness that they felt. This was particularly true of those arrested on entry to the United Kingdom and those who spoke little English, whether they had been living in the UK or not, prior to arrest. Arrest and being processed into the prison meant loss of identity and status for all prisoners, but the process of segregation and isolation for foreign nationals, particularly those charged with drugs importation at Heathrow, was far more acute. In such cases most personal property was taken away by Customs for use as evidence. This included passports, travel documents and any address books and contact names and numbers that the defendant held. Not only was the man arrested suddenly cut off from family and friends, but the means of making contact again from prison was taken away and it was generally months before Customs would agree to return address books. For those who were suspected of swallowing drugs, isolation at the airport could continue for up to a week. For others, being processed into the court and the prison system was more immediate. It was obvious from discussions with prisoners that it was a frightening process and for many, imprisonment was seen in terms of what they would expect in their own country.

The most important goal of the groups was, therefore, to help remove some of this isolation and to bring men together to find some support and solidarity from other inmates. Within the prison one of the main causes of continued isolation was that of language. It was however only in the Spanish speaking group that we were able to lift this barrier. The African group was run in English . However the group included many men for whom English was not the first language and bilingual members were needed to assist others.

The second main goal was that of providing information on practical issues. As our experience with the groups grew, it was obvious that men needed and indeed wanted a better understanding of the criminal justice system. There was tremendous confusion about why they went repeatedly to the magistrates court where nothing seemed to happen, why they never seemed to be seen by the same solicitor and why everything seemed to take so long. There was a great deal of mistrust in relation to solicitors, especially those duty solicitors brought in for initial interviews with customs officers. Many defendants assumed that they must be working for Customs.

There was also the need to explain what they could and could not do in the prison, how they could make international phone calls home and obtain air-mail letters. One of the issues constantly raised was how they could help their families from within the prison. Could they change their cell location to share with a prisoner who shared the same language? Could they ask for support from their embassy or contrary to this, could they be assured that their embassy would not be informed of their imprisonment? Could they send their minimal prison earnings back to their families in countries where there were no state benefits and what rights had they to reclaim money and property confiscated by Customs?

The third goal was to use the meeting as a forum for workers from embassies, consular departments and relevant organisations in the voluntary sector, to introduce themselves and arrange to see those in particular need of their support at a future date. We benefited from regular attendance of London based groups such as Vamos Juntos and Africa Link and talking about their work at the meetings was generally a better way of advertising what help they could offer than posters on the wings. Personal contact always led to greater trust. We were also able to give out information about voluntary groups who did not attend the meetings but who came into the prison on a regular basis or in response to individual requests. As well as benefiting from the support of regular visitors, we also invited guest speakers to give information on particular issues such as immigration and legal aid.

A final goal, which we failed to achieve, was to use these meetings to help break down some of the barriers between prison staff and these prisoners and to help staff to understand the special problems that prison life created for those prisoners coming from other countries.

PRACTICALITIES OF RUNNING GROUPS

In setting up and running these groups we were faced with the inevitable difficulties of working in a secure regime. The initial problems were those of finding a large room where we would be undisturbed for an hour and a half. The second problem was that of arranging for men from different wings to be escorted there and back. Our groups were not an essential part of the prison regime and were viewed by some as a luxury. Our initial meeting place was the Roman Catholic Chapel, the use of which we were kindly offered. However this necessitated the availability of two officers to escort the men from the wings and their attendance at the meeting on security grounds, rather than on the basis of being involved with the groupwork. There were regular problems with the escorts and groups that failed to go ahead or to which only few men were brought. The development and opening of a new education block in 1994 solved this problem in that our group was run as an input in the evening classes. There was a regular escort of all prisoners attending these classes on the education block and we were able to fit into this regime. There was no need for an officer to sit in the room for security reasons. Unfortunately, as with other evening classes, category 'A' or high security risk prisoners were always excluded and the practicalities of getting invited guests into the prison remained considerable.

The second problem was in actually deciding who should be invited to these groups. Initially notices were put up in the wings and men who wished to attend were invited to sign attached lists. This, however was never satisfactory. The lists were sometimes torn down and new inmates, who were most in need of the groups, often did not find out about the meetings for several weeks. We were fortunate however with the development of LIDS (the computerised Inmate Database System) in 1992. This recorded the nationality of most prisoners and through this we were able to update a weekly list of all appropriate inmates to invite to the group. Group attendance was however never compulsory and we often relied on prisoners or probation officers from the Foreign Nationals Unit at Uxbridge Magistrates Court which received all Heathrow arrests, to advise us of any new appropriate prisoners.

Throughout, we aimed at running groups of between 15 and 20 men, so that all those who attended the groups would have the chance of making an input. However as numbers in the prison increased, as did our efficiency at identifying all those who would benefit, we had potential groups of over thirty members. Such groups were not as easy to handle and there was some discomfort from the security point of view. However the solution of restricting membership to newer prisoners was not welcomed by longer term prisoners, who through their time in the prison had developed a position of status within the group, and who took on the role of advisors to newer members.

STRUCTURE OF THE GROUPS

In using the groups to help the Foreign Nationals within the prison, we felt it important to give the group members power in deciding how their time together should be spent and on planning the future agenda. They were also asked to propose guest speakers and where possible we met with these requests, with the exception of the Crown Court judges, responsible for the sentencing decision made on many of the group members. I saw my role as that of organising all the practical aspects of running the groups and then of taking the role of facilitator at the actual meetings, a role taken on in my absence by my Senior Probation Officer. I was regularly joined by one of the two probation staff who worked at the Middlesex Foreign Nationals Unit and by a small group of volunteers from various relevant organisations. As a result each meeting would be made up of on average 18 prisoners and five individuals who worked outside of the prison.

When we gathered for the evening group we would place the chairs in a circle and sit so that prisoners and visitors were mixed. Once all the practicalities of bringing in guests and making sure all members were present we would invite a member of the nationality group to take over the role of chair. We would then start the meeting by introducing ourselves. There was no pressure on prisoners to give their full names and there was often more emphasis on nationality. Seating arrangements were often changed so that those who needed help with interpreting sat beside those who could help them. The formal meeting lasted for just over an hour. We would then break for refreshments and have a final informal session where volunteers could be talked to on a one to one basis, arrangements made for future meetings and prisoners from different wings could talk together.

Throughout the last three years the actual structure of the meetings has varied according to numbers and stability of the prison population. Where there was a stable population and fairly regular group membership, the format of the groups was one of open discussion, where issues and opinions could be debated, and where one of the prisoners would be invited to take on the role of chairing the meeting. At times when there was a higher rate of turnover the role of chair would be taken by a member of one of the voluntary groups and the emphasis was more on giving basic information to new group members. When special guests were invited to the groups the nature of the meeting was more formal and the focus of discussion was narrower.

The structure of the African and the Spanish Speakers groups has been constantly different. The lifting of the language barrier in the Spanish group immediately produced a relaxed atmosphere. The group was chaired in Spanish either by a member of one of the voluntary groups who visited or by a prisoner who had been in the prison for several months. Whenever we had guests speakers who were not bilingual, then interpreting became essential, and it became obvious that bilingual prisoners who could act as interpreters within the group gained status and respect from other group members (because of their language skills they also acted as essential members of the community on the wing). Although I did not have more than a limited understanding of Spanish, I tried not to let this interfere with the progress of the meeting. I would always position myself beside a bilingual member of the group and get assistance with interpreting where necessary. All the volunteers who attended were Spanish speakers.

In contrast, the African group was generally more formal, particularly where we had a higher percentage of older members, and there was less tolerance of different group members talking at the same time. The group members who wished to speak would sometimes stand and this formality meant that it was possible for discussion groups to be dominated by the views of one or two men. The group was held in English, a language used by most of the African prisoners. However language remained a barrier for some prisoners, from countries such as Zaire and Angola, who had difficulties in keeping up with the discussions. The members of the voluntary groups who attended were all of African nationality.

It is obvious that as a British white female who could not speak Spanish fluently I could not be seen as a member or representative of either of these groups and members of the voluntary groups played an essential role in the evenings discussion. Within the Spanish Group the language barrier meant that although I understood an increasing amount of the conversation I took a back seat in the actual running of the meeting. My senior was more fluent in Spanish. Within the African Group the men whom we had worked with knew that both my senior and I had lived and worked in African countries and that we respected the importance of different cultural and social values. We had the personal experience of learning new languages in Africa from scratch and were aware of the frustrations of others misinterpreting ones inability to communicate. However as white workers we had no personal experience of racism and within the African group discussions around this were led by volunteers from Africa Link. What was never lost in either of these groups was mutual respect and the evenings always ended with a handshake and where possible good-byes in the appropriate language.

My role however was always seen as very different from the other visitors in that I was part of the prison culture. My office was on the wing where most of the group members were resident and I was in contact with daily prison life. However there was a danger in this in that I was also seen as part of the establishment and the obvious route of communication between the group members and that establishment, particularly in relation to complaints. In being seen as part of this establishment it was often hard to take a confrontative approach in group discussions and this role was taken over by experienced members of the voluntary groups.

GROUP DISCUSSIONS

Discussion in both groups often focused around the topic of discrimination by Customs, the Police, the Courts and the Prison system. As the majority had been arrested on drugs importation charges, the sentences given were usually between four and ten years, irrespective of the fact that for many this was a first offence and taking on the role of courier was taken under duress. There was astonishment that sentences given were often far in excess of those given to British prisoners who had a list of previous convictions and were found guilty of serious offences such as of grievous bodily harm. Within the African group discrimination within the courts was discussed in terms of racism. However, discrimination within the prison was seen in a different light and much more in relation to their cultural background. Fear and conflicts within the prison were evidently as great with black as with white British prisoners, and many African inmates felt that their cultural norms of courtesy and respect was met by prison officers and prisoners alike with mockery and hostility. For many issues, such as this, we could offer no immediate solutions, but this did not take away the value of expressing opinions in a forum where others from the same cultural background would understand and support you.

Other regular topics were those of shame for arrest on a criminal matter and tremendous anxiety about the survival of ones family, in countries where there was no system of state benefits and where the family could be further harassed when the courier failed to deliver his goods. We had group members who experienced deaths in their families attributable to illness and poverty and at least one murder of a child because of the father, acting as a courier, failed to deliver the drugs. For many the view was expressed that the incarceration in prison was a much harder sentence on the family than on the prisoner and it is perhaps not insignificant that employment in the workshops was sought so that these prisoners could send small amounts home to help families survive. These were not issues that these men would discuss with British prisoners.

Guest speakers provided a valuable input, particularly in relation to immigration issues and the criminal justice system. Unfortunately, we failed to achieve the degree of support we would have liked from prison staff due to other work pressure and lower staff coverage in the evenings. This was a pity, as officers would have gained a new perspective of prison life from attending the group. For those who worked in the criminal justice system coming to a group was often very demanding, as inmates used the meeting to express their frustration at how powerless they felt in what they saw as an unjust system. The benefit was not however just one sided and a clerk from one of the local magistrates courts, who came as a guest speaker every few months, told us that she learnt a great deal about how the courts were experienced from the defendant's perspective.

Where there was a sufficiently large group of Foreign Nationals of one country in custody, we would encourage support from their relevant consular departments, on the basis that group participants from that country would be advised in advance of such a visit and would not be identified by name. This was particularly relevant for those claiming asylum or in fear of return. At one very interesting meeting, when a vice consul from one such country advised his nationals to fully co-operate with customs and name those who had asked them to bring in drugs, there was derision in the group. The prisoners response was that of questioning whether those in positions of authority in their country would like to be named. National solidarity was never absolute!

Group discussions regularly brought home to us that the anxieties about a court sentence did not end on release from prison. Sentencing for drugs importation inevitably included a recommendation for Deportation. This meant that Foreign National prisoners would not be freed in the U.K. at the end of sentence, but would be sent back to their country of origin. This was irrespective of whether or not they or their family had been living in the UK prior to arrest. We tried to keep our group members up to date with different countries' policies in relation to the return of their nationals as deportees. The voluntary groups were particularly helpful in that they regularly brought in national newspapers for the group members. Those about to be deported often promised to write back to us after return and update us on what actually happened. However such letters were rare and it was not an effective way to keeping in touch with developments. What awaited prisoners on their return was particularly relevant for Nigerians because of their Government's Decree 33. This proposed imprisoning and resentencing Nigerians on the charge of exporting illegal drugs, on their return from a country where they had been sentenced for importation. Financial anxieties in relation to deportation were also considerable. Such prisoners were not eligible for discharge grants and would have to find ways of paying their way through Customs and Immigration on return and for their own transport home from the airport. This put prisoners who tried to protect their families by explaining their long absences in terms of 'working overseas' in an impossible situation.

The challenges of groupwork

From the previous sections it is apparent that within the groups we set targets and on the whole met them. However this method of working was not without problems. One of the major ones related to the structure of the drugs world, particularly in South America. Where, as was not unusual, three or four co-defendants were arrested, conflicts often arose in relation to the evidence co-defendants offered that could affect the trial of others. It was not unusual for an inmate who was in need of the support group to be frightened of coming or having much to do with any of his fellow nationals, having been identified as a 'grass' (someone who gave information to the prosecution that could be used against another defendant). Even those, who were not co-defendants on a case, would sometimes be approached and interviewed by Customs officials in the prison, seeking information on co-nationals. A strong defence might necessitate producing evidence of harm to others so that although the greatest support could be given by those from the same country, so could the greatest threat.

A second issue was that some of those who attended the groups saw themselves as outsiders in the prison culture, but not necessarily identifying with other group members. This was particularly so for those in custody because they came into the country with false passports or were being held as immigration detainees. At no stage were participants asked to talk about why they had been arrested, but there was a lot of anger expressed when false assumptions were made by other group members about the degree of involvement in criminal activities. Indeed it was obvious that those who were in custody through legally or illegally trying to find asylum in another country would have benefited from a completely separate group. The problems they needed to discuss, of loss of family and friends, experiences of overseas imprisonment and torture and anxiety about the future, could not be generally be talked about openly with prisoners who had not shared the same experiences.

Perhaps the greatest challenge was however in keeping our goals of the groupwork in focus. Often those attending wanted more than advice and support feeling that the groups should provide an active voice for those who felt they were discriminated against. As probation staff we were seen as part of the prison establishment with more power than the voluntary groups to put right the many wrongs. There were many complaints that we felt in sympathy with, but for which we could offer no immediate solutions. However we were able to take issues and suggestions forward to the prison

Foreign Nationals Liaison Committee and the Race Relations Management Team. This did result in steps being taken to look at and resolve problems. When issues were brought up concerning alleged maltreatment by prison staff these were more difficult to handle. We advised prisoners about the formal complaints procedure within the prison, but prisoners made it obvious that they feared the consequences of putting their name on a complaint form against a particular member of staff. This was understandable but we could not, as requested, make individual complaints on their behalf and it became obvious from resultant discussions with Governors, that they would not support groups whose main focus appeared to be that of an unofficial complaints forum. The group therefore never developed the power that its members sought of putting right the many wrongs of prison life.

A balance also had to be achieved between personalising issues and dealing with them on a group basis. At times group members wanted to talk at length about the details of their own case and discuss issues that would more appropriately be dealt with on a one to one basis. This was particularly so in the African groups and at times it became necessary for me to take a more active role in chairing the groups' process.

The other great challenge was in preventing language becoming a barrier in group participation, for the dependence on interpreters never allowed full or confident involvement. Within the Spanish group to a large extent we prevented this, although differences in dialect sometimes caused problems. There was however a tendency at times, especially where the guest speaker was not a Spanish speaker and where we used an interpreter, for those who were confident in using English to try to dominate the discussions. Within the African group the problems were also present. Within the groups, as within much of my work within the prison, there was no funding for professional interpreters and we were therefore dependant on prisoners to take on this role. However this could give them a powerful position and they had to be prevented from slipping out of role of interpreter to adding their own comment or answering the questions.

GROUPWORK AND THE WAY FORWARD

Feedback on the groups from those who have attended has, on the whole been very positive and non inclusion in an evening meeting due to the pressure of numbers led to strong protests. Attendance has, however, always been voluntary so one could argue that for those not seeing the benefit, opting out was always an option. Our experience has been that voluntary opting out is rare but group pressure against 'grasses' attending could be very strong. The main criticisms were in relation to aspects of prison life, made by inmates who thought that issues raised at the group could and should always be acted on. Important issues raised in the group were acted on, but the positive changes that resulted could rarely be achieved quickly, so that men who raised issues had often moved on before the changes were brought in.

As a probation officer based on the reception wing, I saw many benefits of group attendance. Attending the group was the most immediate way we could begin to inform prisoners and allay fears of prison life. There was an obvious sense of relief when a more confident member of the group talked about aspects of his arrest and imprisonment that were common to many Foreign Nationals. By attending groups, prisoners also had a chance to meet myself and other workers on a less personal basis and decide whether they would benefit from a future interview on the wing. They could also identify those who could and who they would trust to act as interpreters.

This experience was shared in other prisons. It is interesting to note that a similar group was started at High Down prison in Surrey at the suggestion of an African prisoner. This man had played a key role in our group and when he was transferred to this prison felt the lack of such support. Groups have been run by voluntary organisations at The Verne Prison in Dorset over the last few years. This prison receives many Foreign National prisoners transferred on from Wormwood Scrubs. At Holloway Women's Prison in London, separate groups have been run by probation staff and voluntary groups and at Belmarsh Prison, Probation Officers have run a successful Foreign Nationals Group over the last two years with Prison Officer support. (Alfred and Fleming, 1995). No doubt there are many other such groups and those of us, who are members of prison probation teams and who have become involved in such work, have found meeting together to discuss the issues thrown up of great benefit.

Looking to the future it seems inevitable that the number of prisoners from overseas at prisons, such as Wormwood Scrubs, covering arrests at ports of entry, will increase. Therefore ways will have to be found of meeting their needs within a prison system which has not been developed with this in mind. Groupwork is one way of making some progress. However the groups, as with any other form of work, must be flexible and look at where there is potential for the greatest input. In this prison, with the highest percentage of foreign prisoners arrested over the last few years on drugs importation charges, it has proved beneficial to organise the groups on the basis of culture and language. However with changing patterns of arrest, it may prove more beneficial to run separate groups for prisoners arrested for offences which lead to short sentences, but for whom the issue of Immigration Service involvement is more immediate and critical. For example, over the last year there has been increasing number of arrests on the charge of passport fraud. Those arrested are usually asylum seekers trying to reach America or Canada and travelling via Heathrow Airport. In 1995 we received over 400 such prisoners and it seems inevitable that as immigration law tightens up, in the United Kingdom as in other European countries, those arrested for trying to find illegal ways of moving will increase. The issues around for these prisoners usually focus on how to survive their current situation and avoid removal to the country they have fled from. One of the obvious answers is by running a particular group for these men. Indeed, considering their growing numbers, it may be the only way to pass on the relevant information. However the group members would be from countries such as Iran, Algeria, Sri Lanka, India, Pakistan and the former Yugoslavia. The language difficulties might prove an impossible barrier to this form of work.

In their article on Foreign Nationals in English Prisons, Richards et al. (1995) talk of the official invisibility of Foreign Nationals in UK Prisons despite the growing numbers. This is perhaps exacerbated by the fact that they are generally the best behaved and least demanding sector of the inmate population. For the individual Foreign National the experience of imprisonment is often one of unbearable isolation. Groupwork has proved a powerful and effective way of helping to overcome both of these. By working and speaking as a group, foreign prisoners and those who work with them have been able to effect some changes in the prison regime. From the individuals perspective, meeting, talking and identifying with others has been an essential element of surviving prison life. It is an important area of work and one that should be encouraged and supported in all prisons that hold prisoners who do no have U.K. nationality. Such groups however must depend on the development of partnerships between those workers within the prison, who are in daily contact with the prisoners and who can facilitate such group meetings, and those from the voluntary sector, who can offer outside support and be seen by inmates as fellow nationals who can be trusted and turned to for advice and support.

The Dynamics of Groupwork
in a Prison Community

LIZ DIXON

Last week we had a huge success in Holloway in that we made a successful application to the Home Office for Early Compassionate Release on Medical grounds. The last successful applicant I know of was Earnest Saunders (I guess there have been others!!) and I am told it is over ten years since Holloway made their last successful application. I will refer in detail to the process we engaged in to secure the release of the person in question later in the article, but at the outset I want to reflect on why we went ahead and raised the hopes of a woman who had very little real prospect of gaining release.

Our motivation came from the sheer force of her personality and her belief that we as professionals in the system, could make a difference to her situation. She insisted that I would be able to help her go home and quite literally begged that I make sure she did not die in a foreign prison. Josephine (not her real name) implored others to assist and had extraordinary faith in those she felt could assist her in her plight.

The place where she had most effect, and demanded most respect was in our weekly Foreign National Group. One of the Governor grades attended the group on one occasion and on meeting her he was moved to go beyond his normal brief in order to help secure her release.

The theme of my paper is about group influence on the community outside the group. I will be citing the Foreign Nationals Group as an example of how professionals can help raise awareness in an oppressive environment running groups. We are aware that groupwork is an effective and efficient way of working in any community or institution but I am very interested in how it effects and alters the environment of our community.

Many of us were taught about the potential for social and political action as a result of our work and how to make the private ills we witness in clients into public issues. The arenas in which we take these 'ills' and translate them can vary depending on the setting and the issues. As a Probation Officer in Inner London my union identity has, for the last years, been integral to my work. It is the area where I am most clearly a social worker. I am a member of the National Association of Probation Officers (NAPO) working in Britain to influence and affect social policy. NAPO has been a crucial organisation in raising issues of discrimination in the Criminal Justice System and it has been tireless in its campaign to publicise how social problems contribute to criminality and to furnish government with ideas about what needs to be set in place to bring about changes. Using this union forum I give voice to observations of oppression and press for social change - the group experience truth is stronger than the individual witness. There are of course other vehicles that we use. Without that link I would feel that I am merely an observer and technician... maybe even benefiting financially from other peoples misfortune.

In a prison environment our role as Probation Officers is about trying to influence the regime in an enlightened way and again to make the private ills of inmates into public issues. As a worker I (and my colleagues before me) have spent time adjusting to the compromises you make in working in a prison. Having the keys to the prison and sitting on boards to discuss temporary release and writing reports recommending (or not recommending) parole requires that we make decisions and judge the inmates, and this does not rest easily with our traditional role as advisers to the sentencing process. I found that the quality of the case work and groupwork that could be achieved with the women in the prison environment and use of systems to monitor how I manage that power made the compromise manageable. It takes a good six months to get used to the environment and to feel reasonably good about your role. On reflection I realise now that you are not always aware of how much you can achieve when you have come to terms with the compromise and that is what I want to discuss in this article.

I want to look at this potential with specific reference to groupwork.

In Holloway, work with Foreign Nationals has thrown up some interesting observations about the impact of groupwork in the greater environment.

GROUPS

When a group of people (in this instance a group of prisoners) have a common identity, their group presence can become a powerful testimony to their situation. It also operates as a source of support in terms of making links communicating and getting emotional and human support. We are familiar with this dual potential when observing groups in the community, support groups for campaigns and political pressure groups.

In a prison environment there is a pecking order which is often quite brutal if you are low down on the scale. The experience of bullying, which is linked, can be emotionally frightening and physically abusive. We have found that some refuge is to be had in group identity which can have a tremendous impact on the individual and the greater environment. Thus our experience of running weekly groups for young women (16-21) has over the years informed us of the strength the women derive in just belonging to the group which we call 'Choice and Change'. They welcome the sense of identity and hold on to it as something that gives them permission to feel what they feel. It is a common experience for all young women to be bullied and frightened by the more sophisticated and experienced older women in the adult prison. Typically this may mean stealing from the young women and threatening them. It may also involve physical harassment. As a result of being in the group the young women learn that bullying is an experience many young women share, i.e. it is not because they are weak as individuals that they are bullied or vulnerable. They also learn that it is laudable and normal to want to do something about your offending behaviour. It is not always safe to express such desires in the bigger prison where they may be ridiculed, but it is OK to do it in the group with other young women and they thus value their group identity. Aside from the support and the space that the women get there is another dimension. When the group is running we as Probation Officers can discuss the issues around young women with the Prison Officers, be it about bullying, depression and potential suicides or efforts that the women are making to try and change their ways of life. There is thus a real dialogue between the Prison Officers and civilian workers about the issues that effect the women and which enables the Prison Officers to work with the women. Prison Officers are often given inadequate training and are overwhelmed with their jobs. It is hard to engage on a one to one sometimes and the presence of a group can facilitate dialogue and assist us to assist the Prison Officers who are the key workers.

We have noticed a similar process operating as a result of the self harm groups which are now running under the auspices of the psychology department. Prison Officers are greatly affected by the incidents of self harm and tend to trivialise it by labelling it as attention seeking behaviour. The effect and damage is under estimated as Prison Officers collude to deny the prevalence of incidents and there has been a silence about the prisons responsibility in the face of such self abuse. I believe that it is too distressing to take on board, so denial and rationalisation operate as defence mechanisms for the officers. The problem is now more observable as there is a group operating every week and people are beginning to speak more freely about the reasons behind the incidents and the prison response. This is giving rise to common dialogue about the complicated issues of self harm.

This phenomenon, namely that the presence of a group can have the effect of raising awareness and recognition of specific problems thus provoking dialogue discussion and ultimately action, is particularly pertinent to groupwork with Foreign Nationals. I will now address the history and current impact and objectives of the Foreign Nationals group.

THE FOREIGN NATIONALS GROUP

The group was set up following a very successful Foreign Nationals Day (*NAPO News*, 1994, September). We organised the conference with the help and inspiration of the Female Black Prisoners Scheme in an attempt to try and learn more about the problems experienced by Foreign National women in Holloway. It was obvious the Foreign National Women in the prison received a poor service from the Probation Department and the prison itself, the issues seemed to be around language and poor communication, access to services in the prison, lack of credible legal representation, culture deprivation and discrimination, and welfare problems with dependant children abroad. As a department we felt we needed to know more and find a way to work constructively with the problems and the conference served the purpose of establishing the foundation of the group and putting on a day which enabled all the key agencies to address the issues including the Governor and Prison Officers. The group thus started off as a series of meetings with interested foreign national inmates who in the end did most of the work to prepare for an ambitious and constructive day. To hold an open conference in a closed prison was fantastic and it happened because of the power of the partnerships we were engaged in, viz the women themselves and the voluntary sector who were in a way the equivalent of the community in fact. The conference went ahead weeks before the clamp down in prison security as a result of three major escapes from secure prisons and a myth that the prisons were 'too cushy!!' It would be hard to imagine holding such an event in the present political climate.

As a result of that conference we became far more aware of the specific problems facing female Foreign Nationals which were practical, emotional psychological and cultural. There were specific problems which related to the fact that we were dealing with women who were mature and had left dependant children in very desperate conditions. We realised that there was a lot we could do as Probation Officers to make major differences and that we needed to raise specific awareness amongst other prison staff groups. We learnt about initiatives that were already happening, we became aware of community resources that the women should have access to and we learned about the sort of resources that needed to be developed. We worked initially with Black Female Prisoners Scheme (a voluntary group who visit the prison and offer individual casework and consultancy for professionals) and then developed stronger links with Hibiscus a voluntary agency who run weekly advise sessions in prison. They have tremendous expertise with Foreign nationals and offer wide ranging services as a result of their satellite sister offices in Lagos and Kingston.

Both organisations have been extremely productive but Hibiscus has become integral to our development, they often assist us in running the group sessions and also assist the women by giving financial support and welfare support to families at home. They are also in contact with the families of women from Nigeria and Jamaica. Olga Heaven, the Director of the organisation has made a great contribution to the groupwork. The partnership has been innovative and creative adding to the dynamism and development of the group.

HOW THE GROUP EVOLVED

The women who organised the day set about organising the next stage which was following up the various initiatives and workshops and engaging with the agencies who said they would get involved in the various issues. The women were clearly encouraged by the meetings and they encouraged other Foreign Nationals to attend. They were able to reflect how much they had grown and that the meetings had been very empowering. They were aware of subtle changes in the institution as they felt that their differing needs were starting to be acknowledge. Their common pursuit had proved supportive and they had come to rely on the group meetings, they elected to continue meeting as a group. They have since then formed into possibly the most established group in the prison. We have run the group consistently for two and a half years and the average attendance can rise up to 33 as, for example, last week when we had a judge to attend a meeting.

I could not in this paper discuss the complex nature of the group and struggle to find which model we follow. I know it is a very good one but I do not know what you call it!

The group is generally co-facilitated by two experienced officers but the whole team is involved to ensure that it runs every week.

It is an open group in that it is accessible to all foreign national women prisoners. We aim to attract women recently incarcerated to help them cope with the initial horror of imprisonment in a foreign country. As a group we decide on the topics of each week over a two month period and ask the women whom they would like us to invite to attend the group. We have had representatives from Customs, Immigration, Foreign Embassies, Lawyers and Barristers (discussing appeals and representation), specific cultural groups, Black Female Prisoners scheme, Governors, Government Inspectors, representatives from the Home Office Race Relations group and more latterly those loosely defined as motivational speakers. These are religious and spiritual guests whom the women requested as they value their help to strengthen their motivation to survive... we have had prison pastors and the Imam.

We have the continuous problem of interpreters and engage with the problem in an attempt to provide some service. We liaise with an organisation called Groupo Amigo who work with Spanish Speaking women. They run separate groups on some occasions and they attend the big group on occasions and translate. We use other women to translate if they can, which they do willingly. Sometimes we just have to wait until the women in question learn English, which happens incredibly quickly on some occasions and not at all with others. The women have told us that they enjoy meeting as a discrete group in the prison. They say they benefit enormously by attending the group and feel that they gain from their common identity as Foreign Nationals even if they have considerable difficulty in communicating. We understand this to mean that there is something to be gained by attending forum where those in the group appreciate and empathise with the seriousness of their situation and the level and nature of hardship and suffering being experienced. The British women and the Prison Personnel often fail to appreciate the depth of deprivation and difficulties the women have undergone prior to coming to prison and what they are experiencing now. Their problems are often ignored and minimised by the greater environment. They suffer a more profound discrimination and they all receive harsher sentences. They nearly all have children and agonise about their situation and they share the common experience of lack of contact with their loved ones. Often their families undergo further hardships - some learn of fatalities and killings whilst they are in prison. Most of them come from climates where there is a poor or non-existent welfare state system and there are appalling concerns about the children. They try to comfort each other in these situations and are testimony to each other of the harshness of their situations.

Format

We alternate between information groups where we invite a speaker, who addresses the group, answers questions, and gives out advice, and support groups which I will discuss in due course. With regard to the sessions with a speaker, we prepare for these sessions the week before by rehearsing possible questions, this has proved useful and helpful and empowers the women. With groups of upwards of thirty we have to be organised. The groups are always well disciplined but some women are inevitably more articulate than others and will take all the space if not challenged. With regard to the support sessions we invite the women to discuss whatever they want. Sometimes this can be communicating her sadness, sometimes she has achieved something significant and wants to share it. We have a system where we go around the group giving each and every woman space to air her feelings and thus get supported. As group facilitators we are challenged by the size of the group, and the nature of the material which is frequently overwhelming - be it a woman newly sentenced (the sentences can very between 5 and 17 years), or new inmates who are devastated by the implications of their initial trauma of incarceration. We have learned an awful lot and the women trust us to manage the group and challenge speakers who are ignorant or insensitive in their remarks to others. The women often become extremely distressed particularly those at the start of long sentences or following distressing news from home. Guest speakers and prison workers were alarmed at the level of expressed emotion. Having discussed this as workers we feel that women tend to use the group on occasions to start the grieving process and this will involve painful acknowledgements. Such distress is thus appropriate and is rarely sustained. If we have specific worries we alert the prison staff, particularly if we feel that the woman is a potential suicide risk, although such occasions are rare.

The various cultural groups represented demonstrate cultural awareness toward each other and we talk more confidently about the effects of the cultural deprivation they will face and indeed are experiencing. The naming of the effects like double punishment, cultural deprivation and cultural isolation help outsiders get their minds around and understand the processes. We are very aware of how women in particular are stereotyped in sentencing and this is one of the reasons why we get professionals to come to the group so that they can learn about the nature of the women caught up in the drug trafficking trade. A judge who visited recently reflected that although the judges are becoming aware of the need for race awareness training (following the Hood Report, 1992) few acknowledge the discrimination metered out to foreign drug couriers. This judge said that sentencers do not empathise with Foreign Nationals and tend to stereotype. He explained that it did not hurt them to sentence a foreigner to a long sentence in the way it hurt to sentence a British National. One could sense that meeting some 40 women who were strikingly different and thus difficult to stereotype, was having a very strong impact on this particular judge; the speakers often learn more than the group members, another by-product of the group process.

We sometimes use the support sessions to reflect on the previous week. As mentioned previously we use the support session to offer mutual support and advice. All the women introduce themselves and are invited to discuss specific dilemmas. The group will offer comments or advice or life experience and the women report on the usefulness of this process. Sometimes we pick a specific issue and break into small groups to do an exercise. It may be dealing with bullying, it may be about how to be more assertive, it may be about empowerment or it may be about how to find sources of support and how to fight depression. It is on these occasions that we also discuss the complex causes that lead women to be here and when the group is well formed we discuss offending behaviour and possible strategies for change.

We have moved towards a more active acknowledgement of the tremendous spiritual strengths the women possess. We bring our own material, we design questions which we put to the group and the women themselves bring material, poetry and sometimes prayer.

The Prison has come to accept the group albeit that we occasionally meet some hostility from those who deny that there are special needs. The institution itself now relies on it as a useful resource for the women. Prison Inspectors and official prison visitors have been directed to attend and witness the group as an example of good practice. The authorities have also asked the group for guidance with particular policies, e.g. issues in sentence planning for Foreign Nationals and about products they want in the canteen. It is because the group has persisted that we have been able to raise issues with the staff and there has been a culture change in the institution. Foreign Nationals are now more likely to request probation support for a wide variety of issues, they are more able to pursue grievances or make appropriate requests as they are likely to receive a more sympathetic response than in the past. They feel able to work in other parts of the prison as there is a greater cultural awareness. Many of the Foreign Nationals are used as Befrienders, prison inmates who are trained by and work as Samaritans in the prison environment. Staff are more likely to chase up immigration when a woman's sentence has come to an end as there is more knowledge about how to manage the immigration bureaucracy.

The staff are starting to acknowledge the issues and dynamics and there has been the first training day of Prison Officers specifically devoted to the issues in working with Foreign Nationals. There are to be eight officers trained specifically in this area and they have been asked along to the group which is acknowledged as an appropriate learning forum for workers.

The group has a specific energy and vitality which has resulted in excellent attendance over a very long period. It is this energy that keeps the issues alive and has helped educate the prison regarding the needs and issues involved in the incarceration of Foreign Nationals. There was probably always an awareness that Foreign Nationals suffer in the system but little incentive to do anything about it because it was never visible enough. The group has forced the institution to look at its practice and change has occurred.

We are also aware that we as group facilitators can become complacent or unaware of changes we need to make and we have found the introduction of new officers with new energy is vital both as a monitoring process and as a way to tap new expertise. I could talk about the dynamics of the group leaders but I feel this is a separate issue. Suffice to say that the energy created to run such a group is reliant on staff support and Holloway Probation team is and has been an excellent source of energy and expertise which has nourished and enabled the group to run... it is part of the group and the group could not run without that support. The women relate to the group as the Probation group.

I would like to return to the woman I mentioned at the outset whom I referred to as Josephine; she is a powerful demonstration of what the group has achieved. This woman was sentenced to eight years imprisonment for carrying cocaine from Nigeria. She always maintained that she had no knowledge that the parcel she agreed to carry was full of cocaine; she had made no attempt to disguise her package which she carried on top of her suitcase, she was apprehended immediately and arrested.

She had no confidence in her legal representation and was not able to change lawyers, she had applied and the court refused her request. The medical reports were not as substantial as those prepared after her sentence. The author of the Pre-Sentence Report said in his report that her medical difficulties had not been confirmed, which was not exactly true, and the document relayed little of her situation. Josephine had a heart attack when she was sentenced to eight years and spent the first two days of her sentence in a hospital before being transferred to the medical wing of Holloway. This was a miserable experience, she was the only Foreign National on that particular wing, she spoke very limited English and none at all when severely distressed... another common phenomenon with Foreign Nationals. On the hospital wing she was among British Nationals who were predominantly drug users withdrawing from heroin and cocaine and requiring a lot of staff support. She received very little attention as a result, and was worried about asking for any or causing too much fuss and attracting unpleasant encounters.

She attended the group when she could and received tremendous support from the women. Most of the professionals in turn also became appalled at her plight and we launched an appeal. Josephine aged rapidly and had difficulty waking. Her bladder no longer functioned adequately and she suffered the indignity of having to wear heavy padding. Her solicitors said there was no grounds for appeal. We raised an application for early release on medical grounds. It failed at the first hurdle. We invited some new solicitors to the group who were moved by her situation and presence and they took her case on. These new solicitors supported us by supplying independent psychiatric reports which proved extremely effective in the second application. Hibiscus pressurised for official recognition and provided tremendous support on a personal and financial level. Her attendance at the group however had the effect of rousing everybody to do something and not give up. She galvanised one of the Governors and one of the Medical Officers and with a far more robust second application we were ultimately successful. I heard recently that she has reached home and is with her family. It may be that she will not die and recover given that she is in a better place.

The prison staff were clearly pleased along with the rest of us and it has been a good lesson to learn that you can make progress even within a prison setting.

As I said at the beginning of this piece, I was motivated to write this article to explore the notion that groups serve many purposes. After three and a half years in Holloway prison I have made the following observations:

1. That they serve to raise the profile of specific groups of women and their particular problems, be they young women vulnerable to bullying or Foreign Nationals pressing for proper medical service with translators.
2. Groups have the capacity to educate and initiate action. They motivate professionals to act because the problems are much more visible and credible when voiced by a group of people rather than separate individuals. An individuals grievance or condition can be ignored more easily than a group of people expressing the same concern (cf. trade union lobbying).
3. They give the individuals in the group in question the confidence to air their collective private ills in the hope that they will become public matters. They can empower the members - the original group members of the Foreign National Group put on a conference which raised awareness throughout the institution. Subsequent women have earned themselves concessions with regard to customs procedure and canteen stocks. In the self harm groups women feel free to explain what they are experiencing and what would help or hinder them. They too have effected change and educated the workers about ways to monitor and supervise potential suicides.

4. Groups stop professionals becoming complacent, the case of Josephine showed us all what could be achieved. They serve to keep us in touch with the ever changing needs of prisoners in a Criminal Justice System, a system that militates against women, and which is heaving at the seams as a result of the 'prison works' policy. The last six months have seen a huge increase in the numbers of female prisoners, three new units have been opened to accommodate this rise in numbers (The Prison Reform Trust, 1996).

5. Groups can educate the greater environment merely by their presence but also by engaging with those who hold power and are abusing that power by discriminatory attitudes and ignorance. We witness this when we invite speakers who leave the group greatly effected by the women's experience and also by the realisation that they have held prejudiced views, or have been ignorant about the implications of certain policies. This generally inspires useful and constructive change in those individuals, such as customs officials who go away and make changes, or Home Office representatives who proceed to lobby for greater flexibility for telephone calls for these groups of inmates. However it sometimes goes further. The group on occasions been asked to comment on canteen provisions, sentence planning procedures and the effect of changes in the prison following a damming Inspectors report. The presence of the group helps to keep the profile of such a vulnerable group raised, which is a challenging task in a closed institution where the potential for abuse and collusion and denial is rife. By bringing people from the outside in, it acts as a monitor and educates in a way the group acts, as a watchdog.

6. The individuals who have benefited from the prison are empowered and can become a resource as they assist others. The success of an institution is often judged on how the inmates cooperate with the workers and their sense of being valued (The Woolf Report, 1991, p.20).[1] A woman is valued as a reliable and trustworthy person then everybody benefits... the groups enable, assist and empower such individuals who can then practice their new found confidence in an attempt to survive the damaging experience of incarceration.

The Foreign Nationals has had a tremendous impact on institutional awareness and practices as illustrated by the above points. I would conclude by suggesting that they are a source of great inspiration and that they can be extremely profound (if a little overwhelming at times). They provide a professional challenge which informs practice. There is much room for improvement, new workers are ever able to pick up on some of the poorer areas of practice which can improve the overall quality. My experience has lead me to believe that groupwork in a prison is a good way to work.

Note

1. The Report states: 'They must be treated with respect if they are expected to treat staff and other prisoners with respect themselves'. It concluded that one of the reasons for the riot was a genuine grievance on the side of the inmates.

Groupwork with Refugees
and Asylum Seekers

Jeremy Woodcock

One of the themes which all groups address over time is the issue of inclusion and exclusion. In no other group in society does this theme emerge more dramatically than with refugees. To be a refugee means to be forced out of ones homeland, to be an outsider in a place of exile. The experience of atrocity, human rights violations, forcible uprooting and flight mean that issues linked to the theme of inclusion and exclusion such as trust, secrecy and fairness are commensurably very potent. The nature of race, nationality, culture and tradition are also inextricably themes in such a group. Furthermore, notions about what is meant by health and healthy interaction become questionable both because of the cultural context and because as yet there is still no general consensus in clinical work and research findings about the effects of trauma on settled populations let alone on refugees who are forcibly uprooted. This chapter will set out these issues and attempt to draw some conclusions from my own and colleagues' groupwork experience with refugees. Most of the groupwork described has been conducted from a cross-cultural perspective using interpreters because the principal language of the therapist has been English. These matters are discussed in some detail.

Contexts: refugees in international law

Refugee is a generic term used to describe someone who has sought asylum in another country. This popular understanding accords with the terms of the 1951 Geneva Convention which defines a refugee as someone who:

> ...owing to a well founded fear of being persecuted for reasons of race, religion, nationality, membership of a particular social group or political opinion, is outside the country of his nationality and is unable or, owing to such fear, is unwilling to avail himself of the protection of that country (UNHCR, 1988).

In practice, as described in the later clauses of the Convention, there are different terms for refugees depending upon their position in the process of being examined and legally recognised as refugees. Thus, people in flight seeking protection are referred to as asylum seekers and those granted protection are termed refugees. In practice, European countries are increasingly hostile to asylum seekers and have enacted legislation and methods to deter people from situations of conflict and human rights violations arriving and making successful claims for asylum. One of the results of deterrence is that many fewer people are granted full refugee status. Actually, the majority now given protection are granted exceptional leave to remain. This is a less secure status which gives fewer rights, and most importantly, it means that the Home Office will usually not even consider family reunion until at least four years have passed.

Throughout this chapter I will refer to asylum seekers, those granted full refugee status and those with exceptional leave generically as refugees. However, it is very important to understand the asylum status of refugees in a group. Many anxieties may be rooted in the political and legal conditions of their status. For instance, because the political climate is so hostile to refugees and because the immigration authorities take so long to make decisions, many asylum seekers feel very anxious about whether they will be granted protection or returned to their homeland to face further persecution.

CONTEXTS: WAR AND ATROCITY

Political conflict, oppression and war form the backdrop of groupwork with refugees. Since the end of the Second World War and the formation of the United Nations there have been over 170 wars in which 30 million are estimated to have died and of which the greatest proportion have been civilian deaths. Political regimes have used exemplary violence to enforce their rule; community leaders, teachers, doctors, trade unionists, religious leaders and other prominent people have been made the target of oppression (Summerfield, 1992). Oftentimes, whole groups and communities have been subjected to violence. Social networks, systems of lineage, historical links with places and ways of life have been destroyed both deliberately and indiscriminately. The proximity of the individual to these events both literally and in relation to the personal meaning invested in them will shape their resilience or susceptibility to what they have suffered.

Some may identify with a resistance culture; others may feel the hapless victims of oppression. It seems necessary that at some point the existential question of 'why me' needs to be answered and formulations will depend on the interaction of political circumstances with deeply personal themes. Groupwork is well set up to work with those linkages and to enable deeply personal processes to be worked through simultaneously with issues in the political and social domain.

CONTEXTS: ATROCITY AND TRAUMA

Because the field of cross-cultural work with refugees is so complex and also relatively young, choice treatment approaches have not been established with any certainty. Indications are that the frameworks which therapists use need to be open textured and inclusive (van der Veer, 1992) and this chapter will draw on thinking from systemic, psychodynamic and group-analytic paradigms. Furthermore, the chapter will take account of the complexities generated by cultural difference (Fernando, 1991) and the light thrown on our understanding of distress and psychological adjustment by historical studies (see, for instance, Porter, 1987; Farge, 1993). Undoubtedly, the study of both culture and history simultaneously broaden and sharpen our categories of knowledge in this field but they also tend to relativise our understanding. Nevertheless, there is a need for some clarity about what issues should constitute grounds for offering therapy in the light of broadly conceived contemporary understanding and clinical experience.

Undoubtedly, reactions to severe adversity differ enormously, it must not be assumed that every survivor will be traumatised and in need of psychological treatment. Trauma needs to be regarded as a relative term, culturally shaped and open to negotiation about its meaning and equally about the best way of meeting its challenges. Writing a history of the United Services Club, Major General Sir Louis Jackson describes a career soldier who barbarised his way across three different continents. His attitudes are depicted as straightforward and manly with high expectations of reward and honour. Despite being involved in inconceivable horrors there is no thought of trauma (Jackson, 1937). A century later returnees from similar colonial endeavours in Vietnam were ostracised by their country and there were consequently high numbers of psychological casualties as soldiers resettled into a country which rejected their involvement.

Subsequently there was clearly an interplay between the political marginalisation of Vietnam veterans and the incidence of Post-traumatic Stress Disorder which became a popular diagnosis subsequently elaborated in the nosology of psychological medicine. Thus it was medicine that validated veterans' distress, not in terms of spurned valour, but in terms of damage to their individual psychological integrity as a result of their involvement in the war. Occurring at the same time among recent South-East Asian refugees, signs indicative of trauma to western oriented mental health professionals were ameliorated, not by treatment, but by attention to prescribed ancestral rites (Eisenbruch, 1991). Parallels can be drawn with the diagnoses of anorexia nervosa among Ethiopian Jewish adolescents recently settled in Israel. Was this true anorexia or a way of coping with massive transition and unacknowledged losses? (Ben-Ezer, 1992).

Refugees are survivors and associated with all but the most severely affected there is usually a sense of resilience imbued through resistance against overwhelming odds. Michael Rutters' thinking about resilience in the face of adversity is very pertinent (Rutter, 1985). He identifies the distinctive aspects of emotional resilience as being the presence of reasonable self esteem; the presence of secure relationships; the ability to interact positively with ongoing stress and the eventual gaining of mastery over stress which provides a sense of control; a measure of success and achievement and the interaction with others in securing those gains; the ability to process events in a meaningful way and the ability to integrate the stressful event into a personal belief system - in other words, to make sense of what has happened. These are central themes in therapeutic work with refugees and the absence of these qualities of resilience will indicate vulnerability. Vulnerability will also have a particular social dimension when refugees are isolated because their families and networks are not available. Equally, vulnerability will have a cultural dimension when the host culture does not readily support culturally given ways of creating or sustaining the meaning of life events. Vulnerability may also have a predominantly individual psychological dimension because the experience of trauma may have impaired the survivors' ability to access personal, social or cultural forms of resilience. Groupwork offers unique opportunities for the processes of resilience to be brought forth in an accessible way and enhanced. For instance, the group offers a social environment in which practical and emotional strategies for survival can be explored. Opportunities for giving and taking comfort and advice are provided. The group is also in a position to probe the existential dilemmas of refugees because there will be competing understandings of situations which enables events to be deconstructed and the meaning of events can be enriched. An example of this is the African women's group which met each week to prepare and eat a meal from each of the women's homeland. This offered chances for their identity and self esteem to flourish; they were able to offer each other practical and symbolic nurturance in the food that was cooked; the women would always bless the food in their own traditional way before the food was eaten and this stimulated discussion about the meaning of what had befallen them.

CONTEXTS: TRANSITION, LOSS AND BEREAVEMENT

Loss and bereavement is a central theme: group members will present with massive losses, including loss of family members, friends, comrades, community, downward shifts in status and lifestyle, loss of possessions and livelihood; physical pains associated with physical and psychic injuries; severe disruption of normal sleep patterns; thoughts and feelings associated with having lost the meaning of life accompanied by anxiety or hopelessness about the future; a sense that vigour and self esteem have been lost; feelings of desperation and thoughts about suicide; feelings of self disgust arising from humiliation suffered because of torture, rape or betrayal; feelings of being helpless or overwhelmed and trapped by their situation.

In a non-refugee population clusters of signs like these would normally be indicative of acute clinical depression and a group with many members marked by such losses would be very emotionally heavy and difficult to conduct. However, it would be wrong to approach refugees with such symptoms as if they were suffering from typical depression. Although their feelings will have a depressive cast they will be rooted in the massive emotional and concrete losses and therefore, unlike typical depression where causes may be more convoluted and hidden, a predominant aspect of refugees' mental conditions will be more immediately accessible to therapeutic work. It is of course difficult to apportion grief either to personal losses or to loss of homeland and its function as a repository of living values. Thus it is vital to have an understanding of both personal bereavement processes (Murray-Parkes, 1972) and issues of transition and cultural bereavement which should include an appreciation of how losses are dealt with in the traditions and beliefs of group members. Conversations about death and its meaning will need to encompass an understanding of the spiritual dimensions of people's traditions and experience and an understanding of the communal nature of mourning (Some, 1993). For instance, there will undoubtedly be members who have been unable to bury their dead and follow through prescribed funeral rites. The group may be able to offer itself as a refuge in which group members are able to bring forth their funeral traditions in conversation and mourn the fact that they have not been able to follow the prescribed rites. It may also be possible to work out alternative rituals which encompass the group and these may include food, prayers, blessings and invocations.

The impact of transition and cultural bereavement is present in many subtle transactions in the group. For instance the relative status of group members is complex in groups for refugees. Each will have had a certain status in their country of origin and they will have another status in exile. These differences in status will have a dynamic effect as the group negotiates whether to respond to the home or exile status (Al-Rasheed, 1993). Also, the extent to which the group meets a social need may be dependent on the relative isolation of group members and their ability to use the group as a means to enrich their social connections. It is usual to have considerable discussion about what has been left behind and lost and how this impacts on the internal and external worlds of group members. At times the group as a whole may feel at sea, without anchorage, lost in the desert, living on tasteless, insipid food. These are all metaphors of cultural bereavement which sum up the lack of social and emotional connectedness brought about by the transition into exile. By providing the sensibility to focus on these themes the group can help with the incorporation of members into exile, enabling them to integrate aspects of their culture and past life with the culture and demands of life in the host country (Woodcock, 1995).

RESPONDING CREATIVELY TO GROUPWORK WITH REFUGEES

My experience indicates that only small numbers of refugees can be recruited into groups conducted on mainstream group-analytic principles. Not enough is really known about why this is the case, although it can be conjectured that refugee communities are generally not familiar or comfortable with the formality of the group analytic setting; or that at the point of crisis when a group could enable them to process psychological material too few speak English and there are too few therapists available who can work in refugee languages. This area deserves further study and experimentation. Nevertheless, group-analytic, psychoanalytic and systemic ideas used in the group setting are very pertinent to the refugee experience. The group provides excellent opportunities for reparation by reproducing lost and destroyed aspects of social and family life and the contribution of group therapy comes into its own where the social and creative aspects of the group are emphasised and developed as the leading task of the group. Here are three descriptions of such groups.

USING FOOD AND NARRATIVE AS MEANS TO HEAL

This group was run for African women who had suffered massive loss and atrocity which was not resolving naturally over time. The preparation and cooking of a meal was made into a primary focus of the group. Each week a different woman would buy the food and initiate the preparation of a meal from her homeland. The symbolic nature of the hearth and familiar food was used as a resource for this group. Food powerfully communicates identity in differing ways of presentation, the making of hospitality and the marking of kinship which differ between cultures. Food also communicates identity by smell, taste and other subtle aesthetic qualities. The groups brought these issues alive and stimulated symbolic and practical thinking. Friendships were created in the groups which continue to this day.

While the meal was eaten the second focus of the group would be brought into play which was the telling of stories. These consisted of the women's personal stories and also traditional stories and histories from their homelands. Their personal stories enabled the women to realise that they were not alone in their suffering. As trust developed, the stories which emerged were often connected to the vivid existential themes of their lives: separation, loss, death and betrayal. Each woman had aspects of experience which prior to the group had been too painful to recall, or experiences which were so bizarre as to be barely believable, or experiences which were denied because they felt too shameful to admit. An interpreter was not used and the conversation was conducted in various African languages and French and English which were spoken by the group therapists. The group offered a holding environment in which their internal and external worlds were looped together by the therapists' attention to systemic patterns and existential themes. By these means the groups created a matrix of meaning which made sense of their experiences and enabled them to process events by both conscious and symbolic means through the medium of the story telling and the wider therapeutic discourse. Setting the group within the stream of the women's cultures also revivified their connections to the rich symbolic store of meanings within their traditions (David, 1991; White and Epston, 1990). Finally, the group gave a voice to the women which demonstrated their strengths and commitment to life and cried out against oppression.

A MOVEMENT PSYCHOTHERAPY GROUP

This group used the notion that the body is the site of oppression. Therefore the body both literally and symbolically represents the impact that torture, atrocity and oppression has upon its victims. The group was for refugees from differing backgrounds who were suffering the sequelae of torture which included clearly recognisable physical injuries and psychosomatic injuries rooted in the body (Callaghan, 1993). My colleague's understanding is that 'torture exists on a body-mind continuum and cannot be easily separated into physical or psychological categories.' Furthermore, following the ideas of Scarry (1985), she works with the idea that the body is the 'site of creation out of which we construct our symbolic world and invest it with meaning.' Torture, atrocity, loss and exile imply the attempt of repressive regimes to destroy such creative processes and to destroy potency literally and symbolically. The movement psychotherapy group became the site in which reconstruction of meaning and the recreation of a restored relation between mind and body took place. The group was able to work with members with very little common language because movement was the primary means of communication. Materials such as balls were used; these allowed members to express inclusion and exclusion by whom the ball was passed to or whom was omitted; aggression through rough play and also pleasure through skilful and humorous play. Another material used was an elastic loop which could be used to encompass the whole group. At times the loop became a safe house into which the whole group huddled; at other times it was used to express rejection by excluding the therapist. This play with the boundary was common to all the groups conducted by the therapist using this method of group interaction. This seems to illustrate several interlocking themes: the importance of the boundary in all groups as a marker of who is psychologically inside the group and this is particularly relevant to refugees who are exiled from their homelands and live on the margins of the host society. Secondly, it illustrates the importance of the boundary of the body, the space which it moves within and the actual physical skin of the body which gets broken through in torture and atrocity. This group worked with those themes at a very deep symbolic level.

A GROUP FOR REFUGEE CHILDREN

This group meets to enable adolescent refugee children who have suffered significant harm, either because they are unaccompanied children living in unsupported settings or because they have parents or carers who are unable to meet their developmental needs. The theoretical principles upon which the group is based follow developmental psycho-analytic ideas. Adolescence is a phase of development that has its central tasks: developing a new relationship with parents; developing a new relationship with ones body and developing a new relationship with work, learning and friends. It is particularly difficult for adolescents to negotiate these tasks when they have been overwhelmed by experiences of violence, loss and change or when parents are suddenly lost or withdraw emotionally. The group aims to make a space to explore these issues via various modalities including art, drama and storytelling. This enables the group to explore extreme events and extreme feelings connected with those events. It is also a reality that in the lives of some refugee adolescents they often have little time and space for play - either because they have been overwhelmed or because they are forced to take on parental roles to support ill parents. The group aims to provide a place to play in the widest sense of the word - to play with ideas verbally and non-verbally - to have fun and thus integrate difficult painful experiences and good experiences in the process. Thus, the group aims to be fun while pursuing common themes which enable the children to relate to each other and to find a place in which the vulnerable and scary aspects of their experience are held and processed in a meaningful way. The group meets after school on a fortnightly basis and provides snack food both English and from the children's own culinary traditions. The group has drawn on storytellers and musicians from the children's communities and it has also enabled each child to describe their personal story and journey into exile using various media such as Polaroid photography and painting. In the summer the group ventured out to the seaside for the day. It is enriched by being co-run by a child psychotherapist, an Oral History Worker and interpreters from the Kurdish, Somali and Arabic communities.

HOW THE THERAPIST TAKES CARE

At best, any therapeutic work presupposes an understanding of the dynamics of the therapist's personal relationship to the central themes of the work. Perhaps unsurprisingly, working with the uprooted forces an examination of ones own origins and the connections made are part of a very personal story: what experience do we have of marginality, cultural difference, racism, issues of gender, politics and religious belief?

Nevertheless, refugees' experiences of atrocity, massive loss and displacement are beyond the experience of most western health professionals. The horror of what they have endured can be difficult to contemplate and may make us wish to recoil and close ourselves up to them. This is not a shameful response but a rather natural protective reaction we are likely to have when exposed to terrible and unthinkable experiences. Once we understand that we may react in this way we are better prepared to work with compassion and skill. Therefore, before starting work with the group some time should be spent thinking through the issues and emotions they may bring. This mental preparation should include being generous about finding support for oneself and giving oneself sufficient time preparation, for the session and the tasks that will follow. Cultural difference will also have to be thought about and may lead us to question western notions of health, the sick role and ways of helping. However, cultural difference should not undermine our skills if we remain open, curious, and exploratory about what we don't know. Nevertheless, some preparatory information about how such issues as gender, childhood, work, the life cycle and so forth are considered within the group members' home countries are well worth finding out about before the group starts as well as understanding the background reasons why group members have fled into exile. Over time, the group will always become the best informants about these issues and no doubt some of their viewpoints will be controversial both within the group and within their community. Culture is fluid and ever changing, so differences of view should not surprise us.

This basic groundwork will provide the therapist with a sense of the terrain they will be working on and in the same way as the group will shift between levels and pace of work, so will knowing details like this enable the therapist to shift pace as well and find safety and meaning in wider contexts. Furthermore, one of the tasks of the group may be to explore the very damaging aspects of group members experience. This can be terrifying for the uninitiated therapist and for the group, but the therapists' access to group members' resilient qualities enables this exploration to be conducted with the confidence that there is sufficient emotional fortitude in the group to contain the terrifying issues without the group falling apart or going into flight.

WORKING ACROSS GENDER AND ACROSS CULTURE

When running a group with a co-therapist my practice has been for us to consult with each other about the aspects of our own experience which either connect us or distance us from the central themes of the group. For instance, the African women's group presented the challenge of how I would use my gender with women who had suffered rape, violation and humiliation by men (Swiss and Giller, 1993). My colleague and I first had to consult with each other to make our assumptions explicit about how gender issues would affect our way of working together in the group. Out of that we evolved an understanding of how my identity as a white, English man and her identity as a white English woman could be used. For example what did they make of my participation in food preparation and cooking? How did my presence shape and constrain conversation and interaction? In what way did I represent a threat? Was there opportunity for reparation of their relationships with men through their interactions with me or would they idealise me as a non-threatening, possibly de-sexualised and non aggressive male? To what extent in the group of largely single women would there be a sexual interplay in their relationship with me? How did we think they would react to our pairing as group facilitators? Naturally, we were not able to anticipate all these themes in our pre-group discussion but ongoing consultation enabled us to work with both the conscious and unconscious aspects of these matters as the group was running.

Our gender and cultural differences became grist to the mill for the therapeutic purpose of the group. I was able to be curious about them as African women from the standpoint of my

European maleness and the mutual questioning enriched communication and presented challenges which made it possible for us to work with themes about male and female roles in the here and now. Simultaneously, in combination with the group's ability to sustain safety and enable re-symbolising of community, family and creative relations with their inner selves, there was playing out of themes which helped them to review material from the violations they had suffered at pre-conscious and more conscious levels. The group particularly provides a setting in which the deeply personal wounds of individual survivors can be given social recognition. Good therapeutic work also depends upon a recognition that traumatic events strike at the fundamental identity as described by Lifton (1993) and the therapist has to work to sustain opportunities for the group to access insights which permit them to work through the impact on their individual identities. For many survivors this begins when they realise they are not alone. For others, especially where fear and terror are still palpable, or where there is a disassociative defence, the traumatic events may be projected out into the group where they are worked through collectively and then taken back and re-integrated into the individual.

For instance, complex and different versions of male and female interactions were brought into play both from the women's experience and in the present through their interactions with me and my colleague. We hoped I would present a model as a safe, contained and circumspect man who was able to reflect on male behaviour. One woman who had been brutally raped many times described how she had pretended at first that I was a woman in order to cope with my presence. As the group developed she began to understand she could have a non-threatening relationship with me. Nevertheless, because she actually hated men she idealised me as a special man who was different. This changed over time as the group enabled her to work through the trauma of rape at a symbolic level through interaction, discussion, reflection and story telling. The dilemmas of being a woman in situations where she had minimal control in her relations with men were explored. New ways of relating were reality tested both by herself and other women within the safety of the group through their relationship with me. My task was to offer safety, to tackle idealisations and explore alternatives in a frank and open way in the here and now. Eventually, the woman who had been multiply raped was able to envisage a relationship with a man in which her sense of choice and control in relation to men matched her undoubted healthy capacity for life in other domains. This particularly illustrates the ability of the group to offer an environment in which traumatic material can be worked through with the resources of culture, social relations, personal and ethnic identity and the inner self as sources of healing of the individual and the group.

Qualities of gender and culture are woven into each other. Thus, in responding to issues of gender with the women, there was a commensurate sensitivity to cultural difference. The women identified themselves as African women in relation to outsiders. Amongst themselves they took their identity in multi-layered directions, geographically toward homeland, region and village; ethnically through religious, tribal and regional aspects. We encouraged this diversity and curiosity about differing values, ways of being, and notions of justice, moral values and ways of healing by maximising the use of non-intrusive curiosity when opportunities arose for recognising and working with difference and by underpinning our thinking with the recognition of culture and ethnicity not as essential exotic qualities but as relational and reflexive notions which equally defined us.

RACISM

Racism can be made invisible in therapeutic work. Like Kareem (1992) and Thomas (1992) we acknowledged the need to make it explicit. It probably sounds paradoxical to make this point about women who had frequently suffered violation because of ethnic difference. However, it is certainly true that for most racism was a new experience which they needed help to understand and contextualise. Like new immigrants from the commonwealth in the 1950s and 1960s, refugees tend at first to idealise British society; they do not expect racist hostility and often fail to interpret what is happening. One woman thought when white people frequently moved away from herself and her children on the train journey into London they were being excessively polite. In the group the women had to work out strategies for coping with those sorts of encounters and many more dangerous conflicts brought by racism. As therapists we had to be sensitive to our ability to participate in denial because the way the women experienced racism was not readily part of our personal experience. Denial also came from the women in other ways - for instance, because it did not fit into their repertoire of experiences. Or, because it easily became integrated into the already traumatised and denied part of their self identity, it was thus treated as invisible by them. Also, because it was such a frequent, indeed continuous experience, reporting it into the group or elsewhere seemed carping and senseless. We had to make ourselves aware of these interactions and, like the parents of black children settled in Britain, the group had to see that racism was openly discussed and tackled actively in ways that were not damaging to the women's concept of self and in ways which enabled them to relate racism and the denied aspects of their trauma. For instance, one woman living with the constant abuse of her children called the police onto her inner city council housing estate and asked them to intervene. Their response was mild and ineffectual and earned the family even more hostility. She then stormed into the house of one of her tormentors and screamed in an eruption of feeling that she felt imprisoned by their hostility and would kill them if it continued. The police intervened again at that point and called to interview her. In a high state of anger she conveyed with the complete force of her personality that her husband had been executed in her homeland, she and her children had been mercilessly beaten, shot and tortured and they had escaped to Britain where life seemed little better. The racism on the estate was terrifying and imprisoning her and her children and she would kill if it went on. Better, she had said, to be in a real prison here in Britain for striking back than to be in a prison in her homeland for the sake of injustice or imprisoned in her home by hostility. Curiously, the authentic expression of those sentiments made her accepted on the estate. The other women in the group gasped at the vigour of her response. We discussed the matter for some time. Clearly, the hostility on the estate had connected her experience at home with what was going on in Britain. The impact on the other women came about not only because she stood up for herself so effectively but also because she expressed a connection which had been denied in several of them and we talked this out onto a conscious level and discussed strategies for responding and coping in different ways.

PRINCIPLES OF SIMILARITY AND DIFFERENCE IN SELECTING GROUP MEMBERS

As the groups described illustrate, political and social processes are integral to groups with refugees and these factors will need careful thought in relation to the composition and core therapeutic aims of the group. Even though they may have many common experiences which unite them there are enormous differences both between and within refugee communities. Issues of national and political identity, religious belief, gender, language and class both unite and divide and these differences can be very confusing when thinking through a group proposal.

Usually, the idea for a group will spring up from a perceived need. For instance, a group for African women who have similar experiences of loss and atrocity, or a group for Turkish Kurdish parents separated from their children by exile, or a group for woman who are in conflictual or violent relationships, or a group for Iranian men who have similar experiences of imprisonment and torture, or a group for refugee children whose parents are unable to help them cope with atrocity, loss and change. Nevertheless, the perceived need should be thought through in terms of the similarities and differences which the group will have to encompass and also in terms of the similarities and differences which would disrupt the effective formation of the group. Because these aspects are so important it is useful to think in terms of *principles* of similarity and difference. Such principles would indicate that there needs to be sufficient similarity to enable group cohesion and sufficient difference to stimulate curiosity and to allow opportunities for interpersonal learning about alternative ways of responding to personal and social difficulties to come forth. Thus it helps to have a group with a certain proportion of shared experiences and assumptions but also with sufficient difference for assumptions to be challenged. For instance in the group for African women the principle of similarity was a shared identity as African women. This united them around certain shared perceptions and experiences and in terms of the identity ascribed to them by the host community. However, they were also African women from different countries and different regions with differing cultural and family traditions and personal beliefs. The core therapeutic task of the group was to enable women to pursue a process of mourning complicated by multiple loss and atrocity which was not resolving naturally over time. The women found the common elements of identity and experience were supportive. Meanwhile, the ways they dealt with issues such as rape, loss of partners and children left behind were enriched by the variety of responses in the group about these experiences.

Refugee communities are often divided along sectarian lines which reflect exile versions of the political struggles back home. This can sometimes preclude the simple creation of single language groups where there is an assumption that this will unite group members. For instance, the Iranian community has many mutually suspicious factions and attempts to bring together members of that exile community with stark political differences around non-political themes such as common experiences of torture or imprisonment have not been very successful. This means the group facilitator needs to be adept at understanding political differences and their potential to unite and divide.

The idea for the group will be also be shaped by the therapists' orientation and this can serve to offer a theme which over-rides differences which otherwise could cause a group to founder. For instance, in the movement psychotherapy group because movement was the common language of the group the therapist was able to work with members who spoke very little common language and political differences, which in a verbal group could have been very conflictual, did not disrupt the common themes which united members.

COMMUNICATION

By definition refugees are people whose voices have been excluded or silenced. This makes communication a key issue in therapeutic work with refugees. Careful attention needs to be paid to enabling the differing experiences in the group to be expressed so that trust develops and each voice is privileged. Furthermore, understanding that communication is one of the central issue of refugee groups enables groups to be run in which there is no common language. Instead, what is said may need to be translated several times in a chain of communication around the group, from French to Arabic to Swahili to English until each group member and the facilitator understands. Such a group may seem painstakingly slow, yet this works. Respect for what is being said, attention to the polyphony of refugee voices, the understanding that voice embodies culture and tradition means that core elements of identity that are essential aspects of resilience are privileged by this way of working.

WORKING WITH INTERPRETERS

The therapist will need to decide on the basis of their language skills whether to use an interpreter. Acquiring good skills in communicating through an interpreter may therefore be essential. An interpreter should not be regarded as a colourless conduit of the therapists' talk. Rather they are best considered as colleagues who will be useful therapeutic allies who will enrich communication within the group. They may also be helpful informants about group members' beliefs and traditions, although when offering advice on culture, the interpreter and therapist must also recognise that the interpreters viewpoint is only partial, it offers some access but must not be considered to be definitive.

The fact that therapy is essentially a task about communication should be borne in the forefront of the therapist's and interpreter's thinking. Therefore, a good deal of time spent finding a congenial interpreter and involving them fully as a co-worker in the enterprise, including the planning and preparation of the group is time well spent. Their position in the group may be similar to that of a co-therapist. Therapist and interpreter must work out how to translate. In general, interpreting short phrases of translation makes for more precise empathy. However, translation phrase by phrase may not always be appropriate or necessary. Work slowly, create trust, clarify issues, think through dilemmas of translation openly - involving interpreter and the group. Often, as trust develops, group members may start making more use of English and this is to be encouraged, as is cross talk which enables communication to circulate around the group rather than being directed exclusively toward interpreter and therapist.

THE PATIENT ROLE AND ADVOCACY

No matter what the therapist's orientation refugees do not easily take on the identity of patients nor is it easy for the group therapist to designate them as patients. This is because their needs do not primarily arise from a neurotic history of emotional and social difficulty but from human rights violations which have been inflicted upon them. Refugees also tend to have a great many practical needs to settle. By virtue of flight and exile many are materially destitute, live in poor housing and have little access to the job market because of lack of English or ill-health. Their precarious legal and social position may mean that they might look to the group therapist for opportunities for advocacy. This may artificially elevate the group facilitator's status and the therapist must consider how to respond. In a group conducted for Turkish Kurdish refugees separated from their children my co-therapist was a psycho-analyst and doctor who wrote a great many medico-legal reports attesting to physical injuries and psychological harm arising from torture and atrocity. Naturally the refugees in the group knew this and a great number of sessions were spent exploring if my colleague would offer this individual attention to each group member. In the event it was hardly appropriate for everyone because not all had signs, apart from the natural distress at being separated from their children, which could be written up in a report. We initially responded by playing a therapeutically abstinent role which was very hard to sustain over the many weeks as the group argued that we had an absolute duty to represent their needs in reports for them all. Meanwhile, we wrestled with our consciences: would a report, no matter how weak, really make a difference? Would report writing for the group sustain the severely damaged morale of group members, several of whom had been separated from infant children for over four years? The group idealised our capacity to help and we challenged this by wondering with them about the actual efficacy of our reports counterposed against their own sense of failure as parents who had abandoned their children. In the end the group decided that they would write their own reports and they produced some very moving letters which attested very eloquently to their distress at separation and the reasons why they had to abandon their children and take flight into exile. My colleague accompanied the group to the House of Commons where a charter for separated refugee parents was launched and several of their letters were read. Symbolically, we refused to take on the parental/leadership role which they wished to attribute to us, rather we set out to process and digest the greater complexity of their situations and this enabled them to enlarge their capacity to represent themselves.

The outcome actually worked well in that group; nevertheless advocacy represents real dilemmas and an abstinent approach is not always appropriate. In reality the therapist often does wield more influence than refugee group members and at times advocacy can make a difference, not only with the Home Office in painful areas such as family separation, but also with housing, or the Department of Social Security, or with the health services. It always seems appropriate to wonder with the group what advocacy means; what effects will it have on your relations with the group; will it provoke envy in group members who do not have that attention; does advocacy involve healthy idealisation or the relinquishing of group members' adult capacities; what advocacy is available in the community; is it right at that particular time to allow that or not?

POLITICS, HUMAN RIGHTS AND LEADERSHIP

To offer a therapeutic service to refugees presupposes a certain commitment to Human Rights. It may be rather abstract, such as taking an ethical position within the bounds of ones professional identity, which means that one resolves to offer a service because it is needed. It may be coloured by ones political commitment. But Human Rights are not abstract and work with refugees will force an examination of what Human Rights mean, whether this is done overtly in the group or is the preoccupation taken up privately or in supervision. Taking a strong political stance is not usually very helpful because groups are rarely politically homogenous and this will inevitably alienate some members or it may prevent other more complex positions being reflected. At best the therapist should use Human Rights as a concept which can be used to reflect on positions in the group. For instance, what does it mean to have been a freedom fighter? Did this improve people's rights or lead to greater repression? The role of Human Rights in the group is therefore used to privilege all the differing attitudes and opinions in the group, rather than privileging one position. The therapist may find the concept of therapeutic neutrality developed in systemic family therapy is useful. Systemic practitioners are not detached operators but engage equally with all participants and positions. They also employ the notion of the therapist using different lenses. For instance, the therapist may wonder how an issue looks from the perspective of a woman, or of a man, or from the perspective of a child. These ideas permit the therapist to exercise leadership in the group in a style which fits well with non-authoritarian communal forms of leadership more common in non-western social groups. There the leader remains engaged in the arguments and discussion but models a style that does not take sides but allows all positions to come forth (Smith and Bond, 1993).

In groups with quite sharply different political opinions, especially with members from the same country who have literally fought over the same territory, respect for differing political positions will often need to be established by cohesion around other aspects of their identity. In such groups there will need to be a level of trust about basic emotional themes, before frank political discussion emerges. However, in groups with members from different countries politics are often safer to discuss, because despite different ideological leanings there is greater capacity for being dispassionate. Furthermore, in real politic there are often strange bedfellows and western political demarcations may not necessarily be relevant. Politics can also become the currency in the group for expressing challenging and aggressive feelings or alternatively going into flight about emotional issues which feel too painful for the group to face. The therapist will have to monitor political discussion and like any other form of exchange in the group consider the emotional implications of the communication and what is being transacted at other levels.

CONTAINMENT AND VALIDATION

Torture and atrocity confront survivors with extreme experiences which may rupture the psychic shield. Psychoanalytic writers hypothesise that near death experiences cause a catastrophic weakening of the inner boundaries of the psychic structure. There is an influx of primitive material into the more sophisticated social aspects of the personality and defence against the catastrophic destructive intensity of those feelings may lead to disassociation.[1] Furthermore the social aspects of refugee life emphasise the loss of status which has an impact on the inner world: being stripped of possessions, forced out of their homeland, broken away from family and communal networks, having to relinquish meaningful political struggle, being unable to be an effective family member whether this is as a parent, adult child or sibling.

The group is in a unique position to address the themes of weakened identity which arise from these experiences because of its capacity to recapitulate primary life experiences within the family and social world (Yalom, 1985). To achieve the goal of enabling very deep and disturbing experiences to be processed the group needs to develop as a place of safety and become a psychic container which can hold the chaos of primitive feelings without feeling so dangerous that the group will disintegrate. At the same time established assumptions about the validity of psychological theories to group members with cultures and traditions quite different from one's own need to be examined. This challenges the whole concept of containment, for how can the group facilitator offer safety if their basic assumptions are under challenge? It seems best to meet this problem by relativising ones own assumptions as far as they can be disembedded from habits of mind and personal interaction. At best therapists should attempt to use knowledge and traditions as heuristic devices - inviting curiosity about their own beliefs and theories and being equally curious about the beliefs and theories of group members. The sort of interaction which this invites can be very containing. First of all, the facilitator needs to play close attention to the experiences of group members, thinking about their concerns, reflecting and linking to other experiences in the group. As trust develops, contrasts can be emphasised and the similarities and differences in the group may be deconstructed, analysed and understood. The experiences of group members can be looped through their social world, through their inner experiences and reflected by group processes.

The safety of the group and its capacity to hold members is therefore dependent on the capacity of the group to offer validation of identity and experience. This must encompass the culture and traditions of members, demonstrating in the group that culture can be used as a resource and source of resilience; their political beliefs, whether or not these are discussed in an overt way or tied to common themes such as respect for human rights; their social experiences in exile and these are likely to include strategies for reacting to racism, dealing with marginalisation and living with poverty. Finally, when the outer world of the group feels safe, members may start reflecting the difficult and shameful aspects of personal experience.

For instance, in the group for African women, Samira, the youngest woman in the group, had been abducted by soldiers while at boarding school as violence swept across the region and this had also forced her mother and younger siblings to flee to England. Samira was raped and later had a child about whom she felt great ambivalence. She was also enraged with her mother and younger siblings for seemingly abandoning her. In the group there were older women who under similar conditions had been forced to abandon their infant and teenage children and women who brought their pre-school children with them to the group. Samira would often play very delightfully with these children revealing her capacity to offer something less ambivalent like an older sister re-engaging with her siblings. Meanwhile, the dilemmas of the women who had been forced to abandon their children were talked out. The very painful choices and often the lack of choice were confronted. We did not assume that leaving children was necessarily catastrophic, some were in the care of grandmothers, some were in safety in the other countries where they had opportunities for education not available in devastated parts of their homeland. However, some women were bereft and deeply disturbed by leaving their children. The women offered differing reactions to what had befallen them and the aspects of

Samira which were abandoned and angry and envious of her siblings were parented differently by each of the other women. She in turn offered them opportunities for reparation for their situations. The group was therefore capable of processing very deep feelings while offering opportunities for interpersonal learning and acts of respect and kindness which restored the women's sense of self respect and validity as mothers, daughters and siblings.

CHALLENGE AND SUPPORT

When the group is a safe place it develops a capacity to challenge as well as support. It may be assumed that because of extreme experiences therapeutic work with refugees should be largely supportive rather than exploratory or probing. However, refugees ask themselves very probing questions which are often agonising and to overlook the need to probe values, motivations and relationships would be neglectful of the real work that needs to be done. For instance, some of the Turkish Kurdish parents in the group for separated parents questioned why they had put themselves at risk by political activity. The answer to that question is never merely political, it is shot through with themes from personal history and cultural expectations.

SAFETY, CONFIDENTIALITY AND SECRECY

It may be assumed that in order for the group to feel safe to explore disturbing aspects of experience that a rule of confidentiality needs to be absolutely respected. However, members may belong to refugee communities in which the rules of confidentiality are different and perhaps more porous. The group therapist needs to check these issues out and relate to confidentiality in a dynamic way. The group may respect confidence about certain issues but feel freer about other interactions; for instance how will it deal with themes such as sex, including infidelity, or rape as opposed to an issue such as a member working illegally.

As the group becomes more cohesive it may spontaneously take on stricter rules of confidentiality. The therapist may decide that absolute confidence needs to be imposed in order to enhance the containment of the group and the safety of interactions. Therefore it may be wise to suggest that the group has different and special rules about confidentiality which are unlike those in society. Talking about confidentiality also has a special resonance with refugees from repressive regimes in which secrecy has been a necessary habit. Secrecy can be damaging to intimate relations; it can generate damaging fantasies and prevent difficulties being properly processed (Melzak, 1992). For instance, it is common to find that families back home will not pass on information about relatives who have died. This means that refugees in exile are unable to mourn effectively or live in a world that is impoverished by reality and shot through with nagging fantasies about what is really happening. The role of the group is not necessarily to challenge the secrets themselves but to examine the consequences of secrecy. Parents and children in the group will bring these themes into play because of the need of parents to maintain secrets from their children and there will be differing opinions and beliefs about what is legitimate and what is unhelpful. For instance in Angola parents may not tell their children that people have died until they are a certain age and they might expect the child to absorb the knowledge from available social cues as they grow up, rather than being told directly.

Discussion about confidentiality will also promote the theme of the group as a place of safety. For some in the group it may literally be a refuge in which to begin with they contribute very little. The therapist should be overt about the group as a place of safety, promoting discussion about what makes it safe, thinking about how the discussion shifts between topics, perhaps from emotionally difficult subjects to safer ground. In most groups in which there are very difficult themes of atrocity and loss there is usually a sensitivity among the members about the depth to which conversation can be taken. A theme will be pursued and very sad feelings evoked and explored, then the group will shift tempo returning to everyday concerns. This rhythm needs to be understood and respected and also explored. Has the group gone as far as it will; what made the group change tempo? Understanding these issues will help the group to unfold and strengthen its capacity to be a place of safety.

CONCLUSION

The communal nature of the group experience and the facility of psychotherapeutic work to ponder motifs of identity and difference in profound ways means that groups are ideally placed to work with the themes of refugee experience which include loss of identity through overwhelming terror and marginalisation.

This is quite an optimistic note with which to conclude. It suggests that the Western therapeutic tradition has the potential to be developed as one of the milieu in which the savagery and rejection of refugee experience can be encompassed and worked through. This should not surprise us when one considers the work of Foulkes (1964) and others with combat casualties during the Second World War and the ongoing effort of psychotherapy to understand some of the resonant qualities that lie at the heart of humanity. Refugees invite us to enlarge our experience to understand that the qualities of the fantastic and horrible that enter our lives are not only aspects of mental life but may be deeply real. Furthermore, they ought to lead us to wonder what capacity does our groupwork theory possess to accommodate the experience of refugees and what capacity do we and our agencies possess to include refugees in our practice and to learn from, adapt to and imbibe their culture and healing traditions?

Notes
There is a rich history of writing on trauma which trace the consequences of the notion of the psychic shield being pierced. Here are four references: the first from Freud's initial writing on the subject; secondly from the group analytic canon; thirdly, a modern psycho-analytic view and finally a systemic perspective which emphasises social-interactional account of trauma: Freud, S. (1920) 'Beyond the pleasure principle' in *The Pelican Freud Library Volume 11 On Metapsychology: The Theory of Psychoanalysis*. London: Pelican Books; Foulkes, S.H. (1948) *Therapeutic Group Analysis*. London: Maresfield Reprints; Laub, D. and Auerhahn, N. (1993) 'Knowing and not knowing massive psychic trauma: forms of traumatic memory', *International Journal of Psycho-Analysis*, 74, pp.287-302; Bentovim, A. (1992) *Trauma Organised Systems: Physical and Sexual Abuse in Families*. London: Karnac Books.

Acknowledgement
I would like to acknowledge the help of my colleagues at the Medical Foundation in formulating the ideas in this chapter. In particular, my thanks are due to Helen Bamber, Karen Callaghan, Jeanette Campbell-Johnston, John Denford, Annie Ellison, Susan Levy, Sheila Melzak, John Schlapobersky, Penny Smith, Gill Hinshelwood and Derek Summerfield.

Bibliography

Abernethy, R. and Hammond, N. (1992) *Drug Couriers: A Role for the Probation Service*. London: Middlesex Area Probation Service.

ABSWAP (1983) *Black Children in Care.*

Ackers, L. (1993) 'Race and sexuality in the ethnographic process' in Birmingham City Council Women's Unit and University of Central England School of Social Work (eds.) *An Exploration into Counselling Services for Black and Ethnic Minority Women with Mental Health Problems,* March, 1995.

Acton, T. (1974) *Gypsy Politics and Social Change*. London and Boston: Routledge and Kegan Paul.

Al-Rasheed, M. (1993) 'The meaning of marriage and status in exile: the experience of Iraqi women', *Journal of Refugee Studies*, 6, pp.89-104.

Alfred, J. and Fleming, R. (1995) *H.M.P. Belmarsh Foreign Nationals Support Group*. Available from Belmarsh Prison.

Argyle, M. (1969) *Social Interaction*. London: Methuen.

Asch, S. (1956) 'Studies of independence and conformity', *Psychological Monographs*, 70(9), No.416.

Aveline, M. and Dryden, W. (1988) *Group Therapy in Britain*. Milton Keynes: Open University Press.

Balgopal, P.R. and Vassil, T.V. (1983) *Groups in Social Work: An Ecological Perspective*. New York: Macmillan.

Barthes, R. (1986) *The Rustle of Language*. Oxford: Blackwell.

Ben-Ezer, G. (1992) 'Anorexia Nervosa or an Ethiopian coping style? Diagnostics and treatment of an eating disorder among Ethiopian immigrant Jews', *Refugee Participation Network,* 12, pp.16-19.

Benson, J. (1987) *Working More Creatively With Groups*. London: Tavistock.

Bernstein, B. (1971) *Class, Codes, Control*. New York: Routledge & Kegan Paul.

Bertcher, H. and Maple, F. (1977) *Creating Groups*. London: Sage Publications.

Bion, W.R. (1961) *Experiences in Groups*. London: Tavistock.

Birtill, A. (1995) *Rights for Travellers*. London: Irish Women's Centre.

Bollinger, D. and Hofstede, G. (1987) *Les differences culturelles dans le management*. Paris: Editions d'organisation

Breton, M. (1990) 'Learning from social group work traditions', *Social Work with Groups*, 13(3).

Breton, M. (1991a) 'Reflections on social action practice in France', *Social Work with Groups,* 15(3).

Breton, M. (1991b) 'Towards a model of social groupwork practice with marginalised populations', *Groupwork*, 4(1), pp.31-47.

Breton, M. (1992) 'Liberation theology, group work, and the right of the poor and oppressed to participate in the life of the community' in

Garland, J.A. (ed.) *Group Work Reaching Out: People, Places and Power*. New York: Haworth, pp.257-70.

Bricker-Jenkins, M. and Hooyman, N. (1986) *Not for Women Only*. Silver Springs, MD: NASW.

Brower, A., Garvin, C., Hobson, J., Reed, B. and Reed, H. (1987) 'Exploring the effects of leader gender and race on group behaviour' in Lassner, J. et al. (eds.) (1987) *Social Group Work: Competence and Values in Practice*. New York: The Haworth Press Inc.

Brown, A. (1984) *Consultation*. London: Heinemann.

Brown, A. (1986) *Groupwork*. Aldershot: Gower.

Brown, A. (1988) 'Consultation for groupworkers: models and methods', *Social Work with Groups*, 11(1-2).

Brown, A. (1990) 'British perspectives on group work: present and future', *Social Work with Groups*, 13(3), pp.35-40.

Brown, A. (1992) *Groupwork*. Third Edition. Aldershot: Ashgate Publishing.

Brown, A. and Clough, R. (eds.) (1989) *Groups and Groupings: Life and Work in Day and Residential Centres*. London: Routledge.

Brown, A. and Mistry, T. (1994) 'Groupwork with 'mixed membership' groups: issues of race and gender', *Social Work with Groups*, 17(3), pp.5-21.

Brown, J.A. (1984) 'Group work with low-income black youths', *Social Work with Groups*, 7(3).

Brummer, N. and Simmonds, J. (1992) 'Race and culture: the management of difference in the learning group', *Social Work Education*, 11(1).

Bryan, B., Dadzie, S. and Scafe, S. (1985) *The Heart of the Race: Black Women's Lives in Britain*. London: Virago Press.

Butler, S. and Wintram, C. (1991) *Feminist Groupwork*. London: Sage Publications.

Callaghan, K. (1993) *Group Movement Psychotherapy with Adult Survivors of Political Torture*. Paper presented at the 9th European Symposium in Group Analysis 'Boundaries and Barriers,' Heidelberg, 29 August- 4 September.

Canton, R. et al. (1992) 'Handling conflict: groupwork with violent offenders', *Groupwork*, 5(2).

Carby, H. (1982) 'White women listen! Black feminism and the boundaries of sisterhood' in Centre for Contemporary Studies (eds.) *The Empire Strikes Back: Race and Racism in 70s Britain*. London: Hutchinson.

CCETSW (1989) *Requirements and Regulations for the Diploma in Social Work Paper 30*. London: CCETSW.

CCETSW (1989) *Requirement and Regulations for the Diploma in Social Work*. Paper 30. London: CCETSW. Quoted in Thompson, N. (1993) *Anti-Discriminatory Practice*. Birmingham: BASW.

CCETSW Leeds, Northern Curriculum Development Project (1992) *Improving Practice with Children and Families: Social Work Theories and Models. Chap 2 Resource Paper 1: Ethnocentrism in Social Work Literature*.

Cemlyn, S. (1994) 'Health and social work: working with Gypsies and Travellers', *Practice*, 6, pp.246-61.

Cemlyn, S. (1995) 'Traveller children and the state: welfare or neglect?', *Child Abuse Review*, 4, pp.278-90.

Chau, K. (1990a) 'Introduction: facilitating bicultural development and intercultural skills in ethnically heterogeneous groups' in Chau, K. (ed.) *Ethnicity and Biculturalism: Emerging Perspectives of Social Group Work*, New York: Haworth, pp.1-5.

Chau, K. (1990b) 'Social work with groups in multicultural contexts', *Groupwork*, 3(1).

Comaz-Diaz, L. (1984) 'Content themes in group treatment with Puerto Rican women', *Social Work with Groups*, 7(3).

Coyle, G. (1979) *Social Process in Organized Groups*. Reprint of 1930 Edition. Hebron, Conn. Practitioners Press.

Crickley, A. (1992) 'Feminism and ethnicity' in Dublin Travellers Education and Development Group *DTEDG File Irish Travellers: New Analysis and New Initiatives*. Dublin: Pavee Point Publications.

David, J. (1991) *Interweaving Symbols of Individuation in African and European Fairy Tales: A Jungian Perspective*. Cape Town: Kaggen Press.

Davies, A. (1981) *Women, Race and Class*. The Women's Process.

Davis, A. (1975) *An Autobiography*. Hutchinson.

Davis, L. (1980) 'Racial balance - a psychological issue: a note to group workers, *Social Work with Groups*, 3(2).

Davis, L. (ed.) (1984) 'Ethnicity in social groupwork practice', Special Issue of *Social Work with Groups*, 7(3).

Davis, L. and Proctor, E. (1989) *Race, Gender and Class: Guidelines for Practice with Individuals, Families and Groups*. New Jersey: Prentice-Hall.

Davis, L.E. (1984a) 'Essential components of group work with Black Americans' in Davis, L.E. (ed.) *Ethnicity in Social Group Work Practice*. New York: Haworth, pp.97-110.

Davis, L.E. (1984b) 'The significance of color' in Davis, L.E. (ed.) *Ethnicity in Social Group Work Practice*. New York: Haworth, pp.3-5.

Day, L. (1992) 'Women and oppression: race, class and gender' in Langan, M. and Day, L. (eds.) *Women, Oppression and Social Work*. London: Routledge.

Delgado, M. and Humm-Delgado, D. (1984a) 'Hispanics and group work: A review of the literature' in Davis, L.E. (ed.) *Ethnicity Social Group Work Practice*. New York: Haworth, pp.85-96.

Delgado, M. and Humm-Delgado, D. (1984b) 'Hispanics and group work: a review of the literature', *Social Work with Groups,* 7(3).

Delgado, M. and Siff, S.S. (1980) 'A Hispanic adolescent group in a public school setting: an interagency approach', *Social Work with Groups,* 3(3).

Demorgon, J. (1989) *L'exploration interculturelle*. Paris: Armand Colin.

Demorgon, J. (1993) 'Un nouvel appareil à penser et à vivre les cultures', *Reperes et Action*, 2. Paris: CEMEA.

Department of the Environment (1995) *Count of Gypsy Caravans*. 19 July 1995.

Donald, J. and Rattansi, A. (eds.) (1992) *'Race', Culture and Difference*. Open University Press.

Douglas, T. (1976) *Groupwork Practice*. London: Tavistock.

Douglas, T. (1978) *Basic Groupwork*. London: Tavistock.

Douglas, T. (1986) *Group Living*. London: Tavistock.

Dublin Travellers Education and Development Group (1992) *DTEDG File Irish Travellers: New Analysis and New Initiatives*. Dublin: Pavee Point Publications.

Dublin Travellers Education and Development Group (1994a) *Reach Out. Report by the DTEDG on the 'POVERTY 3' Programme 1990-1994*. Dublin: Pavee Point Publications.

Dublin Travellers Education and Development Group (1994b) *Starting Out. A Resource Pack for Trainers of Traveller Women*. Dublin: Pavee Point Publications.

Dwivedi, K. (ed.) (1993) *Groupwork with Children and Adolescents*. Jessica Kingsley.

Edwards, E.D. and Edwards, M.E. (1984) 'Group work practice with American Indians', *Social Work with Groups,* 7(3).

Eisenbruch, M. (1991) 'From Post-traumatic Stress Disorder to cultural bereavement: diagnosis of Southeast Asian refugees', *Social Science and Medicine*, 33, pp.673-80.

Emmerson, A. and Kennett, D. (1995) *LGTU Report of Their Groupwork with Traveller Young Women*. London: London Gypsy and Traveller Unit.

Erickson, E. (1968) *Identity, Youth and Crisis*. Norton.

Etter-Lewis, G. (1991) 'Black women's life stories: reclaiming self in narrative texts' in Gluck, S.B. and Pataik, D. (eds.) *Women's Words: The Feminist Practice of Oral History*. New York: Rutledge.

Farge, A. (1993) *Fragile Lives: Violence, Power and Solidarity in Eighteenth Century Paris*. Cambridge: Polity Press.

Fernando, S. (1991) *Mental Health, Race and Culture*. London: Macmillan.

Forum TV (1991) *Video Letters*.

Foulkes, S.H. (1964) *Therapeutic Group Analysis*. London: Maresfield Reprints.

Freeman, E.M. and McRoy, R. (1986) 'Group counselling program for unemployed black teenagers', *Social Work with Groups,* 9(1).

Freire, P. (1972) *Pedagogy of the Oppressed*. Harmondsworth: Penguin.

Freire, P. (1973) *Pedagogy of the Oppressed*. New York: Seabury.

Gaffey, B. (1992) 'Preface' in Southwark Traveller Women's Group (eds.) *Moving Stories: Traveller Women Write*. London: Traveller Education Team.

Gaffey, B. (1995) *Input from Kathleen Gaffey, Oxford, England*. Unpublished.

Galinsky, M.J. and Schopler, J.H. (1980) 'Structuring co-leadership in social work training', *Social Work in Groups,* 3(4).

Gallagher, A. (1977) 'Women and community work' in Mayo, M. (ed.)*Women in the Community*. London: Routledge and Kegan Paul.
Garvin, C. (1981) *Contemporary Groupwork*. New Jersey: Prentice-Hall.
Garvin, C. (1985) 'Work with disadvantaged and oppressed groups' in Sundel, M. et al. (eds.) *Individual Change Through Small Groups*. Second Edition. New York: Free Press, pp.469-72.
Garvin, C. and Reed, B. (eds.) (1983) 'Group work with women/group work with men', Special Issue, *Social Work with Groups*, 6(3/4).
Germain, C.B. (1991) *Human Behavior in the Social Environment: An Ecological View*. New York: Columbia University Press.
Germain, C.B. and Gitterman, A. (1980) *The Life Model of Social Work Practice*. New York: Columbia University Press. Second Edition in press.
Gilchrist, A. (1994) *Report and Evaluation of the Bristol Festival against Racism*. Bristol.
Gilchrist, A. (1995) *Community Development and Networking*. London: Community Development Foundation.
Gopaul-McNicol, S.-A. (1993) *Working with West Indian Families*. New York: The Guilford Press.
Green, H. (1991) *Counting Gypsies*. London: HMSO.
Greene, B. (1994) 'African-American women' in Coms-Diaz, L. and Greene, B. (eds.) *Women of Color: Integrating Ethnic and Gender Identities in Psychotherapy*. New York: The Guilford Press, pp.10-29.
Gutiérrez, L. (1991) 'Empowering women of color: a feminist model' in Bricker-Jenkins, M., Hooyman, N.R. and Gottlieb, N. (eds.)*Feminist Social Work Practice in Clinical Settings*. Plenary Speech, 17th AASWG Symposium, San Diego California, October 27, 1995. Newbury Park, CA: Sage, pp.199-214.
Gutiérrez, L. and Ortega, R. (1989) 'Using groups to empower Latinos: a preliminary analysis', *Proceedings of the Eleventh Annual Symposium*. Akron, OH: AASWG.
Hales, L. and Connolly, M. (1995) 'Wormwood Scrubs: a local or foreign prison', *Probation Journal*, 42, March.
Handel, W. (1982) *Ethnomethodology: How People Make Sense*. Englewood Cliffs, NJ: Prentice Hall.
Harris, M. (1979) *Cultural Materialism: The Struggle for a Science of Culture*. New York: Random House.
Hawes, D. and Perez, B. (1995) *The Gypsy and the State The Ethnic Cleansing of British Society*. Bristol: The Policy Press.
Hawkin, P. and Shohet, R. (1989) *Supervision in the Helping Professions*. Milton Keynes: Open University Press.
Headland, T., Pike, K. and Harris, M. (eds.) (1990) *Emics and Etics: the Insider/Outsider Debate*. London: Sage.
Heap, K. (1979) *Process and Action in Work with Groups. The Pre-Conditions for Treatment and Growth*. Pergamon Press.
Heap, K. (1985) *The Practice of Social Work with Groups*. London: George Allen Unwin.

Bibliography

Henry, S. (1981) *Group Skills in Social Work*. Itaska, Illinois: F.E. Peacock.

Hill-Collins, P. (1986) 'Learning from the outsider within: the sociological significance of Black feminist thought' *Social Problems*, 35(6), December.

HMSO (1986) *Bangladeshis in Britain*. London: HMSO.

Hobbs, D. and May, T. {eds.} *Interpreting the Field : Accounts of Ethnography*. Oxford University Press.

Hodge, J. (1985) *Planning for Co-Leadership*. Newcastle-upon-Tyne: Grapevine, 43, Vern Avenue, Newcastle-upon-Tyne, NE2 2QU.

Hoffman, L. (1990) 'Constructing realities: an art of lenses', *Family Process*, 29, pp.1-12.

Home, A.M. (1991) 'Mobilizing women's strengths for social change: the group connection', *Social Work with Groups*, 14(3/4).

hooks, bell (1982) *Ain't I a Woman: Black Women and Feminism*. London: Pluto Press.

hooks, bell (1990). *Yearning: Race, Gender, and Cultural Politics*. Boston: South End Press.

hooks, bell (1992) *Black Looks: Race and Representation*. London: Turnaround.

hooks, bell (1993) *Sisters of the Yam: Black Women and Self-Recovery*. London: Turnaround.

Hull, G., Scott, P.B. and Smith, B. (1982) (eds.) *All the Women are White, and All the Blacks Are Men, but Some of Us are Brave: Black Women's Studies*. Old Westbury, New York: The Feminist Press.

Hurstel, J. (1988) *Chroniques culturelles barbares*. Paris: Syron/Alternatives.

Jackson, Sir L.C. (1937) *The History of the United Services Club*. London: Committee of the United Services Club/Gale and Poulden.

Johnson, A. and Lee, J.A.B. (1994) 'Empowerment work with homeless women' in Mirkin, M. (ed.) *Women in Context*. New York: Guilford, pp.408-32.

Joyce, N. (1985) *Traveller: An Autobiography*. Gill and Macmillan.

Kadushin (1972) *The Social Work Interview*. Columbia University Press.

Kareem, J. (1992) 'The Nafsiyat Intercultural Therapy Centre: ideas and experience in intercultural therapy' in Kareem, J. and Littlewood, R. (eds.) *Intercultural Therapy: Themes Interpretation and Practice*. Oxford: Blackwell.

King, P. (1982) 'Race and cultural factors in a casework relationship' in Cheetham, J. (ed.) *Social Work and Ethnicity*. Gorge Allen and Unwin.

Klein, J. (1970) *Working in Groups*. Hutchinson.

Klein, M. (1952a) 'Notes on some schizoid mechanisms' in Rivere, J. (ed.) *Developments in Psychoanalysis*. London: Hogarth Press.

Klein, M. (1952b) 'Some theoretical conclusions regarding the life of the infant' in Rivere, J. (ed.) *Developments in Psychoanalysis*. London: Hogarth Press.

Kumar, Rahda (1993) *The History of Doing*. UK: Verso.

Lacan, J. (1977) *Ecrits*. London: Tavistock.

Ladmiral J.-R. and Lipiansky, E.-M. (1989) *La communication interculturelle*. Paris: Armand Colin.

Lafont, R. (1991) *Nous, peuple europeen?* Paris: Kimé.

Laing, E. (1992) 'Introduction' in Southwark Traveller Women's Group (eds.) *Moving Stories: Traveller Women Write*. London: Traveller Education Team.

Laing, E. (1995) *Personal Communication*.

Lang, N. (1986) 'Social work practice in small social forms: identifying collectively' in Lang, N. and Sullivan, J. (eds.) *Collectively in Social Group Work*. New York: Haworth.

Lau, A. (1988) 'Family therapy and ethnic minorities ' in Street and Dryden (eds.) *Family Therapy in Britain*. Open University Press.

Lawrence, M. (1995a) *Evaluation Study: Gypsies and Travellers Community Development Worker 1994*. Research and Intelligence Unit, Cleveland County Council.

Lawrence, M. (1995b) 'A new approach to gypsies and travellers', Municipal Journal, 1-7 September, 35.

Lebacq, M. and Shah, Z. (1989) 'A group for black and white sexually abused children', *Groupwork*, 2(2).

Lee, J.A.B. (1989) (ed.) *Group Work with the Poor and Oppressed*. New York: Haworth.

Lee, J.A.B. (1991a) 'Empowerment through mutual aid groups: A practice grounded conceptual framework' *Groupwork* 4(1), pp.5-21.

Lee, J.A.B. (1991b) 'Jane Addams in Boston: Intersecting time and space' in Garland, J.A. (ed.) *Group Work Reaching Out: People, Places and Power*. New York: Haworth Press, , pp.7-22.

Lee, J.A.B. (1994a) *The Empowerment Approach to Social Work Practice*. New York: Columbia University Press.

Lee, J.A.B. (1994b) 'No place to go: homeless women' in Gitterman, A. and Shulman, L. (eds.) *Mutual Aid Groups, Vulnerable Populations, and the Life Cycle*. New York: Columbia University Press, pp.297-313.

Liegeois, J-P. and Gheorghe, N. (1995) *Roma / Gypsies A European Minority*. Minority Rights Group International.

Liegeois, J-P. (1986) *Gypsies: An Illustrated History*. London: Al Saqi Books.

Lifton, R.J. (1993) 'From Hiroshima to the Nazi doctors: the evolution of psychotransformative approaches to understanding traumatic stress syndromes' in Wilson, J.P. and Raphael, B. (eds.) *International Handbook of Traumatic Stress Syndromes*. New York: Plenum Press.

Littlewood and Lipsedge (1989) *Aliens and Alienists*. Unwin Hyman.

Lorde, A. (1984) *Sister Outsider*. The Crossing Press. Feminist Series.

Lum, D. (1995) *Social Work Practice and People of Color*. Third Edition. Monterey, CA: Brook-Cole.

Malik, K. (1996) *The Meaning of Race*. London: Macmillan.

Manor, O. (1989) 'Organising accountability for social groupwork: more choices', *Groupwork*, 2(2).

Marshment, M. (1978) 'Racist ideology and popular fiction, *Race and*

Class, XIX (4).

Martin, R. (1994) *Oral History in Social Work: Research, Assessment, and Intervention*. Thousand Oaks, CA: Sage.

Mays, B.E. (1987) *Born to Rebel: An Autobiography*. Athens, GA: The University of Georgia Press.

McCullough, M. and Ely, P. (1968) *Social Work with Groups*. Routledge and Kegan Paul.

McLeod, L.W. and Pemberton, B.K. (1987) *New Men, New Minds*. The Crossing Press.

Melzak, S. (1992) 'Secrecy, privacy, repressive regimes and growing up', *Bulletin of the Anna Freud Centre*, 15, pp.205-24.

Milgram, S. (1963) 'Behavioural study of obedience', *Journal of Abnormal and Social Psychology*, 67(4), pp.371-78.

Mistry, T. (1989) Establishing a Feminist model of groupwork in the probation service, *Groupwork*, 2(2), pp.145-58.

Mistry, T. (1995) 'Hartford Symposium 1994', *Groupwork* 8(1), pp.99-101.

Mistry, T. and Brown, A. (1991) 'Black/white co-working in groups', *Groupwork*, 4(2), pp.101-18.

Mozzaka, N. and Webb, J. (1995) *LGTU Report of their Groupwork with Traveller Girls*. London: London Gypsy and Traveller Unit,.

Mullender, A. (1988) 'Groupwork as the method of choice for black children in white foster-homes', *Groupwork*, 1(2).

Mullender, A. (1990) 'The ebony project - bicultural group work with transracial foster parents', *Social Work with Groups,* 13(4), pp.23-42.

Mullender, A. and Ward, D. (1985) 'Towards an alternative model of social groupwork', *British Journal of Social Work*, 15(2), pp.155-72, quoted in Butler, S. and Wintram, C. (1991) *Feminist Groupwork*. Sage.

Mullender, A. and Ward, D. (1991) *Self-Directed Groupwork. Users Take Action for Empowerment*. London: Whiting and Birch.

Mumford, Whitehouse and Platts (1991) 'Socio cultural correlates of eating disorders', *British Journal of Psychiatry,* 158, pp.222-28.

Murray-Parkes, C. (1972) *Bereavement: Studies of Grief in Adult Life*. London: Tavistock.

Muston. R. and Weinstein, J. (1988) 'Race and groupwork: practice and training', *Groupwork*, 1(1).

Naheed, K. (1990) 'Who am I ?' in Ahmad, R. (ed.)*We Sinful Women*. London: Women's Press.

O'Shea, C. (1972) 'Two grey cats learn how it is' in Berkovitz, I. H. (ed.) *Adolescents Grow in Groups*. New York: Brunner/Mazel.

Padma, P. (1974) 'Spaces of Decision. South India: 1890s to 1970s' in *Birthday Deathday and Other Stories*. London: Women's Press.

Pankhania, J. (1995) 'Benevolent racism' in *Black Perspectives, Youth and Policy*, Summer.

Papell, C.P. and Rothman, B. (1980) 'Relating the mainstream model of social work with groups', *Social Work with Groups*, 3, Summer, pp.5-22.

Parsons, R. (1991) 'Empowerment: purpose and practice principles in social work', *Social Work with Groups,* 14(2), pp.7-21.

Pearson, V. (1991) 'Western theory, eastern practice: social group work in Hong Kong', *Social Work with Groups,* 14(2).

Pedersen, P., Dragun, J., Lonner, W. and Trimble, J. (1989) *Counselling Across Cultures.* University of Hawaii Press.

Perelberg, R. (1992) 'Familiar and unfamiliar types of family structure: towards a conceptual framework' in Kareem, J. and Littlewood, R. (eds.) *Intercultural Therapy Themes, Interpretations and Practice.* Oxford: Blackwells.

Pernell, R. (1986) 'Empowerment and social group work' in Parnes, M. (ed.) *Innovations in Social Group Work.* New York: Haworth, pp.107-18.

Philipson, J. (1992) *Practising Equality: Women, Men and Social Work.* London: CCETSW.

Porter, R. (1987) *A Social History of Madness: Stories of the Insane.* London: Weidenfield & Nicolson.

Preston-Shoot, M. (1987) *Effective Groupwork.* London: Macmillan.

Rack, P. (1982) *Race, Culture and Mental Disorder.* Tavistock.

Regan, S. (1996) Workshop on 'Telephone Groups'. European Groupwork Symposium, Bournemouth, UK.

Reiss, N. (1990) 'The emic-etic distinction as applied to language' in Headland, T., Pike, K. and Harris, M. (eds.) *Emics and Etics: the Insider/Outsider Debate.* London: Sage.

Rhule, C. (1988) 'A group for white women with Black children', *Groupwork,* 1(1).

Rice, M. (1990) 'Challenging orthodoxies in feminist theory : a Black feminist critique' in Gelsthorpe, L. and Morris, A. (eds.) *Feminists Perspectives in Criminology.* Open University Press.

Richards, R., McWilliams, B., Batten, N., Cameron, C. and Cutler, J. (1995) *Foreign Nationals in English Prisons: II. Some Policy Issues.*

Rustin, M. (1991) *The Good Society and the Inner World: Psychoanalysis, Politics and Culture.* London. New York: Verso.

Rutter, M. (1985) 'Resilience in the face of adversity: protective factors and resistance to psychiatric disorder', *British Journal of Psychiatry,* 147, pp.598-611.

Saussure, F. (1974) *Course in General Linguistics.* Glasgow: Collins.

Scarry, E. (1985) *The Body in Pain: The Making and Unmaking of the World.* New York: Oxford University Press.

Schwartz, W. (1974) 'The social worker in the group' in Klenk, R.W. and Ryan, R.W. (eds.) *The Practice of Social Work.* Second Edition. Belmont, CA: Wadsworth, pp.208-28.

Sejdinov, K. (1995) 'Gypsy mediators: training and employment', *Interface,* 17.

Shapiro, B.Z. (1990) 'The social work group as social microcosm: 'frames of reference' revisited', *Social Work with Groups,* 13(2).

Shilkoff (1983) 'The use of male-female co-leadership in an early adolescent girls' activity group', *Social Work with Groups,* 6(2).

Shulman, L. (1984) *The Skills of Helping: Individuals and Groups.*

Itaska, Illinois: F.E.Peacock.

Smith, P.B. and Bond, M.H. (1993) *Social Psychology Across Cultures: Analysis and Perspectives*. London: Harvester Wheatsheaf.

Some, M.P. (1993) *Ritual: Power, Healing and Community*. Portland: Swan and Raven.

Southwark Traveller Women's Group (1992) *Moving Stories: Traveller Women Write*. London: Traveller Education Team.

Standing Conference for Community Development (1992) *A Working Statement on Community Development*. Sheffield: SCCD.

Starak, Y. (1981) 'Co-Leadership: a new look at sharing group work', *Social Work with Groups*, 4(3-4).

Sternbach, J. (1990) 'The men's seminar: an educational and support for men', *Social Work with Groups*, 13(2).

Stiles, E., Donner, S., Giovannone, J., Lochte, E. and Reetz, R.R. (1982) 'Hear it like it is' in Rubenstein, H. and Bloch, M.H. (eds.) *Things That Matter*. New York: Macmillan Publishing Co., Inc.

Sugar, M. (1975) *The Adolescent in Group and Family Therapy*. New York: Brunner/Mazel.

Summerfield, D. (1992) 'Addressing human response to war and atrocity: major challenges in research and practices and the limitations of Western psychiatric models' in Kleber, R., Figley, C. and Gerson, B. (eds.) *Beyond Trauma: Cultural and Societal Dynamics*. New York: Plenum Press.

Swiss, S. and Giller, J.E. (1993) 'Rape as a crime of war: a medical perspective', *Journal of the American Medical Association*, 270, pp.612-15.

Tajfel, H. (1979) 'An integrative theory of intergroup conflict' in Austin, W. and Worchel, S. (eds.) *The Social Psychology of Intergroup Relations*. California: Brooks Cole.

Tarzi, A. and Hedges, J. (1990) *A Prison Within a Prison*. Inner London Probation Service Publication.

Thomas, L. (1992) 'Racism and psychotherapy: working with racism in the consulting room - an analytic view' in Kareem, J. and Littlewood, R. (eds.) *Intercultural Therapy: Themes Interpretation and Practice*. Oxford: Blackwell.

Thomas, L. (1995) 'Psychotherapy in the context of race and culture in Fernando, S. (ed.) *Mental Health in a Multi-Ethnic Society*. Routledge.

Thompson, N. (1993) *Anti-Discriminatory Practice*. Birmingham: BASW, p.1.

Thompson, S. and Kahn, J. (1988) *The Group Process and Family Therapy*. Oxford: Pergamon Press.

Tixier, M. (1992) *Travailler en Europe*. Paris: Liaisons.

Tizard, B. and Phoenix, A. (1989) 'Black identity and transracial adoption', *New Community*, 15, pp.427-37.

Triseliotis, J. (ed.) (1988) *Groupwork in Adoption and Foster Care*. London: Batsford.

Tuckman, B.W. (1965) 'Developmental sequence in small groups', *Psychological Bulletin*, 63, pp.384-99.

UNHCR (1988) *Handbook on Procedures and Criteria for Determining Refugee Status under the 1951 Convention and the 1967 Protocol relating to the Status of Refugees.* Geneva: Office of the United Nations High Commissioner for Refugees.

van der Veer, G. (1992) *Counselling and Therapy With Refugees.* New York: John Wiley & Sons.

Wade, A. and Macpherson, M. (1992) 'Addressing race issues in groupwork', *Probation Journal*, Sept.

Waldman, E. (1980) 'Co-leadership as a method of training' *Social Work with Groups*, 3(1).

West, C. (1993) *Race Matters.* Boston, MA: Beacon Press.

Whitaker, D. (1985) *Using Groups to Help People.* London: Routledge and Kegan Paul.

White, M. and Epston, D. (1990) *Narrative Means to Therapeutic Ends.* New York: Norton.

Willoughby, S. (1995) *Charities Evaluation Services: Evaluation of London Gypsy and Traveller Unit.* Three-Monthly Report to 31 July 1995.

Winnicott, D.W. (1965) *Maturational Processes and the Facilitating Environment.* London: Hogarth Press.

Witt, S.(1995) LGTU *Report of their Groupwork with Traveller Boys* (Fianna Buachailli). London: London Gypsy and Traveller Unit.

Wood, G.G. and Middleman, R. (1989) *The Structural Approach to Social Work Practice.* New York: Columbia University Press.

Wood, G.G. and Middleman, R. (1995) *Constructivism, Power and Social Work with Groups.* Plenary Speech, 17th AASWG Symposium, San Diego, California, October 27.

Woodcock, J. (1995) 'Healing rituals with families in exile', *Journal of Family Therapy*, 17, pp.397-410.

X, Malcolm (1965) *Malcolm X Speaks, Selected Speeches and Statements.* New York: Pathfinder.

Yalom, I.D. (1975) *The Theory and Practice of Group Psychotherapy*, Second Edition. New York: Basic Books.

Yalom, I.D. (1985) *The Theory and Practice of Group Psychotherapy.* Third Edition. New York: Basic Books.

Notes on Contributors

Aileen Alleyne is a psychotherapist and clinical supervisor in private practice. She lectures part-time in counselling at Goldsmiths College, University of London and trains independently in the areas of working with issues of difference and anti-discriminatory practices.

Juliet Amoa is a social worker in a South London Borough specialising in work with people with learning difficulties.

Judith Beaumont is Executive Director, My Sisters' Place, Hartford, Connecticut, USA.

Gail Bourdon is Program Director, My Sisters' Place III, Hartford, Connecticut, USA.

Allan Brown was a Senior Lecturer in the School for Policy Studies, University of Bristol until his retirement in July 1996. He has written extensively on the theory of practice developments in British groupwork for over two decades, as well as being involved in groupwork through a range of training, consultancy and evaluation programmes. He was Co-Editor of the journal *Groupwork* for eight years and the Chairperson of the First European Groupwork Symposium in 1991.

Sarah Cemlyn is a Lecturer in the School for Policy Studies, University of Bristol, England. She has previously worked in practice with Travellers, and is currently engaged in research on the interaction of Travellers and welfare systems, and in the voluntary management of a local development project with Travellers.

Sakhina Dickinson is a youthwork practitioner in Tameside, Greater Manchester, England.

Liz Dixon is Tutor in Probation Studies, Brunel University College, Twickenham, England and a Probation Officer at Holloway Prison.

Marcia Francis-Spence was a Lecturer in Social Work at the Centre for Applied Social Studies, University of Durham, England.

Liz Hales is a Probation Officer at Wormwood Scrubs Prison, England.

Christy King is a Student, Manchester Community College, Manchester, Connecticut, USA

Jean Konon is a Clinical Social Worker, My Sisters' Place II, Hartford, Connecticut, USA.

Judith A.B. Lee is Professor of Social Work, University of Connecticut School of Social Work, USA.

Ruth R. Martin is Associate Dean, University of Connecticut School of Social Work, USA.

B.K. Minhas has been a qualified social worker for over ten years. She has extensive practice experience within child protection and generic case work. Additionally, she has worked to develop policies and implementation programmes in the area of Equal Opportunities, anti-racist and anti-discriminatory practice. She has worked within various organisations at all levels, including managerial, strategic and operational. She has also worked directly with Black Minority Ethnic communities from differing backgrounds in areas of social, community development and groupwork. In recent years she has been working as a freelance training and research consultant.

Tara Mistry is a Lecturer in the School for Policy Studies, University of Bristol. She has been involved in teaching/training social work and probation students since 1988. Formerly a Probation Officer, she has been actively involved with groupwork developments as a practitioner and educator for 18 years. She is currently co-editor of the journal *Groupwork*.

Rosalind Moore-Beckham is Program Director, My Sisters' Place II, Hartford, Connecticut, USA.

Gita Patel has 14 years experience of advice and community work with a variety of client groups, and particularly with children and adolescents. She has a Diploma in Counselling and is furthering her training in Intercultural Therapy. She is the Counselling Coordinator for the Refugee Project at Nafsiyat where she works with refugee children and adults, and with clients from other minority communities, in individual and group therapy. She is a trainer and supervisor for intercultural counselling and therapy. Born in the Midlands, Gita is Indian; her parents migrated to the UK in the late 1950s

Paul Taylor is currently Senior Lecturer in Community Education (*Animation socio-culturelle*), University of Tours, France. With practical experience of cross-national groupwork throughout Europe and West Africa, he has particular responsibility for the management of several international exchange/research programmes.

Evelyn Thorpe, Residential Director, My Sisters' Place II, Hartford, Connecticut, USA.

Jeremy Woodcock is the Principal Family and Marital Therapist at the Medical Foundation for the Care of Victims of Torture. He also teaches at the Institute of Family Therapy and is Honorary Lecturer in Psychology at Birkbeck College, University of London.

Author index

Race and Groupwork

Subject index